# TALES *from* WORLD EPICS

**John Marcatante**
Former Assistant Principal
New York City Public School System

Dedicated to serving

AMSCO
*our nation's youth*

**Amsco School Publications, Inc.**
315 Hudson Street / New York, N.Y. 10013

When ordering this book, please specify:
either **R 515 P** or TALES FROM WORLD EPICS

ISBN 0-87720-786-0

Cover by Don Schlegel
Illustrations by Don Sibley

Printed in the United States of America

# To The Reader

Like the courageous astronauts of modern times, brave men and women of the past accepted the challenge of exploring the unknown. Throughout the ages, daring people have gone forth on difficult and often dangerous journeys in quest of adventure, glory, and more knowledge about the world and its people. Sometimes the questers discovered interesting truths about themselves!

Some struggled to see that justice was done, or to help found a new nation, or to save people from terrible harm. These and other questers usually acted nobly and wisely. However, there were some who, as you will see, didn't always behave so well.

Stories about such interesting characters, some real and some fictional, have been handed down to us in works called the *epics*. Some were written in the years before Christ's birth (B.C.). While some epics are prose works, most are long story-telling poems. In a number of the works, supernatural forces either help or hinder the efforts of some key characters. (To help you more fully appreciate some of these tales, a chart of Greek and Roman gods and goddesses is on page 2.)

Finally, you might be wondering why these tales have lasted for so long, and why they remain so popular. Perhaps it's because they enable readers to learn about life and customs in different times and different lands. Perhaps it's because some characters remind readers of themselves or of people they know. Or perhaps it's because various epics are filled with adventure, mystery, romance, suspense, and humor! But whatever the reasons may be, these stories have lasted through the years, and now it is your turn to enjoy some stirring tales from unforgettable epics.

*John Marcatante*

# Contents

## From Ancient Greece and Rome

## From Later Europe

## From the East

## From Africa

## From America

## Glossary of Names / 247

# From
# ANCIENT GREECE
# and ROME

# Some Gods and Goddesses of Ancient Greece and Rome

| Roman Name | Greek Name | Identity |
|---|---|---|
| Apollo | Apollo or Phoebus Apollo | God of sun, music, archery, healing |
| Discordia | Eris | Goddess of strife |
| Iris | Iris | Goddess of rainbow; messenger of the gods |
| Jove or Jupiter | Zeus | King and ruler of all gods and men |
| Juno | Hera | Queen of gods; wife of Jove |
| Mars | Ares | God of war |
| Mercury | Hermes | God of speed; messenger of the gods |
| Minerva | Athena | Goddess of wisdom |
| Neptune | Poseidon | Ruler of the seas; brother of Jove |
| Parcae (the Fates) | Moirae (the Fates) | Goddesses who control destinies of gods and men |
| Pluto | Hades | Ruler of the land of the dead; brother of Jove |
| Proserpina | Persephone | Queen of the land of the dead |
| Thetis | Thetis | Sea goddess; mother of Achilles |
| Venus | Aphrodite | Goddess of love and beauty |
| Vulcan | Hephaestus | God of fire |

# The Judgment of Paris

You may have heard the old saying, "Mighty oaks from little acorns grow." As you will see, the story that follows (based in part on a summary of the *Cypria*, a now lost Greek epic) is like a small acorn because the events described in it helped lead to the writing of "mighty" Greek and Roman epics now famous throughout the world.

Here then is a little, yet important, story in which a very unusual apple leaves more than one character with a very bitter taste.

## Major Characters

**Discordia**   goddess of strife

**Apollo**   god of the sun and music

**Diana**   goddess of the moon and hunting

**Jove**   king of the gods

**Pluto**   ruler of the lower world

**Neptune**   ruler of the seas

**Mars**   god of war

**Juno**   queen of the gods, wife of Jove

**Minerva**   goddess of wisdom

**Venus**   goddess of love and beauty

**Paris**   a prince of Troy

**Achilles**   Greek warrior

## Vocabulary Preview

**strife**   conflict; disagreement; discord
   Deciding on how much to spend for new uniforms caused *strife* at the meeting.

**vowed**   promised; pledged
   After losing the game, the team members *vowed* to practice more often.

**lyre**   a small, harplike instrument
   While strumming the strings of a *lyre*, the man recited a poem.

**launched**   started off
   The new rocket was *launched* from its pad early this morning.

**immortal**   living forever
   Ancient Greeks and Romans believed their gods were *immortal*.

**A** figure darted quickly into the deepening shadows outside the great hall on Mount Pelion in Greece. "I'll never forget this night!" growled Discordia. "They'll pay dearly for this insult!" Then she watched with narrowed eyes as a couple came marching in to their wedding feast.

The smiling groom was a handsome mortal, Prince Peleus. His lovely bride Thetis was an immortal, a sea goddess. Her large blue eyes were sparkling brightly. Her flowing gown, trimmed with the finest pearls from the oceans and seas of the world, was dazzling to behold.

The great hall was crowded with immortals. All the gods and goddesses were there except for one. Only slim Discordia hadn't been invited, for the goddess of strife always caused problems wherever she went.

"So, they're afraid of a little trouble, are they?" she hissed. Snarling, she clutched angrily at her fire-red cape. "Well, I'll soon give them some trouble they'll long remember!"

Discordia crept up closer to have a better look. Golden-haired Apollo, god of the sun and music, was strumming on a lyre. His twin sister Diana, goddess of the moon and hunting, was nearby. Dancing with Mercury, the swift messenger of the gods, Diana was shaking with laughter at one of Mercury's many jokes.

Seated on a bright throne was Jove, king of the gods. He was stroking his thick beard as he talked to his brothers. One was dark-robed Pluto, lord of the underworld. The other was Neptune, ruler of the sea, holding a huge golden trident (a three-pronged spear) in his mighty fist.

Then Discordia stared hard at a husky god in glowing red armor. It was her brother Mars, the fierce god of war. He was speaking to Juno, queen of the gods. She was known for her sharp tongue, but right now even she was smiling happily.

Indeed, all the guests seemed quite merry. They were enjoying the ambrosia and nectar, the food and drink of the gods. Music, friendly talk, and laughter filled the air.

But all of a sudden, a great hush came over the room. The guests looked up and just stared in silence as a bright object went spinning and flashing through the air over their heads. Finally, the object fell to the ground with a soft thump. It landed right before Jove's feet. And out in the shadows, Discordia laughed in a wicked way.

Jove stretched down and picked up the bright object. "Why, it's a golden apple," he exclaimed, "and there are some words on it!" Then Jove read the words aloud: *To the fairest one of all.*

Juno's large eyes lit up at once. Smiling, she softly patted her wavy brown hair. "Surely this is meant for me," she said, "for I am the queen of the gods."

But dark-haired Minerva stepped forward. Yanking off her war helmet, the tall goddess of wisdom began shaking her head. "No!" she cried. "You may be the queen, but I'm far younger and fairer. Surely the prize is meant for me!"

Quietly then, Venus stepped forward while gently tossing her golden curls. "Please don't argue," said the goddess of love and beauty. "You're both very lovely." Of course, the other goddesses smiled at these words. But their smiles quickly disappeared as Venus went on. "Yet I think that everyone here would agree that the apple should really be mine."

Minerva rattled her heavy shield angrily. Juno stamped her foot and began shouting at Venus. And the goddesses were still arguing when the wedding party broke up.

Up on Mount Olympus, home of Jove and many of the gods, the argument raged on and on. Finally, Juno whirled about to Jove. "Speak up, my husband. You are king here!" she cried. "So you must tell us who wins the golden apple."

Jove frowned. He didn't like the looks in the eyes of the goddesses. Turning away, he began stroking his beard and thinking hard. After a while, he nodded his head. "I've made a decision," he declared. "I've decided to let someone else make the choice!"

This didn't please Juno at all. "But who shall make the judgment?" she snapped.

Jove answered softly. "I want the shepherd boy called Paris to be the judge. He's now on Mount Ida, tending his flock." Then Jove ordered Mercury to take the goddesses there at once.

Now the youth on Mount Ida wasn't just a shepherd. He was truly a prince of Troy. For when Paris was just born, some wise men warned his father, King Priam, that Paris would cause the fall of the city someday. So in later years, the worried king sent Paris to live as a shepherd, outside of Troy.

The goddesses found the curly-haired prince half-asleep. The slim youth began trembling when he saw the strange women staring down at him. "Who are you?" he shouted, jumping to his feet. "What are you doing here?"

Juno was the first to speak. "Don't be frightened," she smiled. "We've come here for your help. Great Jove wants you to make a judgment. He says that you are to award this prize to one of us. You

must give this golden apple to the fairest one here." Then Juno held
up the apple of discord. "Of course, since I am queen of the gods,"
she went on, "I can give you great power and wealth. I can even
make you ruler over all Asia."

At this, Minerva rushed forward. "But I can offer you great fame
in battle," she declared. "For I, Minerva, am also a goddess of war!"

Then Venus just smiled and walked slowly up to Paris. "Do you
know who Venus is?" she asked in a soft voice.

"Yes," answered Paris. "She's the goddess of beauty and love."

Venus smiled sweetly. "Right you are, you clever lad!" she said.
"And I am that same goddess. It is in my power to promise you the
most beautiful woman in the world as your own!"

When Paris heard this, his eyes began to shine. It didn't take him
very long to make his judgment. "The prize goes to the fairest one of
all," he said as he held out the apple. "It goes to Venus!"

At once, Juno and Minerva grew pale with anger. Juno
screamed, "You Trojan fool! I'll never forget this insult!" Whirling
about, she rushed off with Minerva close at her heels. From that
moment on, the two goddesses became the enemies of all Trojans.
And when Discordia heard what had happened, she shook with
laughter. "The trouble has only begun!" she laughed wildly.

Some years later, Paris visited a city in Greece. There he saw Helen, wife of a Greek king, Menelaus. She was so beautiful that before her marriage many other kings had also wished to marry her. So they'd made an agreement to let her choose the one she wanted to marry. They had also agreed to help her chosen husband if she were ever carried off.

Paris couldn't take his eyes off the lovely woman. Her hair was the color of golden wheat. Her green eyes flashed like brilliant emeralds. She wore a flowing yellow gown, and her movements were soft and graceful. To Paris she was the most beautiful woman in the world.

Venus felt she had to keep her promise, so she helped Paris to meet Helen. After that, she helped him escape with the lovely woman to the distant city of Troy.

Grown wild with rage, King Menelaus stamped about. Quickly he sent word to the Trojans, demanding the return of Helen. But Paris refused to release the lovely woman. This further enraged Menelaus, so the unhappy man sent word to all the other kings in Greece. He reminded them of their promise to help him if Helen were ever carried off. And he also asked many famous heroes for their help. Soon a thousand ships were being made ready to sail.

Up on Mount Olympus, Juno and Minerva smiled slyly. They vowed to do all they could to help the Greeks defeat the Trojans. Venus, however, planned to give aid to the people of Troy. And Discordia just laughed wildly as she shook out her long red cape. It was the color of the flames of war!

Among the heroes on the Greek ships was mighty Achilles. Indeed, he was the mightiest of the Greek warriors. Achilles was the son of Thetis, the seagoddess, on whose wedding day all this trouble had started.

Thetis loved her son dearly. From the moment of his birth, the seagoddess feared that he'd grow up only to die young in battle. Her fear was so great that she took him to the underworld when he was still a chubby infant. There she dipped the husky child into the waters of the river Styx.

"Oh, my baby," she cried out on that day. "I now dip you into the sacred waters of the Styx. You can never be harmed where the water now touches your body. This is a gift from the gods!" Then she kissed the baby and wrapped him in a soft blanket. Thetis felt better then. But she didn't know that she'd made an important mistake on that day. Thetis had held her son by his heel, and it had never touched the water! So from that day on, Achilles' heel was his one weak spot.

But now Achilles was a powerful man. He stood proud and tall on one of the fifty ships that belonged to him. His marvelous armor, forged by the lame god Vulcan on Mount Olympus, blazed in the golden sunlight.

Colorful banners fluttered in the morning breezes. Soon the winds started puffing up the sails, and the ships began slicing through the waves.

Many people lined the shore. They waved and cheered as the ships sailed away. Yet there was great sadness in the hearts of these people. For they wondered when, if ever, they'd see their loved ones again.

The people watched from the shore for a long time. They stared hard at the fleet sailing away because of a great problem that had begun with one small, golden apple. And many people cursed Helen's beauty as they watched the ships disappear from view that day, for it was the day on which Helen's face had launched a thousand ships. It was the day on which the terrible Trojan war had begun.

## QUESTING FOR INFORMATION

### A. Getting the Main Idea and Facts

Write the letter of the answer that best completes each statement.

1. This story is mainly about how _____.
   a. Achilles received gifts from the gods
   b. a contest led to war
   c. the gods celebrated weddings

2. Discordia caused strife at the wedding party because she _____.
   a. hated weddings
   b. was jealous of the bride
   c. hadn't been invited

3. Paris had been sent away from Troy to _____.
   a. find a wife      b. save the city      c. judge a contest

4. The golden apple of discord was won by the goddess of _____.
   a. love and beauty
   b. wisdom and war
   c. the moon and hunting

5. Minerva and Juno vowed that they would give help only to _____.

   a. the Trojans      b. shepherds      c. the Greeks

## B. Going Beyond the Facts

Write the letter of the answer that best completes each statement.

1. We may infer that Discordia wanted to _____ .
   a. win a contest
   b. get revenge
   c. help Paris to meet Helen
2. We can see that the three goddesses in the contest were _____ .
   a. humble    b. forgiving    c. proud
3. It would seem that Jove was anxious to _____ .
   a. show that Prince Paris was wise
   b. avoid trouble with the goddesses
   c. help the enraged King Menelaus
4. Probably, the Greek kings kept their promise to Helen's husband because they were _____ .
   a. honorable men
   b. offered good pay
   c. afraid of mighty Achilles
5. The event that took place first was _____ .
   a. Achilles set out for Troy
   b. Achilles was in the underworld
   c. Achilles received special armor

## QUESTING FOR MEANINGS

Write the letter of the word that best completes each sentence below.

a. strife    b. vowed    c. lyre    d. launched    e. immortal

1. The city drive for cleaner parks was _____ with a parade.
2. Mr. Jones _____ to search everywhere for his child's missing puppy.
3. Singing happily, the young lady played an ancient _____ .
4. The youth dreamed of doing great things and winning _____ fame.
5. A move to change club rules caused much _____ among members.

## QUESTING FOR UNDERSTANDING

1. Tell in what way or ways the immortals behaved like ordinary human beings. Why do you think the ancient Greeks and Romans described them as they did?

2. Who seemed more to blame, the mortals or the immortals, for the start of the Trojan War? Support your opinions with facts from the story.

## QUESTING FOR ENRICHMENT

A. *Who's Who* is a reference work found in many libraries. It contains facts about important living people, including some home or office addresses. Identify who's who from the story just read by matching names in column A with facts in column B. Write the number with its letter on your paper.

|  | **A** |  | **B** |
|---|---|---|---|
| 1. | Apollo | *a.* | prince of Troy |
| 2. | Discordia | *b.* | king of gods |
| 3. | Helen | *c.* | goddess of wisdom |
| 4. | Jove | *d.* | mother of Achilles |
| 5. | Juno | *e.* | goddess of strife |
| 6. | Minerva | *f.* | wife of King Menelaus |
| 7. | Paris | *g.* | god of the sun |
| 8. | Priam | *h.* | goddess of love and beauty |
| 9. | Thetis | *i.* | wife of Jove |
| 10. | Venus | *j.* | king of Troy |

B. Including Earth, there are nine planets in our solar system. One is named for Saturn, the father of Jove. Another is named for Uranus, the father of Saturn. Can you list *six* other planets bearing Roman names of gods and goddesses? You may use a science book or another reference.

# The Wrath of Achilles

A Trojan prince named Paris stole Helen, the wife of a Greek king, and took her across the Aegean Sea to the city of Troy. This caused a great war to break out between the Greeks and Trojans in about 1100 B.C. The following tale is based on some events from that war as described in the *Iliad* by the Greek poet Homer, who lived about 850 B.C. The word *Iliad* comes from *Ilium*, another name for ancient Troy.

As the story opens we soon meet the handsome and mighty Achilles, a hero who was both a winner and a loser in the Trojan War.

## Major Characters

**Agamemnon**   king of Greece

**Calchas**   a prophet

**Achilles**   Greek warrior

**Thetis**   sea goddess, mother of Achilles

**Jove**   king of the gods

**Juno**   queen of the gods, wife of Jove

**Hector**   a prince of Troy

**Patroclus**   friend of Achilles

**Ulysses**   Greek warrior

**Neptune**   ruler of the seas

**Apollo**   god of the sun and music

**Priam**   king of Troy

## Vocabulary Preview

**wrath**   great anger
The player's *wrath* caused him to shout at the umpire.

**truce**   a rest from fighting
Both angry brothers agreed to a *truce* to last through dinner hour.

**dread**   to fear; causing terror or awe
Many people *dread* storms, especially the *dread* hurricane.

**fleet**   swift; a group of ships
The *fleet* seabirds flew over the *fleet* of fishing vessels.

**ransom**   payment for release of a captive
A huge *ransom* was demanded for freeing the kidnapped man.

# I. Achilles Takes a Stand

King Agamemnon's dark eyes flashed like fire. Could it be true? Was he to blame for the fall of so many Greek warriors? The long-haired king leaned forward in his seat. Frowning, he listened to old Calchas the prophet speaking in the crowded hut.

"For nine days now the sun-god Apollo has been showering arrows into our camp. Arrows of disease! This dreadful plague will continue until the beautiful Chryseis is returned to her home. King Agamemnon has ignored all the pleas of her father," said Calchas. "Apollo, the lord of the silver bow, grows angrier each day. For Chryseis is the daughter of a priest. A priest of the god Apollo!"

King Agamemnon gripped the arms of his chair. "But Chryseis is a slave now, a prize of war! We raided many small cities for supplies to help us in our war against mighty Troy. Chryseis was taken along with weapons, cattle, and many prisoners," he scowled. "Am I to return her now? Am I to lose honor in the eyes of my men?" Then he looked long into the troubled faces of his officers.

"Very well!" he roared at last. "To save men's lives, I will give her up. But I will not give up my honor! You must find me an equal prize now!"

At this, yellow-haired Achilles stepped forward. "Great king," said the young man. "How can this be? All the prizes have been given out. It wouldn't be right to take them back. Wait until we capture the city of Troy, and you will be repaid with treasure three times over!"

The king jumped to his feet. "No!" he shouted angrily. "I won't be cheated. Chryseis will be sent back. Then I'll take a prize from Achilles or another Greek general!"

"What?" cried Achilles. "For almost ten years now we've been battling the Trojans. We keep fighting to win back Helen, your brother's wife. Many of our warriors have perished since the day she was stolen from Greece by Prince Paris of Troy. These heroes fell trying to help you and your brother. And I, the son of a goddess, fought bravely along with them. Now you threaten to rob me of a prize and my honor? Well, I won't stay here and be dishonored. My men and I shall return to our homes in Greece!"

"Go ahead! Run away with your company of spearmen! I have other warriors here to fight for me," bellowed the king. "But know this! I will take one of your prizes! I'll have the slave girl Briseis taken from you this very day. You may be a great hero with strength from the gods, but I am a king! I will be obeyed!"

Shaking with wrath, the powerful youth clutched his sword. But at that moment, Minerva, the helmeted goddess of wisdom appeared. She was visible only to Achilles. Tugging his golden hair, she said, "Use your reason! I was sent here by Juno, queen of the gods. She cares for you and the king alike. Now unhand your sword, Achilles. Fight only with words!"

Nodding in agreement, the angry youth turned to the king. "Do as you wish, you stuffed wine-skin!" he shouted. "From this day on the Greeks will get no help from me. Nor will they get help from my men. From the doorway of my hut, I'll watch the war. And you, old dogface, will regret the insult you gave me this day!"

When the stars came out that night, Achilles paced beside the dark sea. There he called out for his mother, Thetis, a sea-goddess. Soon she appeared in her silver sandals. Carefully she listened to her unhappy son, whose father was King Peleus, a mortal.

"Mother, help me! Go to the king of the gods for me. Surely Jove owes you a favor. For it was you who brought him the hundred-handed giant for protection. This stopped the gods who were seeking to bind Jove in chains," said Achilles. "Plead with Jove for me. Ask him to give help to the Trojans now. Then the Greeks will see how much they need me!"

Filled with love for her son, Thetis flew up to Mount Olympus. There she pleaded with Jove, the bringer of clouds. "Help the Trojans," she begged. "Help them until the Greeks give Achilles the honor owed to him." And mighty Jove nodded his head in solemn promise, causing all of Mount Olympus to shake.

When Thetis was gone, Juno hurried to her husband's side. "What did you promise her?" she snapped. "Are you settling things behind my back?"

Jove glared at his wife. "Hold your tongue!" he thundered. "Stop nagging me!" And Juno backed away as Jove smiled to himself. He knew it was wise to keep his promise a secret from white-armed Juno. He realized that both Juno and bright-eyed Minerva hated all Trojans. These goddesses were still angry with Prince Paris of Troy. For Paris hadn't chosen either of them as the winner in a beauty contest held years before.

Some other gods sided with the Trojans. Among these were Apollo and Venus, the goddess of love and beauty. Indeed, it was Venus who had been chosen as the winner in the famous beauty contest. And it was she who had helped Prince Paris steal Helen away from her home in Greece.

So the great war continued with the gods taking sides as they pleased. Many brave Trojans and Greeks fell in the terrible battles. Yet Achilles remained true to his word. He lifted no weapon to fight. From the doorway of his hut he just watched the fierce battles raging before high-towered Troy.

There were large stretches of flat land in front of the walled city. Most of the fighting took place on these windy plains. Beyond the plains was the sparkling blue sea. Anchored along the shore were a thousand ships, fifty of which belonged to Achilles. And along the shore were the huts of the Greek warriors who fought the Trojans, who were known as the tamers of horses.

The mightiest of the horse-taming Trojans was Prince Hector. On this sunny morning he stood speaking to his slim wife, Andromache, inside the city gates. A nurse standing nearby held the couple's baby son. Sadly she watched as Hector took his dark-haired wife into his arms. Neither Hector nor Andromache knew that Achilles was no longer fighting.

"Oh, my dear husband! Your great courage will destroy you! Don't go out to face dread Achilles," wept Andromache. "He slew my father and seven brothers. Do not make our little child fatherless!"

The long crest of horsehair on Hector's bronze helmet swayed as he shook his head. "My love, I must go. Am I not a prince of Troy? I must try to win glory for King Priam and for myself, though in my heart I feel that Troy will fall one day. And yet, dear wife, my greatest fear is for you. I'd rather die than see you taken away in chains as a slave!"

Then Hector turned and reached for his tiny son. But the baby began crying loudly. The fiercely nodding plume on Hector's bright helmet had frightened the infant. Quickly the warrior removed the helmet covering his curly hair. Very gently then, he rocked the sobbing child in his powerful arms. Soon the baby began to smile. After that, Hector handed his son to Andromache who was trying hard to smile through her tears. Then Hector, joined by his brother Paris, raced through the city gates and out into battle. And many a young life was lost in the savage fighting before night fell and both sides agreed to a truce for the next day.

The truce gave each army time to burn and bury its dead so that the souls of fallen heroes might enter the underworld. The Greeks also used some time to build a long wall to protect their ships. In front of the stone wall there ran a wide trench with sharp stakes sticking up to hold back Trojan chariots.

On the next day, when Morning in her orange and yellow robes began lighting the world, Jove called a meeting of the gods. With his promise to Thetis in mind, he spoke firmly to the gods standing before his golden throne. "Listen well! You are not to help either the Greeks or the Trojans. Be careful now! Don't cross me," he warned. "Those who disobey me will be hurled down from Olympus!"

Jove then stepped into his gleaming chariot and went racing through the clouds. The lord of the skies stopped at last at his sweet-smelling altar high on Mount Ida, a mountain not far from Troy.

Seated on Mount Ida, he watched the battle between the horse-taming Trojans and the bronze-coated Greeks. Then at noon he lifted a golden scale and held it by the middle. Into a pan on one side of the balance he dropped a weight for the Greeks. Next he dropped a weight for the Trojans into the pan on the other side. The fate of the Greeks went down! For the Fates, three ancient and wrinkled goddesses, who control men's destinies and decide when each person will die, had made their decision. Many Greeks were to perish that day! So mighty Jove pushed back his long sleeves and hurled giant thunderbolts through the air. They went crashing down among the startled Greeks.

Joy filled Hector's heart. "Even the king of the gods is for us today," he laughed. "He'll give us glory in battle. Bring fire! We'll send the whole fleet up in flames!" Then shouting fiercely, Hector and his forces went charging forward. They did very great damage that day, but they didn't succeed in destroying the ships. Night fell, ending the battle. And the Trojans, after building a thousand watch fires that shone like the bright stars in the silent sky above, waited eagerly for the dawn.

That night, King Agamemnon called for an assembly of the Greek leaders. After spilling wine on the ground as a drink offering to the gods, they feasted well and then discussed their problems. Finally, they all agreed on one important point. They needed the help of mighty Achilles!

## II. Hector Makes His Move

Ulysses, a great warrior, was sent with two other men to the young champion's hut. There they found Achilles sitting and playing a lyre. His closest friend Patroclus sat nearby listening to the song about the glory of famous heroes. Dark-haired Patroclus looked sad because he knew that Achilles wanted to be out winning glory in battle. Patroclus was also sad because he had hoped that Achilles would one day marry the beautiful captive Briseis and live a long and happy life with her. But Agamemnon had taken her away from Achilles.

Then Patroclus looked up and saw the visitors. Quickly he and Achilles stood up. "All hail and welcome," exclaimed Achilles happily. However, his joy upon seeing his old friends was not to last for long.

Ulysses, stroking his curly beard, explained the reason for their visit. "Great Achilles, we've come to ask for your help," he said. "King Agamemnon sent us here. He says that the slave Briseis will be returned to you. He asks you to forgive him and accept his gifts. He offers much gold, twelve prizewinning horses, and other treasures! He also offers one of his daughters as your wife, and seven cities in Greece as a wedding present!"

Achilles lowered his thick eyebrows. "I'll hear no more! That hound doesn't dare look me in the face," he exclaimed angrily. "Well, he won't trick me. He can't undo his wrongs with gifts! Nothing will move me until I've had revenge for what he has done to me!"

Achilles paced about as he went on. "Let him keep his treasures and his daughter! If the gods let me return home, my father will find me a lovely bride. And it will be long before death overtakes me there," he said. "My mother, Thetis, has told me that if I stay here, I'll win glory and an immortal name. But my life will be cut short!"

The visitors listened in silence for a while. Before long, however, they began pleading with Achilles to return to battle to help save their lives. But Achilles stood his ground. "Enough!" he shouted. "For as long as I remain here, I will never fight until horse-taming Hector comes to my own ships with fire! Now go back and tell the king all that I've said!"

When Agamemnon heard the news he paced alone beneath the stars for a long time. Tears filled his eyes and he tore his long hair as he prayed to Jove for some help.

The next morning, Hector donned his armor and went to speak to other leaders of companies of men. One of the leaders was the tall and handsome Sarpedon. He was the king of Lycia, and an ally of the Trojans. Sarpedon was also the favorite mortal son of Jove himself!

Soon the Trojan warriors went charging forward like a great storm cloud, and loud were their shouts! Upon reaching the trench, Hector and some others leaped from their chariots and made their way on foot to the wall that the Greeks had built. There they began pounding on the doors in the wall as spears rained down around them.

Glancing down, Jove saw Hector trying to lift a very heavy stone. Smiling, the thunderer filled the tamer of horses with extra strength. Then Hector lifted the stone as though it were just a handful of sheep's wool, and hurled it. The huge stone crashed through, and the doors flew open! Hector and his men roared mightily and went charging toward some nearby ships.

Neptune, ruler of the seas, saw what was happening and felt pity for the Greeks. Besides that, he was angry with Jove, his bossy older brother. So Neptune disguised himself as the prophet Calchas and spoke to some of Agamemnon's greatest warriors, filling them with daring. Then, a while later, Neptune let out a terrible roar! It sounded like the voices of ten thousand Greek warriors! The earthshaking noise filled all the Greeks with new courage, and the battle soon began turning against the Trojans.

All this delighted Juno who was watching from afar. She hoped to keep her husband from giving further help to the Trojans. So she hurried to see Sleep, the brother of Death. She promised Sleep a beautiful wife if he would help her make Jove fall asleep. Anxious for a lovely bride, Sleep agreed. Then Juno rushed off to see Jove and, before long, he was asleep in his wife's arms. However, when Jove awakened and saw what was happening in the war, he became very angry. Shaking his fist, he accused his wife of trickery.

"Don't blame me," cried Juno, trembling. "Neptune's actions have nothing to do with me. Why, if he were to ask me for advice, I'd always tell him to do just as my dear husband commands!"

Hearing this, the furious bringer of clouds grew calmer. Then he sent for one of his messengers, fair-haired Iris, goddess of the rainbow. "Go, fleet Iris," he said. "Tell Neptune to stop interfering or dare to face my wrath!"

After that, Jove sent the healer Apollo down to give Hector back his strength and to help the Trojans. Laughing with pleasure, Apollo kicked down the banks of the trench, filling it with earth. As the Trojans rushed over the filled-in ditch, Apollo smashed down the great wall. It fell as easily as the sand castles kicked down by children at the seashore.

Like a great wave, the Trojans in their chariots went rolling over the remains of the wall. Reaching the ships, the Trojans hurled their double-edged spears at the Greeks who were bravely defending their fleet. And many a Greek wished that Achilles were there to help them!

# III. Achilles Thinks Again

Things were going badly for the Greeks with the Trojans attacking their ships. It was then that a Greek warrior hurried to see his great friend, Achilles, with a bold idea. "Let me wear your famous armor," begged Patroclus. "The Trojans will think you've returned to battle. Surely they'll run off in fear. This will help us gain the time we need to arm ourselves anew. Many lives and ships will be saved!"

Achilles stared out toward the ships. He could see red flames and dark smoke against the sky. He thought about his fallen friends, and about the danger to his own ships. Turning then, he declared, "All right, noble friend! Put on my armor! Take my immortal horses, a gift to me from the gods. Lead my men and strike terror into the hearts of the Trojans! But when you have driven them from the ships, return here. Do not push on to the walls of Troy or a god may destroy you!"

Not long after that, the Trojans saw something flashing in the sunlight. It was the gold, silver, and bronze armor of mighty Achilles. Howling in fear, many Trojans turned to flee. Patroclus and Achilles' fierce spearmen went swarming over them like angry wasps. And Patroclus sprang down from his chariot to face the fearless Sarpedon. Like great eagles they flew at each other as Jove watched from on high. But he lifted no hand to save his favorite mortal son. Jove knew that the Fates had decided that his son was to perish that day. And Jove lowered his head sadly when Sarpedon fell like a tall oak tree in full bloom.

Then Patroclus began pursuing the Trojans across the plains, for Jove had put this into the warrior's mind. Ignoring Achilles' warning, Patroclus did what Achilles had warned him not to do. He pushed on to the walls of Troy! And there he tried three times to climb the walls, but each time Apollo pushed back the man's bright shield.

On the warrior's fourth try, Apollo shouted, "Go back! It's not for you to take Troy, nor for Achilles who is a better man than you!" And so Patroclus returned to his chariot, while Apollo flew off to see Hector.

Hector and his driver were standing in their chariot just outside a distant city gate. Hector was wondering whether to go on fighting or to lead his men back into the city. However, just at that moment, Apollo appeared disguised as one of Hector's uncles.

"Hector!" called the god. "Drive straight toward that man, for it is Patroclus, not Achilles! Apollo may grant you a victory!"

At this, the joyful Hector and his charioteer went racing through the dust. Patroclus, thirsty for battle and glory, saw this and sprang down from his chariot. He hurled a stone and struck Hector's driver. The man tumbled lifeless into the swirling dust.

Hector leaped down from his chariot to claim his driver's body. But Patroclus sprang forward to do battle. Soon Hector and Patroclus were surrounded by many other battling warriors. Wild cries and groans filled the air!

Patroclus was doing very well. But before long, Jove sent Apollo to step in. Apollo covered himself in dark mist so that Patroclus couldn't see him. The god then struck off the warrior's helmet, and smiled as it went rattling across the ground. After that, Apollo snapped the fighter's spear in two and sent his shield crashing to the ground.

Seeing this, a Trojan soldier hurled a spear and struck Patroclus in the back. Then Hector thrust his spear forward. Groaning, Patroclus fell to the earth with a loud thud. Some Greeks immediately rushed forward to carry off the fallen hero. They wanted to give his body to the flames and then hold chariot races and other funeral games in his honor. But the Trojans fought wildly to stop them, and Hector rode off with Achilles' famous armor. And so sad were all these events that tears flowed from the eyes of Achilles' immortal horses.

Upon hearing the news, Achilles was filled anew with wrath. His loud cries were heard by Thetis. The sea-goddess quickly appeared before Achilles. "My son!" she cried. "What sorrow fills your heart?"

The great warrior wept as he spoke. "Hector has slain noble Patroclus! And even now the tamer of horses wears my armor!" he groaned. "Alas, so many of my fine comrades have fallen just because I wasn't there to help them! Oh, mother, I must make peace with Agamemnon and return to the war. Hector and the Trojans must pay for what they have done!"

Tears filled the blue eyes of the goddess. For she knew a terrible truth! She knew that soon after the fall of Hector, her own son must fall. Weeping, she told this to Achilles, but he wouldn't change his mind. Then she sighed deeply, and had Achilles promise not to fight until she returned with new armor for him. Moments later, she flew up to Vulcan, the god of fire, at his blazing forge on Mount Olympus. There Vulcan promised the tearful Thetis new armor for Achilles.

In the meantime, Juno sent Iris to see Achilles. Jove was busy elsewhere so he didn't know the goddesses were acting behind his back.

"You have no armor now," said the goddess of the rainbow. "Yet just your appearance in the field will frighten off the Trojans. Even now they are trying to take away the body of noble Patroclus. The fallen hero must not become meat for the dogs of Troy! Shame on you if you don't do something about it right now!"

Hearing this, Achilles rushed forward on his powerful legs. All about his head and shoulders shone a blazing golden light, placed there by the goddess Minerva. Then Achilles stood near the filled-in ditch and watched the fighting from afar. His glowing appearance caused the Trojans to tremble. And when his voice and that of Minerva roared aloud, the Trojans rushed away in terror.

Later on, some Greek warriors carried the body of Patroclus back to the camp. And there Achilles and the other Greek warriors mourned deeply for the fallen hero.

# IV. The New Achilles

The fighting continued on the wide and windy plains. Achilles, splendid in his new armor, had rejoined the Greeks who now honored him greatly. His armor flashed like streaks of blazing lightning. His great shield, showing scenes of the world in times of peace and war, gleamed as brightly as the moon.

Achilles battled fiercely, as did many of the gods. For Jove had sent word that the gods could now take part in the war. Juno, Minerva, Neptune, and other gods helped the Greeks. Among those aiding the Trojans were Apollo, Venus, and Mars, the god of war.

During one great battle, Achilles struck down Hector's youngest brother. The youth had foolishly run to the front of the battle just to show how fast he could move. Seeing him fall, Hector grew wild with anger and rushed forward like a flame of fire! Bravely he hurled his spear right at Achilles. However, Minerva just breathed lightly on the spear and sent it flying back to land at Hector's feet.

The furious Achilles then sprang forward, thrusting with his spear. But Apollo quickly lifted Hector away, covering him in a blanket of dark mist.

"Dog! You have escaped me this time," roared the angry champion. "But I will seek you out and make an end of you! You shall not escape my wrath!"

After that, Achilles kept striking down one Trojan after another as he made his way ever closer to the walls of Troy. King Priam groaned aloud as he looked down from the walls at the fleeing Trojans. "Open the gates!" he shouted. "Let our warriors into the city!"

Then Apollo disguised himself as a Trojan soldier and rushed onto the plain. He kept Achilles busy chasing after him, and this gave escaping Trojans just enough time to reach the city gates. And every Trojan whose feet could carry him went rushing into the city. Only Hector remained outside.

Priam watched as Achilles came into view. The old king could hardly believe his eyes. As swift as a prizewinning horse, the fleet-footed man came tearing over the plain! In his bright armor, he rushed forward as radiant as a star. A blazing star that threatened Troy with its fire!

"Oh, my son!" Priam called out to Hector. "Don't face dread Achilles! Come into the city!" The king began tearing at his grey hair. And Hector's aging mother Hecuba prayed and cried aloud in her great distress.

But Hector's mind was elsewhere. "Fool that I was!" he groaned. "I should have listened to my counselor's advice. He told me to call back my men when Achilles returned to battle. But I was too filled with pride in my own strength. Alas, I have brought destruction to my people! Now, in all honor, I must remain here to face Achilles, man to man!"

Troubled and alone, Hector then thought to himself, "Perhaps I can reason with Achilles! Perhaps I should offer to have Helen sent back to her people." But Hector soon realized that such thoughts were useless now, for Achilles was racing straight toward him.

Hector's sweat began running cold. Suddenly he turned and ran faster than he'd ever run before. Like a dove pursued by a falcon he flew. But swift-footed Achilles followed close behind as the Greeks, held back by Achilles' command, watched from the plains.

Hector's heart was beating wildly. On and on he ran like a deer pursued by a hound. Three times Hector raced around the city walls. Then he began to slow down. "I can't keep on running," he gasped. "I must stand and fight." Bright beads of sweat rolled down his face and arms.

The exhausted man stood away from the walls, waiting for Achilles. Suddenly Hector heard a friendly voice calling out to him. He looked around in surprise and saw one of his many brothers standing there.

"I've come to help you," said the young man. "I have some mighty weapons. Together we can bring Achilles down!"

Hector was filled with new spirit. "Yes, my brave brother!" he

cried aloud. Then he turned and watched as Achilles came rushing ever closer.

"Achilles! Let us agree on this," shouted Hector. "If I take your life from you, I will send your body back to your people. Do the same for me!"

Achilles stared angrily. "There can be no promises between men and lions," he growled. "Wolves and lambs can only hate each other!" Then Achilles raised his famous bronze-pointed spear. It was so heavy that only he could hurl it. The gleaming weapon went flying over Hector's head as the prince crouched low. Then Minerva, unseen by Hector, swiftly returned the great spear to Achilles.

Hector stood up and sent his own spear whistling through the air. It crashed against Achilles' bright shield and fell ringing to the earth. However, Hector stood his ground.

"Give me another spear, good brother!" Hector shouted over his shoulder. When no one answered him, Hector looked around and discovered that he was alone. At once he guessed the truth! The gods had led him there. And Minerva, wearing a disguise, had tricked him!

Hector pulled himself up tall. "Doomed!" he shouted. "But I won't fall without a struggle!" Raising his flashing sword, he flew forward like an eagle swooping down out of the sky. But it was too late!

Achilles' great spear came tearing through the air and struck the prince. Hector, the tamer of horses, sank to the earth. Groaning, he looked up at Achilles. "I pray you to send my body home," he gasped. "Let the Trojans give me to the funeral flames. Let me enter the underworld with honor."

But Achilles shook his head fiercely. "Dog! That shall never be!" he roared.

At this, Hector groaned anew. "You have an iron heart!" he said as he fell back. Then with his dying breath he spoke some chilling words. "Beware, for I may become the gods' curse upon you! Before this war is over, you will meet Paris and angry Apollo at the gates of Troy. And on that day you too will fall!"

Achilles just stared at the dead man. "So let it be!" he cried. Then he looked back over his shoulder as loud cries came from the walls of Troy. The Trojans were weeping and wailing for Hector. Their sad cries went echoing over the windy plains.

Moving swiftly, Achilles tore the famous armor from Hector's shoulders. Then he tied the Trojan's feet to the back of his chariot. After that, Achilles did something terrible to see. He dragged Hector's body through the dust before the walls of Troy as the Trojans screamed and wept. And the horrified people then watched as Achilles raced back to his camp with the lifeless Hector.

The Greeks cheered for their champion. However, Achilles' actions didn't please Jove at all. For Hector had always given Jove proper sacrifice and all due honor. Greatly angered, the thunderer called Thetis before him. "Tell your son that I am displeased!" he commanded. "Tell him that he is to give up Hector's body. Achilles is to accept the ransom that someone will bring to him!"

Of course, silver-footed Thetis did as Jove ordered. Her son listened quietly to her words. He didn't like what he heard. But at last, he said, "So be it! Jove must be obeyed. I will accept the ransom in exchange for the fallen Hector."

In the meantime, Jove sent for his messenger. He ordered Mercury to bring Hector's father, King Priam, safely into the Greek camp. So Mercury in his winged sandals threw the camp guards into a deep sleep. Then he opened the gates and let Priam and his driver slip through with the wagon heaped with treasure.

A short time later, Hector's father walked alone into Achilles' hut. The young warrior quickly realized that the gods had brought Priam there.

Falling to his knees, Priam kissed the hand of the Greek champion. "Oh, great Achilles, fear the wrath of the gods," moaned Priam. "Think of your own father and have pity on me. Accept the ransom I bring and let me take my fallen son back to Troy."

Achilles stared at the old man. He began thinking about his own grey-haired father who would never see his only child again. Then Achilles wept long with the king, for they were united in sorrow.

After that, Achilles took the old man's hand and lifted him to his feet. "Unhappy Priam, let us now hide our sorrows in our hearts. Weeping will not help us, for the gods spin the threads of life for unfortunate mortals," he said. "Soon, even my aging father must suffer greatly. And I won't be there to care for him as he grows older!"

Achilles sighed deeply and then went on. "Alas, I must stay here at Troy and bring more sorrow to you and your troubled children."

A short time later, Achilles went outside to Priam's wagon. With two friends he took down the great treasure. Then Achilles himself gently lifted the fallen Hector upon the wagon. After that, he went inside to Priam. There he served a meal to the old man, and had a bed with woolen blankets prepared for him.

"Now bear up, Priam," said Achilles. "You may take your son away with you in the morning. I'll give you as many days as you may need for the funeral games." So saying, he took Priam's right hand in his own to calm any fears the aged king might have.

Before daybreak, Old Priam left the Greek camp. In silence he rode in the wagon over the wide and windy plains toward Troy. There the unhappy king would arrange for the funeral games to honor his fallen son, Hector, the tamer of horses.

# QUESTING FOR INFORMATION

## A. Getting the Main Idea and Facts

Write the letter of the answer that best completes each statement.

1. This story is mainly about how _____ .
   a. a Trojan hero's wife feared for her child's safety
   b. a Greek hero defeated a famous Trojan hero
   c. a Greek hero's behavior brought sorrow to many

2. Achilles believed that King Agamemnon was robbing him of ___ .
   a. a wedding gift     b. his honor     c. his fleet of ships

3. Minerva urged Achilles to use _____ and words in his fight with King Agamemnon.
   a. a silver bow     b. his fighting men     c. reason

4. Hector, the tamer of horses, took Achilles' famous _____ .
   a. bronze-pointed spear     b. armor     c. immortal horses

5. Jove sent King Priam to Achilles' hut with _____ .
   a. new armor     b. Apollo     c. ransom

## B. Going Beyond the Facts

Write the letter of the answer that best completes each statement.

1. We may infer that Agamemnon feared _____ .
   a. falling low in his men's opinion
   b. losing seven cities in Greece
   c. taking a war prize from Achilles

2. We may conclude that Jove made his promise to Thetis because _____ .
   a. he wanted to please his wife
   b. Thetis had him bound in chains
   c. he was grateful to Thetis

3. We can probably conclude that Ulysses and the other men who asked Achilles for help felt that Achilles was _____ .
   a. greedy for more gifts
   b. acting wisely
   c. being unreasonable

4. Jove was probably feeling quite _____ when he caused Patroclus to go riding toward the walls of Troy.
   a. merry and playful
   b. angry and unhappy
   c. worried and confused

5. Probably, Achilles held the Greeks back while he was chasing Hector because Achilles _____ .
   a. wished to give Hector a fair chance to win
   b. feared the Trojans would return and attack his men
   c. wanted to win all the glory for defeating Hector

## QUESTING FOR MEANINGS

Write the letter of the word that best completes each sentence below.

a. wrath    b. truce    c. dread    d. fleet    e. ransom

1. In order to discuss peace terms, the generals declared a three-day _____ .

2. The _____ runner almost lost the race when he tripped.

3. A large _____ was demanded for the return of the prize dog.

4. The neighborhood children _____ passing the deserted house at night.

5. Filled with _____ , the fearless man pursued the thief until he caught him.

## QUESTING FOR UNDERSTANDING

1. Explain in what specific ways Achilles' great pride and wrath hurt each of the following:
a. the Greeks    b. the Trojans    c. his parents    d. himself

2. For a while, Achilles was concerned with only his own problems and feelings. Discuss when and why he changed and began to show concern and compassion for the suffering of others.

## QUESTING FOR ENRICHMENT

A. In this story you read this sentence about Hector: "He ran like a deer pursued by a hound." Comparisons between two different things (man and deer) using as or like are called similes. Complete these similes from the story by writing the letters for the following words and phrases.

a. dove    b. tall oak tree in full bloom    c. angry wasps
d. star    e. prizewinning horse

1. Patroclus and his men swarmed over the Trojans like _____ .
2. Sarpedon, mortal son of Jove, fell like a _____ .
3. As swift as a _____ , Achilles tore over the plains.
4. In his bright armor, Achilles rushed forward as radiant as a _____ .
5. Like a _____ pursued by a falcon, Hector flew from Achilles.

    B. Write a diary entry of a paragraph or two as one of the following characters.

1. Achilles after his argument with King Agamemnon
2. Andromache after Hector calmed their child and left for battle
3. A Trojan man, woman, or child after seeing Hector's battle with Achilles
4. Achilles after he spoke to King Priam

# The Horse of Doom and the Ghosts of Troy

Greek and Trojan forces suffered heavy losses in a long war which began in about 1100 B.C. when a Trojan prince (Paris) stole the wife (Helen) of a Greek king. The Trojans lost their chief warrior, Prince Hector. And the Greeks lost their greatest hero, Achilles, when an arrow struck his heel, his only weak spot.

The following tale concerning the end of the Trojan War is based on a story from the *Aeneid,* an epic written about 29-19 B.C. by the Roman poet Virgil. Here now is a tale in which a mysterious fire that does not burn helps save an old man's life.

## Major Characters

**Laocoön** a priest of the god Neptune

**Priam** king of Troy

**Sinon** a Greek soldier

**Aeneas** a Trojan hero, son of Venus

**Cassandra** daughter of Priam

**Pyrrhus** Greek warrior

**Anchises** father of Aeneas

**Creusa** wife of Aeneas

## Vocabulary Preview

**determined** having one's mind firmly made up about something
The girls were *determined* to win the medal for their team.

**suspicious** feeling something is wrong
Mr. Jones was *suspicious* of the stranger near the deserted house.

**prophecy** a prediction or telling of things to come
The wise man's *prophecy* was that a great hero would soon appear and help save the land.

**confusion** a mixed-up condition
There was great *confusion* at the picnic as people ran for shelter from the sudden storm.

**occurred** took place; happened
An eclipse of the moon *occurred* last month.

28

# I. A Strange Gift from the Greeks

Leaning on their spears, the weary guards yawned as they stood on the high wall surrounding their city of Troy. Watching for a night attack, the men peered at the dark plain which stretched down to the sea.

They were glad when the light of rosy-fingered Dawn began to appear. Soon the morning light filled the wide plains between the walled city and the distant sea, and the guards rubbed their eyes in wonder. Where were the thousands of Greek warriors? Where were the Greek ships in the sparkling blue harbor?

"Our enemies are gone!" the men shouted. "At last the long war is over! But what is that huge, horselike creature standing where the Greeks were camped?"

Many Trojans heard the joyful shouts. Suddenly awakened at daybreak, they rushed outside. In their bare feet hundreds of people began climbing stone steps and steep ladders to look out over the walls. "It's true! It's true!" shouted many of them with tears in their eyes. But even as they laughed and cried for joy, they wondered about the huge and unmoving horse that stood in the distance.

Then for the first time in many years, the joyful Trojans opened the city gates wide. Laughing and chattering, they hurried over the great plain until they reached the immense creature.

"Why, the horse is made of wood!" exclaimed an old man, leaning on his walking stick. "A marvelous thing! Let's take it into our city to remember this wonderful day!"

However, some Trojans began crying out against this idea. "Push it into the sea!" cried some. "Burn it!" cried others. And still others shouted, "Tear it apart and look inside!"

At that very moment, a bearded man came rushing through the crowds. People quickly stepped aside to let Laocoön pass, for he was a priest of the god Neptune. The priest's two young sons ran along beside him.

Staring hard, Laocoön was very suspicious of the wooden creature. "Beware! This must be a trick!" he shouted. "It wouldn't surprise me if there were Greek warriors hiding in this monster! I fear these Greeks even when bearing gifts!" Then he lifted a long spear as people gasped aloud. The spear went whistling through the air and struck the horse's wooden belly, and a sound of clashing metal rang out!

For a few moments, the Trojans stood wondering what to do next. But soon they forgot all about the strange sound as two young

Trojans appeared nearby. They were leading a young man with his hands bound behind him. At once, the crowd surrounded these men and began shouting for the stranger to speak.

Shaking from head to foot, the long-haired stranger stood before King Priam. "My name is Sinon. My fellow Greeks wanted to be sure of a safe journey home," he wept. "So they were planning to slay me as a sacrifice to the gods. But I escaped during the night and hid among the reeds in a pond!"

The crowd pressed closer as Sinon went on. "My fellow Greeks were going to kill me!" he groaned. "Now I shall never see my loving family or my home again." At this, the young man began sobbing loudly.

King Priam was deeply moved by Sinon's tears. "Have no fear; you won't be harmed. You may live here in Troy with us," he said. "But now, young man, tell us why your people made this huge horse and left it on our shores."

Sinon smiled gratefully. "The goddess Minerva was angry because some Greek warriors did not honor her properly. So my people made this great war horse as a peace offering for Minerva. They knew it would please the goddess," he explained. "But they made it very large so that you could never take it into your city. For if you did that, your people would surely be protected from harm!"

Upon hearing this, many Trojans began smiling and nodding at each other. "Then let's claim it for our own," a man declared. "Let's take the horse into Troy, even if we have to cut a hole in the city wall!"

The excited Trojans stood talking over the idea, but they soon became silent when a strange sight appeared on the troubled sea. From a nearby island two immense serpents were making their way over the foaming waters. Their heads were raised high above the waves as they raced along, and their blood-red eyes glowed like fire!

The Trojans screamed and ran off in terror as the creatures came slipping and sliding along the shore. But the serpents didn't chase after them. The serpents went racing straight toward Laocoön's two sons!

Swiftly the monsters twisted themselves around the horrified youths. Straining every muscle, Laocoön struggled wildly to save his children. But the serpents just kept twisting themselves ever more tightly around the man and his sons. Terrible screams filled the air! But after a while, the screams grew fainter and fainter until, at last, the victims fell lifeless to the ground. Quickly then the serpents turned

and went gliding up to a statue of Minerva in a temple on a nearby hill. There they hid under the great shield that lay at her feet.

Gasping, the Trojans slowly began recovering from their shock. "Laocoön was punished!" shouted some people. "He dared to hurl a spear at Minerva's wooden horse!"

Feeling better, the Trojans rushed off to get ropes and wheels. Then they worked for hour after hour as the burning sun beat down on them. Sweat rolled down their backs and arms. And more than once as they worked, the sound of clashing metal came from inside the horse. Yet the Trojans, wild with excitement, just kept tugging and pulling at the long ropes until their efforts were rewarded. That evening the giant horse stood inside their city!

Singing and dancing wildly, the Trojans were filled with joy. They gave no further thought to wild-eyed Cassandra, Priam's daughter who had the gift of prophecy. Earlier she had warned them that taking the horse into Troy would bring doom to the city! But a god had kept them from believing her prophecy.

So on and on the Trojans danced until bright stars began filling the sky. Then the tired people settled down to rest with peace in their hearts, and soon they were enjoying the sweet first hours of sleep.

However, there was one man who remained wide awake. It was Sinon! He knew that the Greeks who had been waiting on a nearby island were already sailing back to Troy in the silent moonlight. Watching from the city wall, Sinon saw the signal fire blazing from one of the ships. Quickly then he hurried down to the wooden creature. He climbed the horse of doom, opened a secret door, and watched as fierce warriors came sliding down long ropes. Before long, a few of these men ran to throw open the city gates.

Soon wild screams began to fill the night air. "Wake up! Wake up! The Greeks have returned!" voices called out in terror. "Wake up! The Greeks are destroying our city!"

Mothers clutched their frightened children and searched for hiding places. Old people stumbled about, crying for mercy. There was great noise and confusion everywhere!

Thousands of Greek troops came charging through the open gates. And before long, the city was in flames. Bitter smoke rose toward the stars. And sounds of weeping filled the night air as unlucky Trojans were slain or dragged off in chains.

## II.  A Doomed City

While Troy was being destroyed, one Trojan hero was still asleep. Sandy-haired Aeneas slept on soundly until the spirit of Hector, a fallen prince of Troy, appeared to him in a dream.

"Awake now," called the ghostly voice. "Awake now, mortal son of the goddess Venus! Troy is finished! You must journey across the sea. Build a new Troy there! Farewell, my friend. Farewell. . . ." And the vision of Hector faded away.

Greatly troubled, Aeneas leaped from his bed. "Hector! Prince Hector!" he called. When no one answered him, he seized his armor and ran to the rooftop to look out over the city. Filled with horror, he saw flames sweeping through Troy just as windswept fire goes racing wildly through a field of corn!

Eager for glory, the angry warrior rushed down into the smoke-filled street. There he ran into some brave men on their way to fight the invaders. At once Aeneas became the leader of the Trojans as they went dashing forward.

Before long they surprised a group of Greek warriors and quickly cut them down. Then, disguised in the bronze armor of the fallen Greeks, the band of Trojans again went dashing on like a pack of wild and hungry wolves.

A few minutes later, the Trojans stopped short in their tracks upon seeing a truly pitiful sight. Greek warriors were dragging a young woman with streaming golden hair from a temple. It was the lovely Cassandra, and her hands were bound with chains!

"Cassandra, my love!" shouted one of Aeneas's men. This dark-eyed youth had always hoped to make Cassandra his wife! Filled with rage, he charged forward with his friends close behind him. But then a terrible thing occurred. Trojans on roofs of nearby buildings began hurling spears and stones down at Aeneas and his men, for they were still wearing Greek armor! And the youth who loved Cassandra was the first of many to fall. Before long, more Greeks arrived, and soon there were too many for Aeneas and his few remaining men to handle.

Aeneas realized that all was lost in this street battle. So upon hearing terrible shouts in the distance, he rushed away to see what was happening at King Priam's palace. There he saw many Greeks holding great shields over their heads as they climbed tall ladders. They were trying to get to the roof of the locked palace. And sweating Trojans on the roof kept showering stones and tiles down on the determined invaders.

Quickly then, Aeneas slipped into the palace by a hidden door. He hurried to the roof and began helping to hold back the enemy. At one point, the powerful man helped push over a very tall tower and send it crashing down on some unlucky Greek warriors.

Shortly after that, Aeneas watched helplessly as Greek warriors rushed toward the palace gates. One of these men was Pyrrhus, a mighty youth whose armor shone like a snake's new skin flashing in the spring sunshine. Swinging a huge two-headed axe, Pyrrhus kept hacking at the palace gates until they went crashing down off their hinges.

Once inside the gates, Pyrrhus chopped through a great oak door that led to Priam's inner chambers. And the Greek forces then went rushing into the palace like a mighty river swollen into a raging flood.

Shouting fiercely, the invaders made their way toward a large court, a garden open to the sky in the center of the palace. There stood grey-haired Priam. Shaking with age and grief, the man was wearing the armor he'd worn as a young man. In his wrinkled hand, he held a spear to protect his loved ones. His wife and the other women of his household were huddled together near an altar like a flock of frightened doves in a storm.

At that moment, one of Priam's sons came running into the

garden. The youth was sorely wounded, and Pyrrhus was close behind him. As the wounded man rushed toward the altar, Pyrrhus cut him down before the eyes of his horrified parents.

"May the gods punish you!" shouted Priam, shaking with rage. "Oh, I know you, cruel Pyrrhus! You claim to be the son of the fallen Achilles, greatest of Greek heroes! But I say that you lie! Achilles would never have treated me this way. He showed me respect and honor!" Then the trembling king raised his spear and hurled it at Pyrrhus. But the weapon just struck the youth's shield weakly and fell useless to the ground.

At this Pyrrhus rushed forward. "Go ahead, Priam! Tell Achilles all about my wicked deeds," he snarled. "Tell him all about me when you meet him in the underworld!" Then he slew the unhappy old man, and left him headless and nameless on the ground.

Watching helplessly from the roof, Aeneas was sick at heart. He groaned aloud, and began thinking about his family waiting at home. Moving swiftly then, he climbed down into the palace and hurried through the halls. On his way, he turned and spotted Helen in a small room. She was weeping and hiding in the shadows beside an altar.

At once Aeneas raised his sword and rushed angrily toward her. But just then, a flash of golden light filled the air. In the center of the light stood the goddess Venus, mother of Aeneas. "No, my son," she said. "Helen is not to blame for the war. The gods themselves caused it. You must spare this woman, and fly to save your family! Remember your little son, and your old father. That dear old man cannot walk and needs your help. Go now, my child. I will keep you safe."

Aeneas stared in amazement as Venus disappeared from view. Then he turned and looked out once again at the city. He realized that once-proud Troy was falling like a giant tree hacked down from a lofty mountaintop.

With sorrow in his heart, he traveled swiftly along secret ways until he reached his family at home. "Gather the little statues of our household gods," he shouted. "Prepare to leave!"

But his old father just shook his head. "Leave me here, my son. Let me end my days here in my beloved Troy," Anchises insisted. And he would not listen to his family members begging him to join them in their flight.

However, something very unusual took place that soon made Anchises change his mind. A flame appeared over his little grandson's head and set the child's hair on fire! But the flames hurt neither the boy nor those who tried to put out the fire with their bare hands. At this, Anchises gasped and cried aloud, "Mighty Jove! If this is your work, send us another sign." And moments later, a loud crash of thunder was heard outside. Then a shooting star went gliding down among the trees on Mount Ida.

Anchises was overjoyed. "Surely the gods mean to keep our family line from perishing," he said. "I will follow where you lead, Aeneas!"

Not long after that, Aeneas was leading his family and some other Trojans away from harm. On his broad shoulders he carried his white-haired father, and he kept a tight grip on the hand of his little blond son. In time, the escaping Trojans were outside the city walls and deep into the woods near Mount Ida. They stopped to rest near a little temple among the trees. It was then that Aeneas missed his wife.

"Creusa! My Creusa is not here. She may be hurt!" he cried. "Wait here for me, my friends. I must go back and find her!"

Aeneas forgot all about his own safety. Bravely he rushed back into the burning city. Running through the streets he called his wife's name over and over again. And he stopped only when a white mist suddenly appeared and floated in the air above him. The mist slowly took the shape of a woman. It was Creusa!

Aeneas was too shocked to say a word. He just stood there and listened as the vision spoke softly. "Don't be troubled, my dear Aeneas. The gods decided that I was not to go with you. I was caught while trying to escape the enemy; now I am a spirit," she said. "Be brave, my love. Lead those who are waiting for you. Take them across the sea to the land where the Tiber River flows. There you will find a new wife, a royal bride. Start a new city in that land."

Weeping, Aeneas reached out to touch his beloved Creusa. But his arms passed right through the fading mist. "Be good to our child," sighed Creusa. "Love him always! Farewell." And then she vanished in the darkness.

With his head bowed low, the tearful man stumbled away. The bits of a great mystery were spinning around in his head. Why had he been chosen for this task? How was he to build a new Troy? Aeneas was now more worried than ever. Yet he felt that it was his duty to do as Venus and the ghosts of Troy had commanded.

Upon reaching the meeting place, he was pleased to see that many more Trojans had made their way there. Then looking back once more, he peered at the burning towers and crumbling walls of Troy. After that, he lifted his father onto his shoulders and took firm hold of his little son's trembling hand. "Let us begin our journey," he called out to his followers. And Aeneas sadly led his people away just as the morning star began shining brightly above Mount Ida.

## QUESTING FOR INFORMATION

### A. Getting the Main Idea and Facts

Write the letter of the answer that best completes each statement.

1. A modern-day headline that would best sum up this story is ___.
   a. Hero Leads Family to Safety
   b. Ghosts Appear to Young Warrior
   c. Clever Plan Destroys Great City

2. A young Greek warrior's life was spared by _____.
   a. Priam      b. Laocoön     c. Venus

3. Anchises left Troy _____.
   a. as a prisoner in chains
   b. on his son's shoulders
   c. with Venus

4. Aeneas returned to Troy and saw _____.
   a. Hector's ghost
   b. Helen in the shadows
   c. Creusa's ghost

5. Aeneas was told that he was to found a new city _____.
   a. on Troy's ashes      b. across the sea      c. near Mount Ida

### B. Going Beyond the Facts

Write the letter of the answer that best completes each statement.

1. We may conclude that Sinon _____.
   a. hoped to meet new friends in Troy
   b. wanted Priam's men to find him
   c. hated the Greeks for leaving him behind

2. We may infer that Aeneas had _____.
   a. never been inside the palace before
   b. just discovered the secret door that night
   c. some special knowledge about the palace

3. The word _____ best describes Priam's efforts in the palace garden.
   a. successful      b. heroic      c. amusing

4. The behavior of Venus reveals that this goddess could be _____.
   a. caring and just
   b. proud and selfish
   c. charming and jolly

5. Most probably, Aeneas was chosen to start a new city because he
   _____ .
   a. was kind to his old father
   b. was the child of a goddess
   c. showed no fear of ghosts

## QUESTING FOR MEANINGS

Write the letter of the word that best completes each statement below.
   a. prophecy    b. determined    c. confusion
   d. suspicious    e. occurred

1. The bank guard was _____ of the nervous man near the door.
2. Broken traffic lights caused great _____ on Main Street this morning.
3. "Did you see what _____?" asked the police officer.
4. Many people used to laugh at the _____ that human beings would fly someday.
5. Peter was _____ to break his old track record.

## QUESTING FOR UNDERSTANDING

1. Identify the characters who made the statements below. Discuss how each character was feeling at that time, and why this was so.
   a. "Beware! This must be a trick!"
   b. "Helen is not to blame for the war . . . you must spare this woman."
   c. "Be good to our child. Love him always."

2. Troy might have been saved from doom if the Trojans hadn't made certain mistakes. Recall and discuss in some detail at least three serious errors made by the Trojans.

## QUESTING FOR ENRICHMENT

A. The English language makes use of many words borrowed from other languages, including Greek and Latin. For example, the

English word *flame* was derived from the Latin word *flamma*. Write the letter of the Latin word in column B from which we get the English word in column A. Then do the same for the Greek and English words in columns C and D. Write each number with its letter on your paper.

| **A**<br>(English) | **B**<br>(Latin) |
|---|---|
| 1. temple | *a.* imperator |
| 2. wall | *b.* vox |
| 3. mountain | *c.* templum |
| 4. emperor | *d.* armatura |
| 5. armor | *e.* vallum |
| 6. wine | *f.* ingenium |
| 7. ruby | *g.* vinum |
| 8. engine | *h.* montanus |
| 9. voice | *i.* aequalis |
| 10. equal | *j.* rubeus |

| **C**<br>(English) | **D**<br>(Greek) |
|---|---|
| 1. sandal | *a.* okeanos |
| 2. cube | *b.* electron |
| 3. ocean | *c.* sandalion |
| 4. comedy | *d.* aither |
| 5. prophecy | *e.* kosmos |
| 6. cinema | *f.* kubos |
| 7. mystery | *g.* propheteia |
| 8. ether | *h.* komodia |
| 9. electric | *i.* kinema |
| 10. cosmic | *j.* musterion |

B. Go on a *voluntary quest* to discover if the ancient Troy of the *Iliad* and the *Aeneid* really existed. Check library materials, such as the encyclopedia and other sources, on Heinrich Schliemann's search for Troy. Then write a brief report (a page or two) on your "discoveries."

# The Daring Voyage of Aeneas

The Roman poet Virgil wrote the *Aeneid* about 29-19 B.C. In part, the idea for the epic grew out of an old legend which said that the early settlers of Troy were people from Italy.

The epic's chief character is Aeneas. He was a warrior who escaped with some other Trojans when Greek forces destroyed the city of Troy and ended a great war in the twelfth century B.C. Jove promised Venus, the goddess mother of Aeneas, that he would have her son found a new city elsewhere. So Aeneas and his followers sailed to Thrace, and then to Delos.

On the island of Delos, Aeneas heard the god Apollo's deep voice speaking to him. It told him to go to the land from which the Trojans' ancestors had come.

Anchises, the father of Aeneas, thought Apollo wanted them to go to the island of Crete. But on Crete, the little images of the household gods that Aeneas had taken with him from Troy appeared before him as in a moonlit dream. They told him to sail to Italy. So Aeneas led his people forward.

In this tale we see how at one point some starving travelers have to "eat their tables!"

## Major Characters

**Aeneas**   a Trojan warrior

**Ascanius**   son of Aeneas

**Anchises**   father of Aeneas

**Helenus**   king of Buthrotum

**Juno**   vengeful goddess

**Venus**   goddess of love

**Cupid**   son of Venus

**The Sybil**   a prophetess

**Dido**   queen of Carthage

## Vocabulary Preview

**exiles**   people removed or separated from their homelands
   The *exiles* longed to return to their native land.

**devour**   to eat or consume greedily
   The smiling woman watched her children *devour* the freshly baked pie.

**strait**   a watery passageway which connects two large bodies of water
   The *Strait* of Gibraltar connects the Mediterranean with the Atlantic.

**seer**   someone who predicts events
   The *seer* predicted that there would be a long-lasting dry spell.

**descendant**   someone descended from a particular ancestor or ancestors
   He is a *descendant* of a signer of the Declaration of Independence.

# I.  A Strange Prophecy

"**H**old on! Hold on!" people shouted to one another on the wildly rolling ships that had started out for Italy. Mountainous waves and howling winds kept tossing the ships about, throwing them off course. Dark clouds hid the light of day. The stars remained hidden in the thick mists of night. And flash after flash of lightning came bursting through the darkness!

When the tempest died down, the ships just drifted along in the dark mists on the Ionian Sea for three days. On the fourth day the weary Trojans spotted islands ahead. Quickly then, the sails were dropped and the men manned the oars, churning up the foam as the ships went sweeping over the blue waters.

The travelers were overjoyed as they pulled the ships into a harbor. They could see untended herds of well-fed oxen and flocks of goats on the green fields ahead. "At last," sighed the curly-bearded Aeneas, "my people can rest and fill their empty stomachs."

A short time later, the exiles were sitting around and happily feasting on delicious roasted meats. But then, all at once, huge shadows went sweeping across the ground. The surprised people looked up to see what had come between them and the sun. And their cries of terror soon filled the air when they spied monstrous creatures circling above them. These creatures had the bodies of birds and the faces of starving women!

Aeneas gasped for he realized that the three winged horrors were things of evil known as the Spoilers. "The Harpies!" he shouted. "We're on one of their islands!" Then he watched in terror as they came swooping down, and with sharp claws began tearing into the food. Bits of meat and bone went flying off in all directions as the Trojans drew back. They were horrified by the foul-smelling beasts that polluted the food with their filth.

Before long, the terrible creatures took to the air again. Shrieking loudly, they soon disappeared in a distant forest. And the relieved Trojans moved swiftly to a place of shelter beneath a huge rock hidden by some trees. There they prepared more food. They placed some of it on a small altar as an offering to the gods. Then they began consuming the rest of it themselves. However, within a very short time the ever-hungry Spoilers came flying back with their huge wings clapping loudly.

This time Aeneas and his men felt they were ready for them. With flashing swords they rushed forward and attacked the hollow-

cheeked demons swooping down with their greedy eyes fixed on the food. The men struck fiercely time and time again at the Harpies. But the sharp blades couldn't even scratch the feathers of the powerful beasts!

The Harpies just kept tearing and gulping down the food until they were satisfied. Then two of the three flew off, heavy and full, flapping their huge wings. And some of their foul-smelling feathers drifted down on the food they'd left behind.

Only the leader of the Harpies remained, sitting on the edge of a nearby cliff. There was fury in her flaming eyes! "Do you want war with us, Aeneas?" she croaked angrily. "You killed our cattle and our goats! And you tried to keep us from eating food from our own land!"

Aeneas shuddered as the huge Harpy shook out her huge wings. "Now hear my terrible words and write them in your heart," she said. "I will reveal a prophecy told to me by Apollo himself! You shall reach Italy someday, but you shall not build the walls of your new city until your hungry people devour their tables!" Then, shrieking with laughter, she went flying off into the distant forest as the Trojans stood watching in fear and wonder.

White-haired Anchises, beloved father of Aeneas, broke the silence. Lifting his hands toward the skies, he prayed aloud. "Gods of sea, earth, and sky, hear an old man's plea! Save us from the terrible words of the Harpy! Turn her curse into good for us!"

The exiles didn't waste another moment and went rushing down to the shore. They launched their ships and sailed along the western coast of Greece, until they stopped to rest on a lovely island. After spending the winter there, they eagerly set out again. In time they entered a beautiful harbor and approached Buthrotum, a high-built city.

Aeneas was amazed for the gates and towers of the city reminded him of the gates and towers of Troy. And Aeneas was even more amazed when the king came rushing out to greet him. It was his friend Helenus, a son of the fallen King Priam of Troy! This man had been taken away by the Greeks as a slave. But a number of unusual events gave the lucky man his freedom and a kingdom.

That night Helenus held a great feast for his old friends, and they dined on plates of gold. The travelers were very happy. They were glad to spend the next two days in Buthrotum. But then the dutiful Aeneas, mindful of his mission, said it was time to leave. However, before sailing away, Aeneas asked Helenus for some advice. For it was well known that Helenus was a prophet and a priest of the god Apollo.

"Hear my words, son of the goddess Venus," said Helenus. "You have a long way to go, even though Italy is near. You must not remain on its nearby coast for Greeks dwell in all its towns. Sail away from that coast and head toward the island of Sicily.

"But don't enter the strait that separates Italy from Sicily. For on the side near Italy dwells Scylla, a six-headed creature that snatches men from passing ships! And on the other side near Sicily is the monster called Charybdis! A raging whirlpool which drags passing ships down into the deep!

"So sail around the southern coast of Sicily. Then head north to Italy," said Helenus. "And as you travel be sure to offer prayers to Juno!"

Aeneas stood wide-eyed, and nodded. He listened carefully as Helenus gave him some more advice. Then he shuddered when Helenus added, "And keep this thought in mind, my friend. Apollo and other gods want you to succeed, even though your starving people have to eat their tables!"

"Thank you," said Aeneas. "Now I must say farewell. Be happy here in your little Troy. Be happy for you have accomplished your destiny. Now you can rest. But my people and I must still go on from fate to fate. We must go ploughing through the plain of the ocean as we struggle to fulfill our mission!"

A short time later the fleet of twenty ships went sailing forth with sails puffed out by the south wind. Lost in thought, Aeneas stood in the prow of the lead ship. He was anxious to reach Italy, and he kept wondering about the strange curse of the Harpy. For the time being, however, things seemed to be going well as through the night the fleet moved toward Italy.

Just as Dawn was lighting up the sky with her glowing robes of red and gold, one of the crew shouted, "Italy!" At once, everyone gazed with joy at the distant shore, a part of boot-shaped Italy's heel.

Soon they entered a harbor above which stood a gleaming temple to Minerva. Stepping ashore, the Trojans offered prayers and sacrifices to the goddess. Then, remembering the words of Helenus, they did the same for the wrathful Juno. Shortly after that, they hurried back to their ships and went sailing west toward Sicily.

As they approached the eastern end of the island, they suddenly felt as though their ship were being pulled to one side. Up ahead they could see waves crashing mightily against huge rocks.

"We must be near the edge of the killer whirlpool!" shouted Aeneas. "Man your oars, men! Man your oars and row for your lives!" So with backs bent and muscles aching, the men sent their oars cutting through the roaring waves!

Thankful to have escaped from that danger and others that followed, the Trojans journeyed onward. A helpful wind filled their sails, and in time they came to the southernmost point of Sicily. Rounding the island's tip, they went up to the place called Drepanum. It was a place that Aeneas would never forget. For it was there that his dear father died suddenly, and was buried.

## II. Cruel Tricks of the Gods

After leaving Sicily, the Trojan fleet sailed toward the mainland of Italy. Wrathful Juno frowned as she watched from on high. She was now more determined than ever to prevent Aeneas from succeeding. She hated him and all Trojans because years ago a Trojan prince had not chosen her as the winner in a beauty contest. Also, she didn't want Aeneas to found a city that would become greater than her favorite city, Carthage.

She flew down to a mountainous island to see the king of the winds. There she spoke to Aeolus, who kept the winds locked away in caverns. "Aeolus, some people I hate are now sailing toward Italy," she said. "Release the winds from the caverns. Drown their ships! If you do this for me, I'll give you a beautiful wife!"

At once, the bearded king struck his spear against the gates of the caverns. The winds rushed out and went howling and storming across the sea. Clouds filled the sky, and flash after flash of lightning tore through the air! Mountainous waves tossed the ships about like bits of straw!

Aeneas was filled with terror. "The heroes who died before the walls of Troy were lucky!" he cried. "Better to have perished with them than to die like this!" Then he watched in horror as some ships were smashed on the rocks and many struggling people were drowned.

Neptune, king of the sea, in his palace beneath the waves sensed the storm above. He came crashing up through the waves and saw what was happening to the exiles.

"This is surely the work of Juno!" he said. Then he lifted his golden trident and roared to the winds. "What's this? Do you dare to cause a storm at sea without my permission? Go back and tell your master that this is my kingdom, not his!"

Fearful of Neptune's wrath, the winds rushed back to their prison in the caverns. Sunlight broke through the clouds, and the sea became calm. Then Aeneas led the seven ships that were left to him to the nearest shore. It was in Libya in northern Africa, for they had been driven far off course.

There, Aeneas and a companion went out hunting. They slew some deer, and fed the weary survivors of the terrible storm. And Aeneas made a speech praising his people and urging them not to lose hope. Yet in his heart he was grieving deeply for the many Trojans who had been lost at sea.

Later on, Aeneas and a friend went exploring further inland. Before long, they arrived at Carthage, a new and growing city. And they marveled at the many workers who were busy as bees in summer.

The ruler of the city was the beautiful, golden-haired Queen Dido. The lovely widow was a wise ruler. She spelled out laws, and made judgments to see that justice was done. She also assigned tasks to those building her city. One of the major tasks had already been completed. This was the construction of a great temple in Juno's honor.

Dido was seated on a throne under the great arch of the temple. It was there that Aeneas walked up to her. She smiled at the handsome man and his friend. She welcomed them warmly, just as earlier she had welcomed many of the Trojans that Aeneas had believed to be drowned. And that night, the generous queen held a great banquet for the travelers.

Aeneas wanted his son to be there with him. So he sent someone down to the ships to bring back Ascanius. Venus, keeping herself invisible from the mortals, saw this and had an idea. It was a plan to be sure that Juno wouldn't be able to turn Dido against her son.

Venus called another son, Cupid, to her side. He was the god of love. "I want you to disguise yourself as Ascanius and sit with the queen," she told him. "While you're close to her, fill her heart with love for Aeneas. In the meantime, I'll keep the sleeping Ascanius with me."

Of course, Cupid did as his mother asked. In no time at all, Queen Dido was in love with the handsome man. He, in turn, soon cared deeply for her. And both Venus and Juno approved of this. Venus hoped that this would protect her son. And Juno hoped that it would keep Aeneas away from Italy and shift his future to Libya.

As a result, the happy Aeneas and his people stayed on in Carthage. After some time, however, Jove decided that Aeneas should get on with the task he'd been given. So Jove called over his messenger, the god Mercury. He had him put on his winged sandals and fly down to remind Aeneas about his mission.

The Trojan leader was again filled with a strong sense of duty. He truly cared for Dido, yet he felt he couldn't remain in Carthage any longer.

When Dido heard that Aeneas was getting ready to leave, she begged him not to go. "How can you do this?" she sobbed. "Have you forgotten our love for one another?" Then she wept, and Aeneas was filled with pity for her. But neither her pleadings nor her furious outbursts could get the unhappy man to ignore Jove's command.

One night the troubled man lay slumbering on one of the ships being made ready to sail. Suddenly, yellow-haired Mercury appeared before him again. "How can you rest like this?" sneered the trickster as he prepared to fool the startled man. "Don't you know that the crazed queen is planning to burn your ships before dawn? You must escape from here right now!"

Aeneas was shocked by Mercury's warning. At once, he jumped to his feet and ordered his men to get ready to sail. Then with his flashing sword, he cut the cable that held back his ship. "We follow the commands of the gods!" he cried. "On to Italy!"

In the morning, Dido glanced out her tower window. She spied the sails of the ships disappearing in the distance, and grew wild with sorrow! Then, by her own hand, the crazed and tragic queen ended her days.

Unaware of this, Aeneas sailed on with his mind troubled about many things. He was concerned about his beloved Dido, and about what lay ahead for him in his travels. He wanted answers to the mysteries in his mind. And the strange prophecy of the Harpy kept bothering him. "How can my poor people devour their tables?" he muttered to himself again and again.

The fleet was headed toward Italy. But before long a ferocious storm began whipping up the ocean. The chief pilot of the fleet hurried over to Aeneas on the wildly rolling ship. "We'll have to stop at the nearest shore," the pilot shouted through the howling wind. "I'll order the men to drop the sails and put their backs into rowing for nearby Sicily!"

Aeneas was relieved when his ships pulled into the safe harbor at Drepanum. He was also pleased to be back in the land where his dear father was buried. There he had his men honor the memory of Anchises with footraces and other funeral games.

According to custom, women were not allowed at these contests. They just sat on the shore, weeping and praying for Anchises. Staring down at them from on high, the wrathful Juno decided to try once again to prevent Aeneas from going on. So she sent down Iris, the rainbow goddess, disguised as one of the Trojan women who was ill and not at the seashore with the others.

Wrinkled and white-haired under her shawl, Iris stood among the women and wept loudly. "We have been traveling now for seven years! It's time for us to rest," she cried to the travel-weary women. "Let's set up home here! Let's burn the ships right now!" Then she picked up a flaming branch from the women's fire and hurled it onto a ship.

Just then one of the women pointed excitedly at Iris. "Look at her glowing eyes! See how nobly she moves! She's not one of us," cried the woman. "She must be a goddess!"

Hearing this, Iris went flying up toward the sky, leaving a glowing rainbow beneath the clouds. Then the women, crazed by what they had seen, began flinging blazing branches onto the ships!

Aeneas and his men were shocked when they caught sight of the ships burning in the distance. "Mighty king of the gods!" Aeneas cried out to Jove. "Save our fleet, or else send down your thunderbolts and destroy us now!"

Almost before he had finished speaking, dark storm clouds filled the sky. Floods of water came pouring down and put out the raging fires. This saved most of the ships.

Stunned and confused, Aeneas wondered whether to sail on or to settle in Sicily. And that night as he kept wondering what to do, the spirit of his father glided down out of the darkness.

"Jove has sent me to you, my son," said Anchises. "Lead the bravest of your people on to Italy, where you must fight some hardy foes! Upon landing in Italy, go first to see the Sibyl at Apollo's temple in Cumae. The Sibyl is a prophetess, and Apollo speaks through her lips. She will reveal some amazing things to you!

"Then come to see me in the underworld. There in the land of the dead you will see some astounding sights and learn some marvelous secrets about the future! Now go to seek the Sibyl. Ask for her help in reaching the land of the dead!"

Having spoken, Anchises' spirit melted away like a vapor in the air. And Aeneas, wide-eyed with wonder, stood peering into the darkness.

## III.  Prophecies Fulfilled

Aeneas was anxious to see his father in the lower world. He wondered what secret things would be revealed to him there. So he soon had his ships on their way again. Cool breezes filled their sails, and their crews swept the ocean plain with flashing oars.

Aeneas was relieved when the ships safely reached the bay at Cumae in Italy. Before long, he struggled up the steep and rocky hill to Apollo's temple. There he met the long-robed and hooded Sibyl. She pointed the way into a nearby cavern, the place where people came to seek Apollo's help.

Raising his arms, Aeneas prayed to Apollo, a god who had always favored the Trojan people. Moments later, the Sibyl's voice went echoing through the air.

"You and your people will reach the land of Latium," she said. Her voice was like the sighing wind, for the god Apollo was sending his prophecies through her lips. "There you will be plunged into war," she went on. "The Tiber River will run red with blood! Wrathful Juno will rage against your forces! And a fighter as fierce as the Greek warrior Achilles will battle against you!

"A woman, an alien bride, will be the cause of much woe for your people. But you must not give up, Aeneas. You must be braver and bolder than ever!"

Aeneas nodded gratefully. "I know there's more strife ahead for me," he said wearily. "But now, great priestess, I need a favor from you. Help me to enter the underworld! My father is waiting there to see me."

The aged seer stepped back and stared into his eyes. "First, go into the nearby wilderness," she said. "Find a golden bough, pluck it from the tree, and bring it back here. If you succeed, it will mean that Fate has called you. Only then can you enter and return safely from the land of the dead!"

As Aeneas searched in the dark forest, he prayed for some help. Suddenly, two doves came gliding down out of the sky, and kept flying before him. Aeneas smiled because he realized that they were the doves of Venus. And soon they led him to a dark grove where he spotted a yellowish light gleaming through the thick leaves on a tree.

Pleased, he rushed back and handed the Sibyl the gleaming bough. The branch was thick with golden leaves. The Sibyl nodded in approval, and led the anxious man to the opening of a dark cave. Birds that tried to fly through the mists drifting from the mouth of the cave fell dead to the ground. But Aeneas and the Sibyl remained safe because of the golden bough.

After offering prayers and sacrifices to the underworld gods, the two mortals entered the cave. Aeneas followed the priestess down long and winding passages. She soon led him to the edge of a dark and dismal river. He saw many souls crowding along the shore, begging a ghostly man to let them enter his dark blue boat. The Sibyl explained that these were the souls of the unburied dead, and that they'd have to wait a hundred years before they could cross the river. And in spite of his own great problems, Aeneas was filled with pity for these troubled souls.

The ghostly man was Charon, the ferryman who took souls across the River Styx. His cloak was dirty and torn. He had a grizzly beard and his eyes blazed like fire. Turning, he spotted Aeneas and pointed his bony finger. "Stand back!" he cried. "I won't let living people into my boat!"

At this, the Sibyl stepped forward. "Don't worry. This is noble Aeneas," she said. "He's come to see his father." Then she showed the ferryman the golden bough.

Charon said no more. He slowly and steadily poled the boat, now heavy with Aeneas's weight, to the opposite shore of the River Styx.

Suddenly, a giant dog with three heads leaped out of the darkness. This was Cerberus, the beast that guarded the gate to Hades, Pluto's kingdom. Barking wildly, it blocked the visitors' way. However, the Sibyl was ready for this. She quickly threw a sop to Cerberus. It was a specially prepared cake that caused Cerberus to fall asleep almost immediately.

The Sibyl continued to lead the amazed Aeneas along. As they traveled they saw many unusual sights. At one point, the Sibyl pointed straight ahead. "Look, there the road splits in two," she said. "To the left is Tartarus, a land of tortures for those who were wicked in life."

After that, the Sibyl led Aeneas in the opposite direction. There on the right side of the road was the entrance to the Elysian Fields, a place of peace and happiness. Aeneas entered it with a joyful heart.

The air in the Elysian Fields had a rosy glow. It was a beautiful place of green meadows, rolling hills, and sparkling streams! The happy souls there were busy enjoying themselves. Some were playing at sports such as wrestling, while others were dancing or chanting old tunes. Among the happy spirits was Dardanus. He was an ancestor of the Trojans. He was a son of Jove who had gone from fair Italy to settle in the land where great Troy would someday rise.

Before long, Aeneas spotted his father sitting in a green valley. And when Anchises saw Aeneas running toward him, he jumped up. "My son," he cried with tears streaming down his face. "At last you've come to me!"

Aeneas joyfully reached out to his dear father. But three times the arms of Aeneas passed right through his father's spirit! Aeneas recalled where he was, and began looking around once again.

Deeper within the valley, he saw a river. It was the Lethe River. There was a huge crowd hovering around it like bees swarming over a field of flowers. Aeneas watched these souls and said, "Father, what are they all doing there?"

Anchises explained that these were souls that were to live in the upper world another time. "They were not terribly wicked. They must spend a thousand years in the underworld making up for past wrongs," he said. "Then they are called to the Lethe River. There they may, if they desire, drink the waters of forgetfulness and gain their wish for a second time on earth."

After saying this, Anchises led his son to the top of a mound. From there they could easily see the forms and faces of the passing souls. Smiling, Anchises pointed to a handsome youth who was yet to be born.

"That is Silvius, your future son. He will be the child of Lavinia, your next wife," said Anchises. "She is the princess of the land you have yet to reach. Silvius shall be a king and the father of kings!"

Staring hard, Aeneas watched in astonishment as his father kept pointing out great descendants of theirs who would be born in Italy. At one point, Anchises said, "Many years from now, a woman from your family line will have a son called Romulus. He will found a great city to be called Rome. It will be the center of a great empire!"

"Look there, my son," Anchises went on. "Those are Romans! People of your own race! See, there is noble Julius Caesar in his toga. And there stands Augustus Caesar, a great ruler who will bring a Golden Age to Rome!"

Aeneas had endured many hardships over the years. But now he was filled with new hope and confidence as his father told him more about great descendants and future events. For the moment, he was not even troubled about the strange prophecy of the terrible Harpy. Indeed, his mind was ablaze with thoughts of fame and of the glory of Rome as he and the Sibyl passed through an ivory gate and stepped into the upper world.

Aeneas quickly rejoined his people and began sailing north along the Italian coast. On a misty dawn, some days later, the wind suddenly died down. So the exiles went ashore on a grassy bank at the mouth of the Tiber River. They didn't know exactly where they were, but they were hoping to find some food there. Starving, they had only some thin wheatcakes left to feed themselves and their children. But after searching for a while, they found fresh fruit and piled these on their wheatcakes. Smacking their lips, they sat under the trees and began devouring the tasty food.

Soon the still-hungry people had finished all the fruit. Laughing, curly-haired Ascanius held up a wheatcake to make a joke. "We've eaten all the fruit," he said. "Now all we have left to eat are these tables!"

Aeneas jumped to his feet upon hearing these words. "What's that you say?" he exclaimed. "Now I understand it all! We must be in the land where we are to build our new city! And surely it's here that I'll meet my new wife!"

Aeneas was right. He soon began raising the walls for his new city. In time he would call it Lavinium in honor of Princess Lavinia. He married this beautiful dark-eyed woman, but first he had to fight in a great war caused by the furious Juno. And the terrible war ended when Aeneas defeated mighty Turnus, prince of a nearby country.

This warrior, fierce as Achilles, had hoped to marry Lavinia and gain her father's kingdom. The words of the Sibyl had all come true!

Many kings and famous men sprang from the line of Aeneas. Then, about four hundred years after Aeneas had set foot in Italy, Romulus founded the city of Rome along the Tiber River. It became the center of a great empire. Many of Aeneas's descendants ruled over it through the years.

And the seeds of all these marvelous things began taking root on one very special day. It was the day when some starving people had to devour their tables!

## QUESTING FOR INFORMATION

### A. Getting the Main Idea and Facts

Write the letter of the answer that best completes each statement.

1. A quotation that brings out the story's main idea is _____ .
   a. "A woman, an alien bride, will be the cause of much woe for your people."
   b. "We must go from fate to fate to fulfill our mission."
   c. "The heroes who died before the walls of Troy were lucky."
2. The Harpy claimed that Aeneas had tried to deprive the Harpies of their _____ .
   a. island home    b. freedom    c. food
3. Queen Dido fell in love with Aeneas because of _____ .
   a. Iris and Mercury
   b. Juno and Jove
   c. Venus and Cupid
4. Aeneas was filled with greater confidence as a result of learning things from his father in _____ .
   a. the Elysian Fields    b. Latium    c. Tarturus
5. _____ was to found a great city that was to be the center of a mighty empire.
   a. Ascanius    b. Romulus    c. Turnus

## B. Going Beyond the Facts

Write the letter of the answer that best completes each statement.

1. Probably, Buthrotum was built as it was because Helenus wanted a city that would be _____ .
   a. like old Troy
   b. greater than Carthage
   c. close to Italy

2. We may conclude that Aeneas's prayers and offerings to Juno were _____ by Juno.
   a. demanded
   b. accepted
   c. ignored

3. Statement _____ tells which of the following happened *first*.
   a. The Trojans were welcomed into Carthage.
   b. Neptune calmed a storm at sea.
   c. Juno offered a bride to Aeolus.

4. We may infer that Charon said no more after seeing the golden bough because he _____ .
   a. realized that Fate approved of Aeneas's visit
   b. hoped to gain some of the gleaming gold for his work
   c. feared being struck by the unusual branch

5. Sentence _____ is really a statement of opinion.
   a. Aeneas had to put his duty before his personal happiness.
   b. Juno must have caused Anchises' sudden death in Sicily.
   c. Juno couldn't really change Aeneas's destiny.

# QUESTING FOR MEANINGS

Write the letter of the word that best completes each sentence below.

a. exiles    b. devour    c. strait    d. seer    e. descendant

1. A lady used a crystal ball in her act as a _____ at the community fair.

2. My friend is a _____ of a famous writer from the past.

3. Many of the _____ quickly learned the customs of the new land to which they had been sent.

4. Our ship sailed through the narrow _____ .

5. Hungry deer sometimes _____ the bark of certain trees.

## QUESTING FOR UNDERSTANDING

1. The heroic Aeneas was not only a brave man, but also a compassionate man. Discuss two or more times in the story when he was concerned about the sufferings or misfortunes of others.

2. The Greeks and Romans believed that gods and goddesses sometimes behaved like mortals who played tricks on others. From the story, tell about tricks played on mortals by the following:

a. Iris     b. Cupid     c. Mercury

## QUESTING FOR ENRICHMENT

Latin was the language of the ancient Romans. Several languages developed from Latin, and are called *Romance* languages. (Can you see why?) Among these are French, Spanish, Portuguese, Rumanian, and Italian.

Below in column A are words which English has borrowed or derived from words in the Italian language. All but the second and tenth words have their roots in Latin.

Match the words in column A with their meanings in column B.

|  **A** | **B** |
|---|---|
| 1. antipasto | *a.* copy; duplicate; reproduction |
| 2. balcony | *b.* selection of Italian appetizers, usually served before a meal |
| 3. cameo | |
| 4. lava | *c.* stringed instrument played with a bow |
| 5. malaria | *d.* raised stone or shell carving, usually small, set on another stone or shell and used as jewelry |
| 6. replica | |
| 7. studio | *e.* molten or hardened volcanic rock |
| 8. tempo | *f.* platform projecting from a wall |
| 9. trio | *g.* group or set of three |
| 10. violin | *h.* place where artists create |
| | *i.* disease passed on by bite of mosquito |
| | *j.* time; rate of speed |

# Ulysses Meets the Cyclops

After the long Trojan war ended in the twelfth century B.C., Ulysses and his fellow Greeks gladly began sailing home to Greece. However, Ulysses' voyage was to last for ten years because of the many troubles he met along the way.

Ulysses' name in Greek is Odysseus. That is why people call any long, adventurous journey an "odyssey."

One of Ulysses' famous adventures took place in the lawless land of the one-eyed giants called the Cyclopes. The story is based on an episode from the *Odyssey*, the epic poem written by the Greek poet Homer in about 850 B.C.

In this tale we find out how Ulysses is promised a very unusual gift which he hopes he will never receive.

## Major Characters

**Ulysses**  Greek warrior and king of Ithaca

**Ulysses' warriors**

**The Cyclops**  a ferocious one-eyed giant

## Vocabulary Preview

**loyal**  faithful
The fans remained *loyal* to their team.

**startled**  suddenly surprised or frightened
Several deer were *startled* by the sound of gunfire.

**conceal**  to hide
The thief tried to *conceal* the stolen goods.

**fleece**  wool that covers a sheep
White, fluffy clouds look like *fleece* in the sky.

**jeer**  to make fun of; mock
Some people began to *jeer* at the speaker who couldn't answer their questions at the town meeting.

# I. Unwilling Guests

The moon was hidden behind thick clouds. The weary travelers stared out into into the darkness. "We can't see anything at all," groaned a worried man. He and the other Greek warriors were on their way home after the long Trojan war. "We've had so much trouble along the way. Maybe this is a punishment from angry gods. Some of them wanted us to lose the war!"

A troubled old sailor nodded. "Yes, we've been through more than we bargained for," he said. The other warriors agreed with him. They, too, wished the gods would help them reach their homes in Greece. Then the men closed their parched lips and listened to their stomachs growling from hunger.

King Ulysses of Ithaca sighed deeply. He knew how his men felt. He too was starving and wanted to be with his family again. There was great sadness in his eyes as he turned to peer into the thick mist hanging over his ship and those behind it.

But just a moment later, something strange happened. The ship stopped moving! What was it? What was holding the ship still in the inky darkness?

Ulysses quickly called for a torch and hurried to look over the ship's prow. "We've been driven ashore!" he shouted. "We're on an island. Lower the sails and follow me. Tonight we'll rest our heads on dry land!"

The tired men did as they were told, and soon were fast asleep on the mysterious island.

When Dawn appeared, the men sat up and rubbed the sleep out of their eyes. They were surprised to find themselves in a beautiful place. Fresh water gushed nearby and herds of goats were running free on the green hills.

Before long, the men were feasting on roasted meat and on juicy, wild fruit. Together the men from Ulysses' twelve ships ate and laughed and relaxed. That night they went back to their ships where they slept well and dreamed of home. And on the next morning, the bright-eyed men waited eagerly for sailing orders. However, Ulysses' command surprised them all.

"Don't raise the sails," he said. "We're staying here a while. Beyond this green island are some rocky ones. I think they're the islands of the Cyclopes! I've always wanted to meet these creatures to learn if they are a kindly race!"

The men just stared at each other. The very thought of the giant

creatures made their blood run cold. But they were a loyal crew, and
soon some men were ready to row Ulysses' boat toward a rocky
island. Ulysses sat in the prow of the boat, holding a huge goatskin
filled with wine.

Long oars struck the grey sea mightily as the boat moved swiftly
along. Suddenly, Ulysses raised his muscular arm. "Up there, on the
face of that cliff! There's an opening to a cave!" he shouted.

The silent men drew the boat ashore. Then twelve of them went
along with their chief who led them up the rocky hillside. Rocks broke
loose under their feet and went splashing down into the dark sea.

Trembling, the men followed Ulysses into the cave. It was quite
dark inside, with the only light coming from a small fire deep within
the vast cavern. In time, the men's eyes became used to the dim place
and they saw pens filled with lambs at the far end of the cave. They
also saw cheeses piled on racks along the wall, and milk brimming in
huge bowls on the ground.

"Let's take some lambs and cheeses, and get away from here!"
said one nervous man. "We can be gone before the giant creature
gets back!"

At once his companions agreed with this idea, and began begging Ulysses to lead them away. But Ulysses refused to listen to their
pleas.

"No," he said forcefully. "I want to meet the owner of this huge
cave, and I want the fine present he might give to a stranger visiting
his home!"

Seeing that they could not change their leader's mind, the men
turned their attention to the cheeses. They smelled so good that the
men soon began grabbing fistfuls of the delicious food. Their eyes
rolled with pleasure and their lips made loud smacking noises as they
stuffed their mouths!

Enjoying themselves, the men forgot about their fear. Then, all
at once, the air grew darker. Something was blocking the light from
the cave opening! The ground began shaking and an immense creature came thumping into the cave, driving many sheep before him.
The startled Greeks dropped their food and rushed to find hiding
places.

The Cyclops, huge and hairy, stood in the center of the cave.
He was even huger than the travelers could have imagined! In silence,
they watched as he rolled a great stone over the mouth of the cave.
Ulysses could see that it would take over a hundred strong men just
to budge that stone!

The giant squatted, put some sticks on the fire, and fanned the growing flames. Then, in the light of the blazing fire, he caught sight of the Greeks huddled near a wall. "Strangers!" he roared. His deep voice echoed like thunder through the cave. "Come forward!"

The Greeks stepped out slowly, one by one. Then they stood quietly before him. But not too close! The Cyclops moved his head slowly from side to side, staring at the small creatures. His single eye was dull green and the size of a very large fist. It peered out at the men from the center of the Cyclops' forehead.

"What are you doing here? Are you pirates?" he growled. "Where is your ship? Is it near here?"

At this, Ulysses stepped forward. "We are Greek warriors on our way home from the great war at Troy. Our ship hit some rocks and sank!" he said. "We pray for kindness. The kindness due to travelers! For it's the will of Jove, king of the gods, that visiting travelers be treated well."

The Cyclops slammed his great fist on the ground, sending a cloud of dust swirling into the air. "I don't care about Jove's wishes!" he shouted. "My own father is Neptune, ruler of the sea!" Then the Cyclops suddenly reached out and seized two men. He dashed them against the ground, killing them. Then he cut them up and ate them greedily, swallowing bones and all. When he was through, he licked his fingers with pleasure.

The remaining Greeks howled and ran to hide. Only Ulysses stood his ground. Filled with anger, he watched the creature wipe his mouth on his hairy arm and then settle down to sleep.

"I could slay him now," sobbed Ulysses to himself. "But if I do that now, we'll never escape from here. We could never move that stone!"

That night the Greeks hardly slept at all. In the morning they watched carefully as the Cyclops stirred. And they jumped back quickly when he sat up, yawning and stretching. But before the men knew what was happening, the Cyclops lunged forward and reached out swiftly. Two screaming men soon became the monster's breakfast.

A short time later, the Cyclops stood up and rolled back the stone at the cave's mouth. "Shoo! Shoo!" he called as he drove his sheep outside into the morning sunlight. Yet he kept his eye fixed on the strangers. Finally, he backed out of the cave and rolled the great stone into place.

Ulysses, scratching his curly beard, sat apart from his men. They didn't bother him, for they knew their clever leader was busy thinking. Then they smiled with hope when he jumped to his feet, grinning.

"Listen well, men!" said Ulysses. "I have a plan."

## II.  A Crafty Plan

Ulysses explained his escape plan to his anxious men. Then he studied a long club that was lying near one of the sheep pens. The club was as long as the mast of a ship. He knelt and began chopping away at it, and soon he had cut off a piece about six feet long. After that Ulysses had his men chop the edges at one end of the pole. Then he himself brought the end to a point and charred it in the fire to make it strong.

That evening, the Cyclops returned home, rolled back the stone, and drove his flock inside. The huge wooly animals hurried to their pens. Some men quickly ran to hide behind the animals as the Cyclops laughed aloud. He reached roughly through the flock and soon had two howling men thrashing about in his huge hands. They looked like frightened puppies. Groaning, the other Greeks turned away. And they pressed their hands hard over their ears as the giant crunched away on his dinner.

Ulysses gasped. He tried hard to conceal his disgust and anger. Forcing a smile, he strode right up to the monster. "You must be very thirsty now," he exclaimed. "Surely, a son of great Neptune should have rich wine. I have some excellent wine in this goatskin."

The Cyclops' dull green eye stared down as Ulysses poured some dark red wine into a huge bowl. Then the Cyclops snatched the bowl and threw back his head. With greedy gulps, he drank until the bowl was empty. "Mm, good!" he grinned, licking his lips. "I thank you for this gift. Now give me some more, and tell me your name. I wish to reward you well, stranger!"

Ulysses smiled slyly as he refilled the bowl. "No-man," said the crafty warrior. "My name is No-man!"

"Very well, No-man. You've given me a fine present. Now I'll give you something in return," said the dizzy Cyclops. "My gift to you is this. I'll eat you last!" Then the giant roared with cruel laughter. After that, he gulped down the last drops of wine and fell asleep.

Grinning, Ulysses turned and quickly thrust the pointed end of the club into the flames. When the point glowed brightly, he and his men lifted the heavy pole. Then at Ulysses' signal, they all went charging toward the sleeping giant.

A terrible scream filled the air! The sheep began bleating and thrashing about wildly. Then more cries rang out as the Cyclops stomped around, clutching his injured eye. His roars alarmed other Cyclopes resting in their caves. They came rushing up to the stone blocking the entrance to the Cyclops' home.

"What's wrong?" they called. "Is someone trying to harm you?"

The Cyclops answered, "No-man's in here! No-man is trying to slay me!"

The Cyclopes outside wondered at these words. "If no man is harming you, you must be ill!" said one Cyclops. "Try to get some rest!" Then the speaker and the other Cyclopes hurried back to their warm caves.

The wounded creature dragged himself to the mouth of his cave and sat down heavily. "You won't escape me," he warned the Greeks. "You'll never get past me alive!"

This caused the six remaining warriors to turn with troubled looks toward Ulysses. But he didn't notice them. He was too busy scratching his beard and thinking over the next step in his clever plan.

The wounded Cyclops moaned all night. He was still in pain when he began driving his sheep out of the cave the next morning.

And he carefully stroked the fleece on the backs and sides of each sheep as it went by.

The last animal to leave the cave was a great ram, the largest male sheep in the flock. This surprised the Cyclops. "Why are you the last to leave today?" he asked. "Usually you lead all the others. Can it be that you're sorry for what No-man and his men did to me? Well, don't let it bother you now. I'll find where they're hiding and dash their brains out!"

After driving the ram outside, the Cyclops laughed wildly. "Now I have you, No-man!" he roared, and began inching his way forward on his hands and knees. But after a while, he froze in his tracks. He couldn't believe his ears. Ulysses' voice was coming from outside the cave! In fact, it was coming from Ulysses who was already out in the boat with his men and some of the Cyclops' sheep!

The clever leader and his men had tied the huge wooly sheep together in threes before the animals were driven out. Under each of the middle sheep, a man had crawled to safety.

Ulysses had buried himself in the thick fleece under the belly of the great ram. Hanging on, face upwards, Ulysses had been carried right past the Cyclops!

"Cruel Cyclops! The gods have punished you!" Ulysses shouted over waves. "You should have been kinder to your guests!"

Shaking with rage, the Cyclops tore the top off a crag and hurled the boulder in the direction of Ulysses' voice. The huge stone almost hit the ship, so Ulysses commanded his men to begin rowing for their lives.

When the boat was a greater distance away, Ulysses stood up to jeer at the Cyclops. His men begged him not to do this, because they feared that the Cyclops might yet sink their boat. But Ulysses wouldn't listen to them.

"Cyclops!" he shouted. "If anyone asks who harmed you, say it was Ulysses, King of Ithaca!"

The Cyclops was crazed with anger. Standing at the edge of the cliff, he raised his arms toward the heavens. "Father Neptune! Lord of the waves! Punish Ulysses for what he has done to me!" he cried. "Grant that he not reach home alive! If the gods refuse this wish, then grant that he may lose all his men. And let him find great trouble at home!"

Then he lifted another rock, much larger than the first, and hurled it with all his strength. It missed the ship and caused a wave that drove the boat closer to the green island and safety.

Neptune was watching and listening from beneath the crashing waves. He felt great pity for his son, so the mighty lord of the sea began causing Ulysses many problems. Indeed, the weary traveler was to suffer greatly. His troubles were only beginning.

## QUESTING FOR INFORMATION

### A. Getting the Main Idea and Facts

Write the letter of the answer that best completes each statement.

1. This story is mainly about how _____.
   a. wine made a monster helpless
   b. brains won out over muscle
   c. Ulysses used a false name

2. Ulysses had his ships wait because he wanted to see if the Cyclopes were a _____ race of creatures.
   a. huge     b. rich     c. kindly

3. Ulysses didn't slay the sleeping Cyclops because Ulysses _____.
   a. felt pity for him
   b. knew his men couldn't move the stone
   c. was still hoping for a present

4. The other Cyclopes believed the Cyclops was screaming because of _____.
   a. illness     b. anger     c. hunger

5. Ulysses' men escaped by _____.
   a. crawling out under the sheep
   b. riding out on the sheep
   c. hanging on under the wooly sheep

### B. Going Beyond the Facts

Write the letter of the answer that best completes each statement.

1. We may conclude that Ulysses' main purpose for taking wine along when he set out to visit the Cyclops was to _____.
   a. make the Cyclops dizzy
   b. present it as a gift
   c. trade it for some fine cheeses

2. Probably, some lives would have been saved if Ulysses had ___ .
   a. not given a false name
   b. told the Cyclops the truth about his boat
   c. listened to his men
3. Probably, the Cyclops asked about the ship because he wanted to
   ___ .
   a. sail away with the visitors
   b. search it for good wine
   c. capture more travelers
4. It would seem that the Cyclops believed the ram was behaving in
   a ___ manner toward him.
   a. friendly    b. stubborn    c. suspicious
5. We may conclude that the Cyclops had ___ .
   a. an uncaring father
   b. a cruel sense of humor
   c. a great fear of Jove

## QUESTING FOR MEANINGS

Write the letter of the word that best completes each sentence
below.
a. fleece    b. startled    c. jeer    d. loyal    e. conceal

1. Good friends remain ___ to each other.
2. The shepherds began shearing the ___ from the sheep.
3. The team's faithful fans didn't ___ when the team lost the game.
4. The child tried to ___ his fear of the storm.
5. Everyone was ___ by the loud pounding on the door.

## QUESTING FOR UNDERSTANDING

1. Ulysses has long been admired as a very clever man. However, as the story shows, he sometimes behaved in a reckless manner.
First, discuss some examples of his crafty thinking and behavior. Then
discuss one or more examples of his rather foolish behavior.

2. Ulysses asked the Cyclops for the kindness due to travelers.
Indeed, in ancient Greece it was the custom for hosts and visitors to
exchange gifts.

Try to think of one or more specific reasons why the Greeks and other people in ancient times thought that hospitality (treating visitors kindly) was so important for everyone concerned.

## QUESTING FOR ENRICHMENT

In the story of the Cyclops, some groups of words didn't mean exactly what they said. For example, we read that the Cyclops "froze in his tracks." This just meant that he suddenly stopped moving.

Below in column A are expressions that don't mean exactly what they say. These figures of speech are called idioms. Write the letter for the meaning in column B next to the number for its expression in column A. Write each number with its letter on your paper.

| A | B |
|---|---|
| 1. burn the candle at both ends | a. make peace |
| 2. burn the midnight oil | b. wear oneself out |
| 3. bury the hatchet | c. act grouchy |
| 4. cool one's heels | d. study late into the night |
| 5. earn one's salt | |
| 6. get out on the wrong side of the bed | e. understand how things work |
| 7. hit the ceiling | f. wait |
| 8. know the ropes | g. work for one's pay or reward |
| 9. pull the wool over someone's eyes | h. let the truth slip out |
| 10. spill the beans | i. become furious |
| | j. fool a person |

# Clever Penelope and the Return of Ulysses

At the end of the Trojan war in the twelfth century B.C., Ulysses and his men set sail for their homes in Greece. During their travels, Ulysses blinded a giant Cyclops, son of the god Neptune. As a result, the wounded Cyclops prayed to his father to cause Ulysses as much trouble as possible.

When the Greeks stopped to rest on the island of the sun-god, Ulysses warned his men not to touch the sun-god's cattle. But before long, the starving men killed and ate some cows. This greatly angered the sun-god, who then complained to Jove. So, as the Greeks sailed away, Jove sent down a thunderbolt that destroyed their ship. Only Ulysses survived, and he alone reached the shores of home. But his troubles were far from over.

The following story is based on episodes from the *Odyssey*, the epic written by Homer in 850 B.C. In this tale we see why Ulysses, a very rich man, had to beg for food in his own home.

## Major Characters

**Ulysses** Greek warrior and king of Ithaca

**Penelope** Ulysses' wife

**Minerva** goddess of wisdom and war

**Eumaeus** Ulysses' faithful servant, a swineherd

**Telemachus** Ulysses' son

**Antinous** troublemaking suitor of Penelope

**Several other suitors of Penelope**

## Vocabulary Preview

**identity** who a person is
Each person wore a mask to hide his or her *identity* at the costume party.

**transformed** changed in appearance, use, or form
All John's hard work *transformed* the old car into a showpiece.

**applauded** showed approval by clapping hands
The crowd *applauded* the appearance of the famous astronaut.

**construct** to make; build; create
Will they *construct* the new school near the park?

**deceive** to mislead; fool; trick
Jane's friends had to *deceive* her in order not to spoil her surprise party.

64

# I. A Surprise Reunion

The king sank to his knees and kissed the ground of Ithaca, his island kingdom. "Home at last," he sighed. "Home after the long war at Troy and ten more years of travel!"

Minerva, goddess of wisdom and war, stood beside him. She had a special liking for King Ulysses because he, like Minerva, was crafty and fond of fooling others. Now leaning on her shield, the bright-eyed goddess nodded at the man.

"Yes, you're home," she said. "But there is danger waiting here. There's much for you to do before you can take your rightful place as king." Then she helped Ulysses hide in a cave some treasures he'd brought back with him. After that, she sat down with him to talk things over.

"Right now your home is filled with strangers," she said. "About four years ago, many chieftains from nearby islands decided that you must be dead. Now they go to your home each day. These greedy men eat your food and drink your best wine. Each day they play at throwing spears and at other sports. They mean to keep on doing all this until Penelope chooses one of them as her new husband. But your wife is very clever. She keeps finding ways to delay making her decision."

Ulysses jumped to his feet. "They must be punished!" he shouted, clenching his fists. "Oh, tell me what to do, great goddess!"

Minerva nodded. "Go to the home of your swineherd, the man who minds your pigs. Wait there," she said. "The little son you left behind when you went to war is now a man. I promise you he'll arrive at the swineherd's hut before long. After he arrives, I'll tell you what to do next."

Smiling, Minerva then touched the king with her spear. At once, his sandy hair disappeared. His face became wrinkled, and a torn cloak covered his stooped body.

Ulysses thanked the goddess, and then hurried along to the home of the swineherd. There he saw his ever-faithful servant sitting outside. And when the swineherd's dogs spotted Ulysses they began barking and rushing toward him with teeth bared! But Eumaeus called out and made them stop before they could attack the disguised king.

"Welcome, stranger!" said the strong, middle-aged man. "You just escaped from great harm. Come in and have some food. All travelers are welcome here, for such is the will of Jove himself!"

Sighing deeply, the tired king sank down on a pile of soft goat-skins. And as he ate, he made up a tall story in answer to the swineherd's question. It was a tale about who he was and where he'd come from. Indeed, crafty Ulysses really enjoyed spinning tall tales.

At one point he said that he'd heard that the famous Ulysses was safe and on his way home. However, the swineherd didn't believe this at all. "Stranger, you're just telling me lies to make me feel better about my lost master," he said with a trembling voice.

A little while later, Ulysses covered himself with a blanket and lay down to sleep near a crackling fire. "Home," he mumbled to himself as he fell asleep.

Ulysses remained with the swineherd for a few days. On the third day, a slim young man with sandy hair and brown eyes entered the hut.

"Welcome, kind master! How are you?" said Eumaeus with joy. Ulysses said nothing, although he realized that the youth was his son. And Ulysses was touched to see that Eumaeus truly loved the young prince.

Smiling, Eumaeus had the young man sit down and served him some warm food. And as Telemachus ate, the kind swineherd asked the prince to give some help to the old beggar who was visiting his hut.

"I can't take him home to the palace with me," said Telemachus. "My mother's suitors would mistreat him. Let him stay here with you for now. I'll see to it that he gets some clothes, new sandals, and money for travel when I return home."

Eumaeus nodded happily, and the prince went on. "But for now, my good friend, I must remain here. Go to the palace for me. See my mother," he said. "Tell her that I'll be staying here awhile. Say that I've learned that some of her suitors are even now plotting to kill me. They believe that I am now in my ship at sea. They are busy sailing around looking for me, and hoping to slay me where there is no one to see them commit their crime!"

Moments later, the alarmed swineherd set out as Telemachus watched from the door. Then Telemachus returned to his seat and sat there quietly with a faraway look in his eyes. In the meantime, Minerva appeared at the door. Visible only to Ulysses, she called him outdoors. There she told him that it was time to reveal his true identity to his son. Then she touched Ulysses with her spear and sent him back inside.

Tall, strong, and young in appearance, Ulysses stood before the amazed prince. Trembling, the youth fell to his knees. "Forgive me," he cried. "I didn't know you were a god! Have pity on me!"

The king of Ithaca shook his head. "I'm not a god," he said a bit hoarsely. "I am Ulysses, your own father, returned from the war at Troy!" With that, he reached out to his son. And tears of joy streamed from the eyes of both father and son as they embraced.

Ulysses then told the youth about the goddess Minerva. He explained that she would help them punish the evil suitors. "But for now say nothing about my return," he warned. "Don't even tell your mother!" And the prince, filled with new courage, promised to obey.

Later on, just before Eumaeus returned to the hut, Ulysses was once again transformed into an old beggar. And when Eumaeus reported that he'd seen unhappy looking suitors stepping out of a boat, Ulysses and his son secretly smiled at each other. Then the three men had dinner and were soon fast asleep.

Before leaving the next morning, the prince spoke to Eumaeus. "My mother is probably worrying herself sick about me," he said. "I'm going to the palace now. Bring the stranger there today."

Later on, Ulysses and the swineherd slowly made their way to the huge palace. The king, still in disguise, pointed to a dog sleeping near the gates. The poor beast was very old. It was thin and covered with fleas. Ulysses groaned at the sad sight, for he knew this poor creature well. It was Argus, his own hunting dog!

The swineherd shook his head. "Servants can be so cruel," he sighed. When a master is away, some become very lazy. See how they've ignored this poor beast!"

Ulysses just stared at the dog. It should have died a long time ago, but it seemed to be waiting for something. Then as Ulysses knelt beside it, the old dog stirred. Slowly it lifted its head and stared through very weak eyes. Moments later the old dog whined, and its thin tail began wagging feebly. Argus had recognized his master! And a tear rolled down Ulysses' face as the now happy dog closed its eyes for the last time.

The sorrowful king stood up. The sounds of music and laughter filled his ears. "The suitors!" he growled. Then, angrier than ever, he entered his own home to beg for food. For such was the order of the invisible Minerva.

## II.  Secret Preparations

Ulysses stared at the richly dressed suitors. Some were lying about on plump cushions; others were strolling about, laughing and talking. Many were greedily stuffing themselves with food, and juices from roasted meats went dripping down their chins.

Controlling his rage, Ulysses walked from suitor to suitor with his arms outstretched. "Pity an old man," he pleaded. "I am weary and hungry."

Some men laughed and tossed him bits of food. But there was one man who just sneered. The thin man refused to give him anything. This was Antinous, a troublemaker. This leader among the suitors didn't really care who won Penelope. All he really wanted was to see Telemachus slain so that Ulysses' kingdom could be taken over more easily.

In fact, even Penelope had heard something about the evil plottings of Antinous. And she had bravely stood up to him about these reports. As the suitors listened in silence she'd told Antinous that he should be deeply ashamed of wanting to hurt the son of Ulysses. "For you well know," she insisted at that time, "that when your own father was in serious trouble years ago, he came running to Ulysses to save his neck. And he got all the help he needed!"

However, the evil Antinous would not admit to any guilt. And now this same man stood scowling as he watched Ulysses begging for food.

"Who brought you here, you dirty old beggar? These other men give you food because they're generous with what doesn't belong to them!" shouted Antinous. "Now stay away from me!"

Ulysses shrugged his shoulders. "It's too bad your manners don't match your fine appearance," he said.

"What's that?" answered Antinous. "Here, beggar, now I'll give you something to pay you for those words!" Saying this, he picked up a stool and sent it flying across the room. The stool struck Ulysses on the shoulder, but the disguised king didn't stumble or strike back.

Some of the other suitors began shouting at Antinous. They warned him that the gods might punish him for treating the traveler so poorly.

Soon the news of how the beggar had been treated reached Penelope in her upstairs chambers. She was very upset and sent word to Eumaeus to come up to her. When he did so, he told her all about the stranger who claimed he had some news about Ulysses.

Upon hearing this report, Penelope became very excited. She was determined to see the stranger. So it was arranged that she would meet him after all the suitors were gone for the night.

Later that afternoon, another beggar arrived at the palace. He was a husky young man who was just too lazy to work. His name was Irus, and he considered the palace his private territory for begging.

Irus became furious upon seeing Ulysses there. "Get out of here, or I'll drag you out by your feet!" he yelled. "This is my place for begging!"

Of course, Ulysses refused to leave, saying that there was enough for both of them. But Irus disagreed and began threatening him all the more.

Ulysses just slowly shook his head. "Don't start a fight now," he said. "Be careful, or I may have to hurt you!"

At this, Irus raised his fists. "You poor old thing," he laughed. "Do you think you can stand up to a sturdy young fellow like me?"

Antinous was delighted at the thought of the old beggar being beaten by Irus. "Oh, the gods are treating us to a merry show," he said to the other suitors. "Come, let's make a ring around these fighters. The winner will share in our feast tonight. And he shall be the only beggar allowed in the palace from now on!"

However, when Ulysses took off his raggedy long shirt and wrapped it around his waist, everyone gasped. They were amazed at his powerful thighs, chest, and arms. And the invisible Minerva then gave him extra strength.

Pale and trembling, Irus wanted to back out. But the cruel suitors insisted that the battle begin. Then with one crashing punch, Ulysses knocked Irus to the ground! After that, he threw him out into the yard.

Ulysses thrust a stick into the loser's hand. "Now sit there in the dust. Keep the dogs and pigs away!" he said. "And don't try to make yourself king of the beggars or you'll really get it from me!"

Word of what was happening reached Penelope. She was angry and sorry about the treatment that beggars were being given in her home. And the invisible Minerva then put it into Penelope's mind to face the cruel suitors. However, before sending the queen downstairs, Minerva caused her to fall asleep for a while.

A short time later, a hush came over the suitors as Queen Penelope appeared at the top of the stairs. She looked quite lovely. For Minerva had restored the queen's youthful beauty while she slept.

Her hazel eyes flashed like the gems in her necklace. Her long brown hair gleamed reddish in the glow of the flames in the fireplace. And the train of her pale green gown made a soft, swishing sound as she slowly descended the stairs.

The dazzled suitors stood watching as she spoke to her son. She made it clear to him that she didn't approve of beggars being ill-treated in her home. Then one of the suitors interrupted her and praised her great beauty.

Shaking her head, she turned toward the suitors. "All my beauty was lost the day my dear husband sailed to Troy. Now he is gone," she said. "And soon I will have to choose a new husband. Now each of you says he wishes to marry me. Yet not one of you courts me properly. Instead of eating up all my property, you should be trying to win me with magnificent presents!"

At this, Antinous stepped forward. "Beautiful lady, you shall have as many presents as you please," he said. "But remember that we will keep returning each day until you choose one of us as your new husband."

The other suitors applauded at these words. Then they sent their servants to bring back wonderful gifts. In the meantime, Ulysses just sat quietly in a corner, smiling to himself.

"How clever she is!" he thought. "She's managing to gain many rich presents from these greedy fellows."

Before long, there were earrings, necklaces, dresses trimmed with gold, and many other fine gifts presented to the lovely woman. Smiling, she then went up to her room, and her maids carried the presents after her.

When she was gone, the suitors began teasing Ulysses again.

Telemachus, filled with new courage, asked the suitors to leave for the night. And, to the youth's great relief, they did as he asked.

When the last suitor was gone, Ulysses had Telemachus help him clear the large room of all weapons. This was to get the room ready for a surprise being prepared for the evil suitors. And before long, all helmets, spears, and shields were locked in a nearby storeroom.

A short time later, Penelope came down from her room. She was anxious to speak to Ulysses, who was waiting for her. She took a seat near the fire, and had a soft fleece placed on a chair set out for the old stranger.

"You have many rich suitors," Ulysses said politely. "Each seems very eager to marry you."

Penelope sighed deeply. "In truth, I am unhappy," she said. "I still hope for my Ulysses to return. I've had to use many a trick to keep the suitors from forcing me to choose one of them as my new husband.

"For the first three years I worked at weaving a funeral robe. It was for my father-in-law. Each day I did some weaving, and each night I pulled out some stitches. By doing this, I never completed my task. Alas, however, my trick became known when one of my disloyal servant girls revealed my secret."

The warrior's heart beat faster. He was filled with joy over his wife's bravery and cleverness. And when Penelope asked if he could tell her anything about Ulysses, he wanted to shout the truth about himself, but he held back. Instead, he said that he'd seen Ulysses. And he even described the warrior's clothes and the golden clasp he used to fasten his cloak about him.

Penelope's face lit up with joy. "I prepared those clothes and gave him that gold clasp!" she cried.

Ulysses just nodded and went on to say that he'd heard that the man was even now on his way home. And at this, Penelope's eyes began sparkling like stars. She couldn't thank the stranger enough for his welcome words. Then smiling and humming, she sent for Ulysses' old nurse.

Soon the gray-haired woman appeared carrying a large basin of water. "The queen says you will sleep here tonight," she said. "So I've come to wash the dust from your feet." And Euryclea set about doing just that.

Suddenly, the woman looked up into Ulysses' eyes. "It's you!" she gasped. For Ulysses' old nurse had recognized a childhood scar above his knee!

"Be silent!" Ulysses whispered. "Say nothing of this to anyone!" Of course, the delighted woman promised to hold her tongue. But she couldn't stop the singing in her heart!

# III. The Contest

Early the next day the suitors returned and gathered in the great hall. Before long, Penelope appeared carrying a huge bow, for Minerva had put an idea into the woman's head.

Standing near a pillar she spoke to the wondering men. "Hear me, you men that seek my hand in marriage. You keep coming here day after day, waiting for me to choose a new husband. So now I'll arrange a contest," she said. "I shall leave this house with the winner."

Nodding their approval, the suitors pressed forward. They listened eagerly as the queen went on. "Twelve ax heads will be placed in a row down the center of this room. I'll marry the man who is strong enough to string this bow, the bow of mighty Ulysses, and shoot an arrow through the holes in the ax heads!"

The suitors agreed to this, and soon all was ready for the contest. Then one stout suitor stepped forward and eagerly reached for the bow that stood against the wall. For a long time he continued struggling to get the string onto the weapon. However, he couldn't bend the bow at all. Finally, he gave up in disgust and put the bow down.

Then other men stepped forward, one at a time. Puffing and sweating, each tried his strength. But not one of them could bend the bow.

Grinning, the next suitor helped rub lard on the wooden bow, and then warmed it by the fire before trying to string it. And when he failed to bend the weapon, he began grieving aloud, "Oh, people will talk about us in years to come," he groaned. "They'll say our strength wasn't as great as that of Ulysses! We'll be laughed at and disgraced!"

Hearing this, Antinous quickly stood up and began waving his arms. "No! That won't be!" he cried. "Who can string any bow on a day like this? For today is a feast day of the god Apollo. All weapons should be put aside! We can go on with the contest tomorrow!"

The suitors gladly agreed to this, and soon began laughing and calling for huge bowls of wine. And after they had been drinking for a while, they heard Ulysses calling for their attention.

"Listen to me, suitors! You have stopped the contest now. In the morning, Jove will surely give strength to the right man," he said.

"But for now, let me try the bow. I just want to see if I have any of my old strength left."

Antinous shook his fist angrily. He, like the other suitors, secretly feared that the old stranger might shame them by somehow managing to string the bow. "You old fool!" roared Antinous. "How dare you ask a thing like that?" And Antinous would have gone on, but Penelope silenced him.

"I see no harm in this," she said with a smile. "Allow him to try bending the bow. If he succeeds, I'll reward him with new clothes, sandals, and a spear to drive off dogs and robbers as he travels along."

Then Telemachus spoke up. "Mother, there is no man here with a better right to say who shall use this bow," he said. "This is a man's business. So please, dear lady, go to your rooms and see to your servants. Let me tend to matters here."

These words amazed Penelope. Never before had her son spoken to her in such a way. Yet somehow the queen felt that now she should do just as her son asked, so she turned and went up to her chambers.

The words of Telemachus and the departure of his mother both angered and amazed the suitors. And they were even more amazed when they saw the man in rags easily bending and stringing the bow. Then they gasped as one when Ulysses reached for an arrow and, with a single pull, stretched the mighty bow.

*Twang!* The arrow went whizzing through the air. It went speeding straight through the holes in the ax heads and tore into a wall! Bits of stone went flying through the air while the shocked suitors dodged and ducked.

Ulysses threw off his rags. He stood revealed as his true self. "Dogs!" he roared. "Did you really think I wouldn't return? Did you think the gods would let you go unpunished for the evil you've done here?" Then he let fly another swift arrow. It struck Antinous who was holding a golden goblet filled with wine. The troublemaker went spinning about. Then he fell forward, sending a table heavy with food crashing to the ground!

Shaking with fear, the others looked around for weapons in the room. But there were none to be found except for the swords being worn by some suitors. One man who had his sword began rushing forward, but Ulysses brought him down with a fleet arrow. Then another suitor rushed forward with his sword held high. But Telemachus hurled a spear that stopped him before he could harm Ulysses.

After that, Ulysses kept firing arrow after arrow while his son hurried off and soon returned with more weapons. Telemachus armed himself and two men who quickly took their stand next to Ulysses. These men, one of whom was Eumaeus, were faithful servants. Earlier in the day Ulysses had revealed his identity to them and told them about the plan. And now the king and his small band stood together, fighting the evil suitors who'd just taken some weapons from the nearby storeroom. For in his haste, Telemachus had forgotten to lock the door.

Now the fighting was fiercer than ever. So Minerva disguised herself as one of Ulysses' friends and helped in the battle for a while. Then she transformed herself into a swallow and flew up to sit on a lofty rafter. From there she watched as six suitors came charging forward together, hurling their spears at the same time. Swift as eagles, the six weapons flashed toward Ulysses. But they missed their mark because the goddess turned them away.

The battle raged on. However, it was a hopeless one for the suitors. Within the hour, the terrible deed was done. Breathing hard, Ulysses stepped back and looked about the room. Just then a man rushed over to him and fell to his knees.

"Spare me, great Ulysses!" he cried. "I am just a harpist who was forced to play for the suitors. If you slay me, who will there be to honor your name in song? Have pity, my lord!"

At this, Telemachus stepped forward. "Father, don't kill this innocent man," he said. "And if Medon the messenger is still alive, spare him also. He always treated me well as a child."

These words brought Medon out from under a seat. Covered with an oxhide, he had been hiding there. Now trembling and weeping, he prayed for mercy.

Ulysses smiled. "Have no fear. My son's sense of justice has saved you," he said proudly. "Go now with the harpist and tell people that good deeds are better than evil ones!"

Ulysses looked around once more at the sorry sight. The men who hadn't escaped lay sprawled about in heaps like fish caught in a net. Sighing deeply, Ulysses then set about having any servants who had been disloyal to his family punished for their crimes.

When this was done, he sent for Euryclea. "Nurse, have this place cleaned up," he said. "Then ask Penelope to come down here to me."

The old nurse obeyed the king and had the room made fresh and bright again. Smiling, the woman stood for a moment before the golden flames dancing in the fireplace. Then she turned and hurried upstairs as though her old knees had become young again. She bent over Penelope and laughed, "Wake up, my dear child! Come downstairs and greet your husband. Ulysses has returned, and the suitors are gone!"

A short time later, Penelope stood at the top of the stairs. Her face was quite pale. Yet she looked quite lovely as she began walking slowly down the steps.

Her mind was greatly troubled. Could what the nurse had said be true? Were the suitors really gone? Was this man really Ulysses? Or was he someone playing a cruel joke arranged by wicked people?

The troubled woman didn't hurry over to Ulysses. Instead, with her eyes lowered she sat quietly near the fireplace. This bothered Telemachus greatly. "Mother, why do you keep away from my father?" he cried out.

Penelope answered, "My son, I am numb with surprise. Still, if this man is really Ulysses, I shall soon know. For only my dear Ulysses would know about some secrets he and I shared." Then turning to Euryclea, the clever queen went on. "Nurse, have Ulysses' bed taken from my room. Put it into the hall for tonight. This man shall take his rest there for the time being."

Hearing this, Ulysses grew angry. "Only Jove could move that bed by himself!" he shouted. "I constructed it myself! There was a thick olive tree growing in the courtyard. I built our room around that tree. Then I cut off the tree's branches and made its trunk a bedpost! Penelope, has anyone dared to move my bed by cutting down the olive tree at its roots?"

The queen's face lit up with joy upon hearing these words. She looked up at the man that Minerva had made tall and strong again. "My husband!" she cried. "It's you! Oh, my Ulysses, don't be angry with me for testing you. I was so afraid someone might be trying to deceive me!"

Sobbing with happiness, Penelope flew to her husband and threw her arms about his neck. Again and again she kissed the happy man who wept as he embraced his loving wife.

"My wise and brave Penelope," he sighed. "We are together at last!"

# QUESTING FOR INFORMATION

## A. Getting the Main Idea and Facts

Write the letter of the answer that best completes each statement.

1. This story is mainly about how a man _____.
   a. begged for food in his own home
   b. punished a great troublemaker
   c. regained his family and kingdom

2. On the day of his return to Ithaca, Ulysses immediately _____.
   a. spoke to his wife
   b. made plans with a goddess
   c. strung a bow

3. Ulysses' _____ recognized him because of a scar above his knee.
   a. swineherd     b. nurse     c. son

4. Two innocent men were saved from Ulysses' wrath by _____.
   a. Telemachus     b. Penelope     c. Euryclea

5. Ulysses proved his identity to his wife by explaining how he had

   _____.
   a. fought at Troy
   b. won the contest
   c. constructed a bed

## B. Going Beyond the Facts

Write the letter of the answer that best completes each statement.

1. We may infer that the suitors Eumaeus saw stepping out of a boat were unhappy because they had _____.
   a. been sent to get presents
   b. failed in a plot
   c. become seasick

2. We can tell that the main reason Argus held on to life was to

   _____.
   a. see Ulysses again     b. find a new home
   c. go hunting

3. We may conclude that a suitor brought the bow to the fire in order to _____.
   a. examine it in better light
   b. keep it away from Ulysses
   c. make it easier to bend

4. Most probably, the main reason Telemachus ordered his mother to leave was to _____ .
   a. keep her from harm
   b. frighten the suitors
   c. embarrass her
5. We can guess that the suitors feared that Ulysses might be able to string the bow because they _____ .
   a. knew he'd had plenty to eat
   b. had watched him preparing for a fight
   c. believed Minerva was helping him

## QUESTING FOR MEANINGS

Write the letter of the word that best completes each statement below.
a. transformed  b. identity  c. deceive
d. applauded  e. construct

1. The happy crowd _____ the good news.
2. The thief's story didn't _____ the police.
3. That old building was _____ into a modern youth center.
4. Plans were made to _____ a new hospital downtown.
5. The _____ of the gift-giver was never revealed.

## QUESTING FOR UNDERSTANDING

1. Through the years many readers have applauded Penelope as a woman greatly to be admired. Discuss story events that prove that she was each of the following:
a. clever  b. courageous  c. kind  d. loyal
2. Minerva liked crafty Ulysses because she herself was crafty and enjoyed playing tricks on people. Discuss three or more ways in which she used her powers to help Ulysses or members of his family.

## QUESTING FOR ENRICHMENT

Assume that a classmate has written a summary of this story, and has asked you to help him select the correct *homonyms* for the following sentences. Sharpen your own skills by making a numbered list of the homonyms he should use.

1. Ulysses' voice was (hoarse, horse) with emotion.
2. Ulysses enjoyed telling a tall (tale, tail) to Eumaeus.
3. Evil suitors had set (sale, sail) to find and slay Telemachus.
4. Argus, the old dog, was too (week, weak) to get up.
5. Antinous (threw, through) a stool and hit Ulysses.
6. Greedy Irus was (throne, thrown) out into the yard.
7. Penelope's face was very (pail, pale) and yet beautiful.
8. The queen slowly came down the long flight of (stairs, stares).
9. Of (coarse, course), the happy nurse held her tongue.
10. Ulysses said that Jove would give strength to the (right, write) man.

From
**LATER EUROPE**

# Beowulf and the Creatures from the Burning Lake

Among the Germanic tribes that settled in Britain in the fifth century A.D. were the Angles and the Saxons. In time, they produced a great poem called *Beowulf*. It was written in the Anglo-Saxon language, which is also called Old English.

This epic, written about 725, was not about the Anglo-Saxons, but about their Scandinavian ancestors. The story concerns the Geats (from Sweden) and the Danes (from Denmark).

In this tale, we learn about two very unusual battles fought by young Beowulf. We also learn how he really won a great swimming contest though he was the last to reach land.

## Major Characters

**Beowulf** heroic nephew of king of Geatland (Sweden)

**Grendel** ferocious creature

**Grendel's mother** more ferocious than her son

**King of Daneland (Denmark)**

**Unferth** Danish warrior

## Vocabulary Preview

**tentacles** long growths on a creature's head or around its mouth, used for holding or moving
The octopus used its *tentacles* to catch the passing object.

**mail** armor made of small metal rings linked together, or of metal scales that overlap
Before rushing into battle, the knight put on his coat of *mail*.

**vast** huge; enormous; gigantic
The Atlantic and Pacific oceans are *vast* bodies of water.

**enabled** made able; given the power to do something
The telescope has *enabled* scientists to study the heavens more closely.

**dissolving** becoming liquid; melting
Intense heat was *dissolving* wax into liquid form.

# I.  Out of the Shadows

"The hairy beast is twice as tall as any man," the husky warrior mumbled with fear in his voice. He was sitting with his fellow travelers on the deck of the long ship from Geatland, the country now called Sweden.

"Yes, and its arms are as thick as the trunks of trees," groaned another man. "And it's said that no weapon is strong enough to stop Grendel, the creature from the burning lake!"

The fourteen warriors began shivering, and pulled their thick cloaks more closely about themselves. Sitting in silence, they fixed their eyes on their leader, Beowulf. The young man was standing near the curved prow of the ship. Huge black wings swooped up from the sides of his bright helmet, and chill breezes from the North Sea kept blowing back strands of his blond hair.

Beowulf's gray eyes were staring out over the dark and rolling ocean waves. "I must win this battle, even at the risk of losing my life," he was thinking to himself. "The people of Daneland must be helped to live in peace and safety!"

Beowulf stayed awake all night, watching for the shore. He was eager to reach the land now called Denmark. And he caught sight of Daneland just as dawn was breaking. Not long after that, he and his men pulled their boat ashore and were met there by a friendly watchman.

Soon the travelers were following the watchman, trudging up the rocky beach toward the dark green forest of pine trees. Swords and heavy shields clanked noisily as the men continued their long march inland. On and on they struggled until they reached a huge town and were led to the doors of the king's great meeting hall.

With swords and spears at the ready, the king's guards quickly surrounded the strangers. Then they led them into a very large room.

About two hundred noblemen were busy eating and drinking at long wooden tables. The new arrivals walked past the staring nobles and soon stood before the white-haired king and his queen. They were sitting in huge carved chairs near a roaring fire. Their long robes were edged with fur, and golden bands gleamed around the queen's long braids. Huge dogs, growling softly and watching the strangers, sat at the feet of the royal couple.

"Welcome, visitors!" said the king. "Be at ease, and tell us the reason for your journey here."

At this, Beowulf bowed low and began explaining his mission. "I am Beowulf, a nephew of the king of Geatland," he said. "I've come to slay the monster from the burning lake!"

The king shook his head and smiled a bit sadly. "Ah, young nobleman, I fear that you'll be unable to help us," he sighed. "No one has ever been able to stop Grendel, that fierce enemy of mankind. No weapon has ever been made that can stop the deadly creature!"

Beowulf looked around, for the room had suddenly become very quiet. All the noblemen had put down their food and drinking cups to hear what his answer would be. Seeing this, Beowulf answered in a voice loud enough for everyone to hear.

"I'll slay the beast, or I'll die trying! And since no weapons can harm the monster," he declared, "I'll fight him with my bare hands!" Then he raised his powerful hands high into the glow of the firelight for all to see.

Beowulf's men smiled and nodded to one another. For they knew that in all the world there was no man with a mightier grip.

But just then a deep voice filled the room. "Boaster!" cried a well-built man as he jumped to his feet. The angry man's name was Unferth, and he was one of the mightiest warriors in Daneland. "How can you slay Grendel?" he shouted. "You're no hero! Why, even in this land we've heard how you lost a swimming contest to Breca, a youth in your own land! Isn't that true?"

Beowulf stared hard at Unferth. "Yes, Breca reached land first," he answered. "But I proved myself the mightier man, and a man of honor!"

Unferth laughed aloud. "How can that be?" he sneered for all to hear.

Beowulf pulled himself up tall. "Well, my friend, drunk with beer, you will soon know," he said. "Breca and I went out into the sea to see whose strength was mightier. We carried swords in our hands to fight off any whales or other sea monsters we might meet. The sea was rough but we swam on for many days. Breca couldn't pass me by, though he tried hard. And I chose not to swim ahead and leave him behind.

"Then one day the waters became very rough. The waves crashed and rolled, and we were separated by the surging tide. Breca was swept along and finally swam to shore. But in the meantime, I was attacked by monsters from the deep!"

Now many listeners began leaning forward. They wanted to catch every word of Beowulf's story.

"The creatures with long tentacles tried to pull me under. But I kept swinging and thrusting my sword with all my might," said Beowulf. "The battle was fierce and long, and more than once I found myself fighting underwater! But in the end I was the victor! And when all was through, I realized that the surging tide was sweeping me far off course. Finally, then, I swam to shore in a distant land!

"So, you see, Unferth, my strength was the mightier! And my honor was great for I hadn't deserted a friend at sea. Now I ask you what you have done that can match my deeds!"

When Unferth heard this, his face grew red. He said not another word and quickly sat down. From the corner of his eye he watched as the king shook Beowulf's hand. "So be it!" exclaimed the king. "You're a worthy young man. You shall have your chance to stop the beast from the burning lake. We shall speak more of this tomorrow. But for now, we'll leave you and your weary companions to eat and then rest here through the night."

An hour later, Beowulf and his men were alone in the great hall. They had eaten well and were beginning to settle down for some rest. Stretched out on their great cloaks, all the men but Beowulf were soon sound asleep near the comforting warmth of the fire. But little did any of them know that a terrible figure was already moving through the shadows in the woods.

Beowulf sat up and stared into the leaping flames in the fireplace. He was busy going over his daring scheme. Could his plan succeed? Could he stop Grendel just by using his bare hands? Beowulf stretched mightily, yawned, and kept on thinking.

Everything was very still, except for the crackling sound made by the burning logs. Then suddenly a noise like a crack of thunder filled the air! Long pieces of the wooden door went flying by like spears. And Grendel, the hater of mankind, rushed in out of the darkness!

Grendel's eyes gleamed red in the firelight. Stomping heavily, he came slouching into the room. His hairy arms and legs, thick and powerful, knocked over tables and benches as he moved closer and closer to the men.

Beowulf didn't run to hide. He just stood his ground, waiting for the beast to attack him. But then Beowulf stared in horror as the creature suddenly seized a screaming warrior and began devouring him, clothes and all!

"Don't touch my men!" Beowulf shouted.

At this, the monster turned and stared at the youth who stood shaking a fist at him. Then Grendel gave an earsplitting yell. Stretching out his long arm, he went rushing toward Beowulf.

The youth waited until the monster was almost upon him. Then, like a cat, Beowulf instantly leaped aside. Reaching out, he gripped the beast's thick arm and held on for dear life. Tightening his mighty grip, he leaned heavily against Grendel's arm in a powerful wrestling hold.

Beowulf's plan was working! Grendel stomped about wildly, tugging to break the hold. And the building shuddered as the fierce struggle went on.

In the meantime, Beowulf's men struck at the monster with their swords. However, Grendel was not harmed at all because an evil spell protected him from such weapons.

Then Beowulf increased the pressure of his mighty grip, and the monster roared in pain and anger. Soon the pain became so great that Grendel tried to pull his arm away by using all his remaining strength. With one mighty tug he yanked himself free. But in doing so, Grendel's arm was torn right out of its socket!

Roaring in agony, Grendel went stumbling out of the hall. He went howling and crashing through the dark forest. His arm, however, lay at the feet of the young hero from Geatland.

On the next day, the king and his joyful subjects gazed long at Grendel's arm. It had been nailed to the wall. The happy king then gave a great feast, and he rewarded Beowulf with many fine gifts. Beowulf smiled at the sight of new armor, several fine rings, and a great collar of bright gold.

The feast went on late into the night, until at last the king and queen rose to leave. Beowulf and his men left, too. They were going to spend the night as guests in the homes of grateful noblemen. Indeed, all the people were happy that night as they lay down to sleep. Of course, they didn't know that once more a terrible figure was slouching through the shadows of the forest.

## II.  Beneath the Burning Lake

Early the next morning, the king heard the terrible news. Quickly he sent for Beowulf. "Another creature, one that we all thought was dead, came out of the burning lake last night," he moaned. "The thing of evil slew one of my closest friends and took Grendel's arm away. The creature is Grendel's mother. She's even more dangerous than her son!"

Beowulf listened quietly, clutching at his sword. "Show me the way to the monster's lake," he said with anger in his voice. And at once the king ordered his men to get things ready for the trip.

Before setting out on the journey, Beowulf put on his war shirt, a thick coat of mail. And as Beowulf put on his helmet, Unferth walked up to him and handed him a sword. "Take this," he said. "It's the strongest weapon in Daneland. You may need it."

Beowulf nodded, took the famous battle-sword, and clasped the warrior's hand. After that, the young hero mounted a horse and rode off with the king and a party of frightened men.

On and on they went, cutting through the tangles in the thick and lightless forest. It took them several hours before they caught sight of the lake which indeed was a very strange one. The lake was steamy and bubbling. And it had a bloody red glow as if fires burned beneath its troubled surface.

The blond youth dismounted and walked to the edge of the lake. For a while he just stood there, peering into the restless waters. Finally, he turned to speak to the king.

"I may not come back," said Beowulf. "If I fail to return, please send all the treasure you have given me to my noble king in Geatland. See that my men are taken care of, and give my own sword to Unferth. Please, my lord, do these things for me."

Then, after whispering a prayer, he plunged into the lake. The men on shore trembled at the thought of what might happen to him. Silent, they stared at the bubbles in the water as he sank out of sight.

Almost immediately, sharp claws struck at Beowulf. But the claws of Grendel's mother failed to harm him because of his thick war shirt, and this made the hag angrier than ever!

With fierce tugs she dragged him deeper and deeper into the lake. Strange creatures with long teeth began circling him and tearing wildly at his arms and legs. But he fought them off, jabbing and thrusting at them as he sank lower and lower. And finally, just as his lungs were aching for air, he felt himself being dragged into a dry cave.

Beowulf was startled to see the vast underground cavern and the flames leaping in pits near its entrance. But even more startling was the sight of the horrible creature gripping him.

Her thick green hair looked like tangles of dripping seaweed. Her skin was gray as stone and twice as hard. And her deep-set eyes seemed to be circles of swirling fire!

Beowulf took a very deep breath and swung Unferth's mighty sword. The weapon struck the creature's head, but did her no harm at all! Beowulf's mouth fell open in surprise.

Quickly then, he reached out, seized her shoulder in his powerful grip, and hurled her to the ground. But as she fell, she clutched at his legs and caused him to stumble. He hit the floor with a crash, and at once she pounced on him!

Kneeling on his chest, she drew a dagger and raised it overhead. Shrieking with cruel laughter, she struck at the youth. But the blade failed to pierce his thick coat of mail.

Then Beowulf pushed the surprised monster to one side and jumped to his feet. His eye caught sight of a huge sword hanging on a nearby wall. It was a weapon made in the days when giants roamed the earth!

Yanking the weapon down, Beowulf swung it mightily toward the dangerous beast. The blade struck the monster in the neck, and she fell moaning to the ground.

"Your days of evil are over!" shouted Beowulf. Then he struck at the creature until she moved no more.

After that, the light in the cave grew brighter. In time it blazed as bright as heaven's candle that shines in the sky.

The light enabled Beowulf to spot Grendel's body lying near the back of the cave. He rushed over to the lifeless beast and cut off its frightening head.

The blood of Grendel and the hag was so hot and poisonous that the sword blade began dissolving like an icicle in the summer sun. Soon it was completely melted away. All that was left of the weapon was its golden hilt that sparkled with colorful jewels.

"The king shall have these beautiful gems!" cried Beowulf as he stuck the hilt into his belt.

The men waiting on shore were certain that their friend had been slain. Sick at heart, they were just turning to leave. But just at that moment, something came crashing up through the waters. The men gasped in horror.

"Run! Run!" the terrified men cried at the sight of Grendel's head. But suddenly the men broke into cheers! Beowulf, smiling broadly, rose to the surface of the now calm and peaceful lake.

That night there was a great celebration; it was the greatest feast ever given in Daneland. Many rich gifts were piled high before the young hero. And though Beowulf was truly happy, his thoughts kept turning homeward.

Soon after that night, Beowulf sailed back to Geatland. His own people gave him a hero's welcome. Overjoyed, Beowulf did all he could from that time forward to keep his land free from all harm.

Years later, Beowulf was hailed as the new king. And it is said that he ruled wisely and well for fifty years.

## QUESTING FOR INFORMATION

### A. Getting the Main Idea and Facts

Write the letter of the answer that best completes each sentence.

1. This story is mainly about how Beowulf _____ .
   a. sailed to Daneland
   b. fought beneath the burning lake
   c. freed a nation from terror

2. Beowulf declared he'd fight Grendel with _____ .
   a. help from Breca      b. his bare hands      c. a dagger

3. Beowulf was saved from great harm by _____ .
   a. his men      b. a coat of mail      c. a magic spell

4. The fierce hag was finally slain by a weapon _____.
   a. from her own cave
   b. brought from Geatland
   c. belonging to Unferth

5. A sword _____ because of the monsters' poisonous blood.
   a. rusted     b. shattered     c. dissolved

## B.  Going Beyond the Facts

Write the letter of the answer that best completes each statement.

1. Unferth probably felt _____ after Beowulf told the story of the swimming contest.
   a. amused     b. foolish     c. pleased

2. We may infer that Grendel's mother left the lake that night in order to seek _____.
   a. revenge     b. safety     c. food for herself

3. It seems correct to say that, in time, Unferth began to _____ Beowulf.
   a. hate     b. respect     c. ignore

4. Probably, Beowulf's main reason for his unusual behavior toward his opponent during the swimming race was to _____.
   a. gain greater glory than his opponent
   b. be sure of his opponent's safety
   c. reach land before his opponent

5. The event which occurred *first* was _____.
   a. a sword melted away
   b. Unferth gave Beowulf a sword
   c. a sword failed to slay Grendel

## QUESTING FOR MEANINGS

Write the letter of the word that best completes each sentence below.
a. mail     b. vast     c. dissolving     d. tentacles     e. enabled

1. Hairlike _____ of the sundew plant help it to trap insects for food.
2. We could see the sugar _____ in the glass of water.
3. Lots of practice _____ the player to score many points in the game.

4. Bulletproof vests and coats of _____ were invented to protect people from harm.
5. A _____ amount of money was spent to improve the city's parks and playgrounds.

## QUESTING FOR UNDERSTANDING

1. Recall Beowulf's requests made to the king near the lake, and tell what they reveal about Beowulf's feelings concerning _____.
a. his own king    b. his men    c. Unferth

2. Unferth became angry with Beowulf for boasting. Discuss one or more other possible reasons the great warrior might have had for becoming so angry with the youth who had claimed he'd slay Grendel or die trying.

## QUESTING FOR ENRICHMENT

Modern English contains some words borrowed or derived from the languages of Germany, Holland, and the Scandinavian countries. For example, *waltz* (a type of dance) comes from German. *Stoop* (a step or entrance stairway of a house) comes from Dutch. *Law, sky* and pronouns such as *they* and *them* come from Danish.

Match the borrowed or derived words in column A with their meanings in column B.

**A**
(Words and Sources)

1. kindergarten (from German)
2. easel (from Dutch)
3. meek (from Danish)
4. fiord (from Norwegian)
5. smorgasbord (from Swedish)

**B**
(Meanings)

*a.* stand or support for artist's painting
*b.* mild and patient
*c.* large variety of dishes set out and from which diners make choices to fill their plates
*d.* class for children, usually between ages of four to six
*e.* long, narrow body of sea-water between steep cliffs

# Roland's Fateful Decision

The *Song of Roland* is the French national epic. It dates from about 1100. The epic grew out of reports of events that took place in 778 when the forces of King Charlemagne (Charles the Great) were at war with Saracen forces in Spain. The Saracens were men of North Africa who invaded Spain during the Middle Ages.

Roland was the son of Charlemagne's sister. The story that follows concerns this young man and a fateful decision he had to make. His choice was one that could mean life or death for thousands of men.

In this version of the tale, we see why the young warrior tries hard to *destroy* his mighty sword on a famous battlefield.

## Major Characters

**Charlemagne**   king of the Franks (France)

**Roland**   Charlemagne's nephew

**Oliver**   Roland's best friend

**Ganelon**   a baron and Roland's stepfather

**Marsilies**   king of Spain

## Vocabulary Preview

**vassal**   a man in the Middle Ages who owed loyalty to a king or lord who had given him some land to hold
> The king called each *vassal* to bring some men to join him in a war against an enemy lord.

**tribute**   a forced payment or an award to show respect or thanks to someone
> Some kings expected *tribute* each year from nearby weaker nations.

**hostage**   a person kept as a pledge by an enemy until certain conditions are met
> The *hostage* was released when his general agreed to a truce for new peace talks.

**desert**   to abandon; leave someone or a place that shouldn't be left
> That soldier didn't *desert* his post.

**retreat**   to withdraw; fall or move back
> Our dog's barking made the burglar *retreat*.

# I.  The Traitor

**T**he richly dressed man had no love for his stepson. Over the years Ganelon had grown very jealous of young Roland's fame. The baron nervously gripped the sides of his fine cloak of sable skins. His eyes burned with hatred for the youth standing with the other nobles before their king in his army camp.

Roland, the king's nephew and favorite vassal, was bright-eyed and muscular. Standing next to this sandy-haired youth was the young man known as Oliver the Wise. He and Roland had been the best of friends since boyhood days.

Leaning on his favorite sword called Durendal, Roland watched the king who was lost in thought. Charlemagne, King of the Franks and Emperor of the West, was a very old man. Yet the white-haired lord was still a powerful leader of men. Now on this sunny morning in Spain, he sat quietly in the cool shade of a huge pine tree.

Looking troubled, the ancient one kept thinking over a message that had been delivered to him from an enemy king. Finally, Charlemagne looked up at the nobles gathered around him.

"For seven years now we've been fighting here in Spain. We are punishing this king for helping my enemies during my last war," he said. "Now King Marsilies has made me an offer to bring about peace in this land."

Many nobles were pleased to hear this. They longed to return to their homes in France. Smiling with hope, they listened as the king went on.

"Marsilies says that if I agree to return to France now, he'll send me rich tribute. He promises me seven hundred camels, along with four hundred mules carrying bags filled with gold and silver. He also promises to send twenty hostages, including the sons of nobles, to show he means all he says. And, finally, he pledges that within a month he will come to France and obey my wish that he accept my faith as his own. What shall I do?"

Roland quickly spoke up. "Be careful, my lord," he declared. "Marsilies tricked us the last time he asked for a truce. That cruel tyrant cut off the heads of our messengers!"

At this, Ganelon pushed his way through the crowd. "Close your ears to Count Roland's words! We've been fighting a long time. We all yearn for peace!" he argued. "Perhaps Marsilies is now truly ready to do as he says!"

Charlemagne sat silent for a few minutes. Then he slowly nodded his head in agreement, bringing a sly grin to Ganelon's lips.

"But whom shall I send to Marsilies? Who will see that the promised tribute is brought here to me?" asked the king. "The mission may be dangerous!"

Roland swung his bright sword into the air. "Let me go and face that false man!" he cried. "I have no fear of the Saracens."

At once, dark-haired Oliver raised his strong arm in protest. "No, my friend. You might lose your temper and be harmed. Let me go in your place!"

Charlemagne smiled with pleasure at this display of courage and friendship. However, he shook his head. "You are two of my twelve peers, my chief vassals," he said. "I won't allow either of you to go. Now you and the other Franks must choose someone else to make the journey."

Hearing this, Roland nodded. "Well, then," he said, "there stands Ganelon." And at once, many of the Franks agreed with this choice.

Flinging his fur cloak to the ground, Ganelon glared at Roland. "You would send your own stepfather on such a mission?" he snarled.

This brought a frown to Roland's face. "Never mind," said the youth. "If the king will allow it, I'll go in your place!"

Ganelon's thin face grew red with rage. "No! You won't go for me!" he snapped. "I'll obey the king's command, for my fellow Franks have chosen me. But I won't forget that this is all your doing, Count Roland!"

Later that day, the king held out a sealed letter and a glove to Ganelon. Charlemagne's glove was to show Marsilies that the baron was his messenger. However, Ganelon dropped the glove as he reached for it, causing all the Franks to gasp.

"Surely this is a bad sign," one noble whispered to another.

A short time later, Ganelon was on his way with Charlemagne's sealed letter to the Saracen lord. Marsilies' messengers went riding along with him as he made his way to Saragossa. And as they rode along, Ganelon spoke freely to Marsilies' chief messenger, a great nobleman.

The Saracen messenger listened with interest as Ganelon revealed his feelings about Roland. Ganelon claimed that Charlemagne depended heavily on his nephew, and that there could be peace only when Roland was gone. And before long, Ganelon and the Saracen noble agreed that Roland should be slain.

Later that day, the riders entered Marsilies' camp outside the walls of Saragossa. The Frank was led up to the king. He was sitting on a gold-trimmed chair in the shade of a pine tree. Nervously, Ganelon bowed to the powerful lord.

Marsilies sat tugging gently at his stringy black beard. "Speak!" he commanded. "What is Charlemagne's answer? Is he ready to go back to France?"

Ganelon pulled himself up tall. "My king has conquered all the cities in Spain, except Saragossa. He says he won't attack it if you agree to obey all his wishes," said Ganelon. Then, smiling slyly, he went on. "Charlemagne will then allow you to rule half of Spain for him. If you don't agree to his offer, he says you will be seized with force. You will be bound and flung onto the back of a dirty pack animal. Then you will be taken to France to be judged, and surely you will be put to death!"

Marsilies grew pale with both fear and anger. Quickly he raised a short spear. And just as quickly Ganelon reached to pull out his sword. However, neither man attacked the other. For Marsilies' tall uncle, one of his most trusted advisors, whispered something into his nephew's ear.

"Don't kill him," said the wise man. "Slaying him won't help us to be rid of Charlemagne. Let the man speak on."

Soon after that, the sly Ganelon rubbed his dark beard and went on speaking. "Why are you so filled with rage?" he asked. "Charlemagne says he will allow you to rule half of Spain for him. The other half will be ruled by Roland, his favorite vassal. Remember now, if you don't agree, you'll be seized and bound. You'll be flung onto a common pack animal and taken back to France to be judged. And there you'll die in shame!"

Ganelon then handed the angry king the letter from Charlemagne. The king quickly broke the thick wax seal and read the letter. Then Marsilies' eyes narrowed to slits.

"This letter just complains about my treatment of Charlemagne's other messengers," he said. "So he wants me to send my uncle as one of the hostages. Charlemagne says he will not trust or honor me otherwise."

"My lord," said one of Marsilies' men. "The letter makes no wild threats against you. Perhaps this baron spoke falsely. Let me right this wrong for you!" And when Ganelon heard this, he gripped his sword.

However, the king just shook his head and walked away lost in thought. The king's chief messenger then hurried over to speak to him.

"Ganelon is very angry with the Franks, and especially with young Roland. He hates Roland," said the nobleman. "He told me he wants to see him dead! Ganelon will gladly serve us now!"

Now Marsilies grinned slyly. He was quick to see that his messenger was right. So the king walked back to his seat and sat down.

"Noble baron, I was only tricking you with my false anger," he said. "We mean you no harm. You were only delivering your king's message. It took great courage to come here. Come, take these fine furs from my shoulders as a gift!"

Ganelon smiled greedily at the sight of the expensive furs. And he listened carefully as the king went on.

"Now tell me more," said the king. "It's said that Charlemagne is already a very old man. When will he stop fighting his endless wars?"

Ganelon frowned. "Never!" he cried. "Charlemagne fears no one with Roland and his men to protect him. The wars won't end so long as Roland lives!"

Tugging at his beard, Marsilies nodded slowly. "I understand, noble baron," he said. "But how can we rid ourselves of Charlemagne's great protector?"

Ganelon's heart was beating faster now. "I have a plan," he hissed. Then the traitor explained his plan to the grinning king.

After that, Marsilies' nobles presented Ganelon with a costly sword and a new helmet. Marsilies' wife gave the pleased baron two jeweled bracelets worth a great fortune. And Marsilies promised that each year he'd send Ganelon a mule carrying sacks heavy with gold.

Then the happy king gave Ganelon the keys to the city of Saragossa to present to Charlemagne. And he had his men prepare the tribute that had been promised to that king. Soon after that, Ganelon began leading twenty hostages away. For Marsilies and his advisers were willing to risk the lives of these men in order to be rid of Roland and Charlemagne.

Behind the hostages came four hundred mules carrying sacks of gold and silver. They were followed by seven hundred camels. And Ganelon, smiling, rode along with the jeweled bracelets in his pocket and an evil plan in his heart.

## II. The Trap Is Set

Early the next morning, Ganelon entered Charlemagne's camp. He found the king sitting before his great tent. His nobles stood nearby, staring at the hostages, the camels, and the four hundred dusty mules carrying the treasure.

"Good news!" exclaimed the baron, bowing low to the king. "I present you with the keys to Saragossa! Marsilies was truthful. He meant all that his messengers told us," he said. "Within a month he will follow you to France and be ruled in all things by you. He has sent you the promised tribute and hostages. However, he couldn't send his uncle, for that man is now dead. A victim of drowning!"

Charlemagne nodded with understanding. Then he quickly began issuing orders. He commanded that his great army should begin preparing for the long journey home.

The king was pleased, yet that same night he dreamed of Ganelon seizing and splintering the king's own spear. And he dreamed of being attacked by a bear and a leopard. In the morning the king rose tired and troubled. Yet he went on with preparations for the march.

"There's one more thing," he said to his chief officers. "A rear guard must ride behind the main army to protect it from surprise attacks. Now, whom shall I put in charge of the rear guard?"

Brushing dust from his fur cloak, Ganelon looked about. His gaze rested on his stepson. "Well, then," he said, "there stands Roland. Your nephew should have the honor of protecting you!"

Nodding, Charlemagne quickly decided that half of the whole army should ride with Roland in the rear guard. He wanted to be sure that his nephew would be safe. However, the youth bravely refused the offer of so many men.

Then Charlemagne and the main body of the army began moving slowly forward, heading toward a pass in the mountains between Spain and France. Several miles behind rode Roland, Oliver, and twenty thousand men in the rear guard.

The two young peers rode side by side, talking and joking like schoolboys. There was peace in their hearts. In truth, the hearts of all the men were at ease. For the golden sun was shining above, and they were on their way home.

Suddenly, Oliver stopped speaking and looked toward some high hills not far off. "I thought I heard a trumpet blast," he said. "I'll be right back!"

Oliver raced to the great hills, and rode to the top of the highest one. What he saw in the green valleys below made his blood run cold! For as far as the eye could see, the valleys were filled with armed warriors! Thousands upon thousands of them! Their swords and helmets blazed in the sunlight.

"Why are they here?" gasped Oliver. "Why didn't these Saracens attack the main army as it went by? Why did they remain hidden?"

Swiftly then Oliver turned. "Ambush! They mean to ambush the rear guard!" he cried as he raced down the hill.

"We're greatly outnumbered," Oliver told Roland and his men. "This will be the most terrible battle we've ever had to fight!"

Hearing this, some Franks began shouting loudly. "Let great shame fall on those who desert! Shame on deserters! On to battle, even if we must perish!"

Oliver raised his hands for silence. "Hear me!" he shouted. "I tell you we are greatly outnumbered!" Turning then, he pointed to a great ivory horn hanging from Roland's saddle. The magnificent horn, called Oliphant, had been carved from an elephant's tusk.

"Sound a blast on Oliphant! The king will hear it!" he pleaded. "He'll return to help us!"

Roland threw back his head. "Never! I would be called a fool! My family's honor would be ruined," he declared. "People would speak evil of dear France! Besides, these Franks are good men. They'll fight bravely!"

Oliver stared right into Roland's face. "I know our men have great courage, but the Saracen army fills the valleys," he argued. "Sound a blast on Oliphant and call Charlemagne back!"

Roland shook his head. "Friend, say no more about sounding Oliphant! A man should be willing to suffer all things for his king. So we shall not desert our post!" he said. "We shall stand firm and begin the attack!"

At that moment, a stocky man rode up. He was an archbishop who was riding with the rear guard. "Charlemagne is our king!" he called. "Well may we die for him!" Then all the men, twenty thousand of them, knelt for the holy man's blessing.

A short while later, Roland raised his good sword Durendal. Then he went charging forward with all his men bravely following him. And the hooves of twenty thousand horses pounded on the earth, making a sound like rolling thunder.

"*Mountjoy!*" the Franks shouted. Again and again they repeated Charlemagne's battle cry as the rear guard surged swiftly forward. It went crashing into the front ranks of the Saracens like a tidal wave hitting the shore. Swords and shields clanged and clashed! And the cries of unlucky men echoed through the valleys as the battle raged on and on.

Marsilies stared in disbelief. "These Franks are amazing! They fight like cornered lions!" he exclaimed. "They don't let up for a moment!"

As he spoke, silver trumpets sounded. Thousands of them! Another part of the Saracen army had just arrived. Roland saw this and gasped. He quickly realized that now there was no hope of winning.

"Oliver!" he shouted as he called his friend aside. "I'll sound the horn and Charlemagne will return! Some men may yet be saved!"

Oliver shook his head. "It's too late!" he cried. "You should have done it when I begged you to sound a blast on Oliphant!"

Roland was confused and weary. He didn't know what to answer. Before long, however, the archbishop rode up. His cloak was covered with dirt and blood.

"Don't be angry with each other! Remember your friendship!" he called. "Yet I must agree with Oliver. It's too late to save us now."

With gloom in his heart, Roland listened as the archbishop went on. "And yet I believe the horn can still do us some good," said the holy man. "Surely the horn will bring Charlemagne back. The Saracens would flee upon our king's return. Our people could then give

us decent burial! And our bones would be safe from wolves and wild pigs!"

To this, Roland and Oliver agreed. So, with blood running from the corner of his mouth, the wounded youth raised Oliphant to his lips. Then with all his might he sounded a long blast. The mournful sound filled the air. It carried for miles and finally reached Charlemagne's ears.

Ganelon began laughing softly. "That's not Oliphant you hear. It's only the wind," he said. "Besides, Roland would be too proud to call for help!"

But soon the mournful wail of the ivory horn sounded through the air again. "The rear guard is in trouble! Roland has been betrayed!" shouted the angry king. Turning, he glared at Ganelon. "You alone spoke to Marsilies! You set up an ambush to destroy my nephew!"

The furious king ordered his men to seize and hold the trembling man for severe punishment later on in France. So some men seized Ganelon with force. They cut off his beard, beat him, and bound him with a chain around his neck as though he were a bear. Then they flung him onto the back of a dirty pack mule to carry him back to France for judgment.

In the meantime, Charlemagne quickly wheeled his horse about. Riding hard, he led more than three hundred thousand men back toward Roncevaux, the scene of the battle.

A Saracen scout spied the huge army. At once, he raced ahead to warn his master. Marsilies, upon hearing the news, turned pale. Moving fast, he ordered the trumpeters to sound retreat! And so the Saracens rode off toward Saragossa.

Later on, the seriously wounded Roland dragged himself through the battlefield searching for wounded men. It was then that he fell to his knees beside the fallen Oliver. "Oh, my dear comrade," he wept bitterly. "You gave your life! You stood by me to the very end!"

Still weeping, Roland took out his fine sword and struck it against a great rock. He did this again and again, hoping to destroy Durendal. For the wounded youth knew that he would soon perish. He meant to keep any remaining Saracens from claiming his famous sword.

Then the dying youth lay on a grassy hillside. Beneath him was hidden his unbroken sword. His face was turned in the direction of the departed Saracens. He wanted to die facing the enemy!

Moments later, he groaned softly. He raised his right-hand glove to the sky. "May Heaven have mercy on me!" he gasped. And his hand fell limp to the ground.

Arriving at the battlefield, Charlemagne wept bitterly and long for his nephew and his fallen men. Then he had all but three of the honored dead taken from the field and buried with honor. After that, he had the bodies of Roland, Oliver, and the archbishop lifted gently into carts and covered over to be taken back to sweet France.

Later that day, Charlemagne sat up tall on his horse and pointed into the distance. "Ride!" he commanded. "We shall destroy the armies of false Marsilies!" And the tremendous army of Franks went thundering forward as trumpets blared and the sound of Oliphant once again filled the air!

And so ends this tale of Roland. However, it's said by many that Roland's story is not yet over. They say that his spirit dwells in the caves of the mountains between France and Spain. Some even claim they've heard the mournful sound of Oliphant in the hills. They say that whenever sweet France is in danger, Roland appears on the hills. And the ghostly sound of Oliphant can be heard wailing through the night.

## QUESTING FOR INFORMATION

### A. Getting the Main Idea and Facts

Write the letter of the answer that best completes each statement.

1. This story is mainly about how _____ .
   a. tribute and hostages were brought to a king
   b. jealousy and pride caused great suffering
   c. Roland and others chose Ganelon as a messenger
2. The Franks felt it was a bad sign when the king's _____ fell to the ground.
   a. sealed letter    b. splintered spear    c. glove
3. The archbishop wanted Roland to sound a blast on Oliphant so that _____ .
   a. lives would be saved
   b. the dead could be buried
   c. Oliver would be pleased
4. The sound of Oliphant caused Charlemagne to _____ .
   a. retreat to France    b. turn back    c. seek a truce
5. To save his famous sword from falling into enemy hands, Roland _____ .
   a. hid it    b. broke it    c. gave it to Oliver

## B. Going Beyond the Facts

Write the letter of the answer that best completes each statement.

1. We may infer that Marsilies' real reason for giving Ganelon fine
   furs was to _____ .
   a. reward his bravery
   b. keep him warm
   c. gain help from him

2. It seems correct to conclude that Ganelon was feeling _____ when
   he returned to Charlemagne's camp after meeting with Marsilies.
   a. ashamed of himself
   b. pleased with himself
   c. sorry for himself

3. We may conclude that Marsilies' uncle didn't appear as a hostage
   because _____ .
   a. he had drowned
   b. Marsilies wanted to keep him safe
   c. Ganelon didn't trust him

4. It seems certain that Ganelon was sure that Charlemagne would
   ask for _____ .
   a. more tribute      b. the keys to Saragossa      c. a rear guard

5. The statement, "_____ ," is true about Roland.
   a. He deserted his post
   b. He was willing to suffer for his king
   c. He always trusted Oliver's advice

## QUESTING FOR MEANINGS

Write the letter of the word that best completes each sentence
below.
a. vassal      b. hostage      c. desert      d. retreat      e. tribute

1. It is unkind to _____ a family pet on the street or anywhere else.
2. The new _____ pledged to serve the king who had given him land
   to hold.
3. The general didn't order his men to _____ even when the battle
   seemed hopeless for a while.

4. After both sides came to an agreement, the _____ was released unharmed.

5. In ancient days, some weak kings sent _____ to more powerful ones in order to be left in peace.

## QUESTING FOR ENRICHMENT

English has borrowed words from the French language. Some of these are listed below in column A. In some cases there is more than one acceptable pronunciation for certain words. You might want to check your dictionary for the other acceptable pronunciations.

Match the words in column A with their meanings in column B.

| **A** | | **B** |
|---|---|---|
| (French words) | (Pronunciations) | (Meanings) |

| | | |
|---|---|---|
| 1. ballet | (ba LAY) | *a.* kitchen; a style of cooking |
| 2. chef | (SHEF) | |
| 3. corsage | (kor SOJ) | *b.* flowers worn on shoulder, waist, or wrist |
| 4. cuisine | (kwee ZEEN) | |
| 5. debris | (day BREE) | |
| 6. deluge | (DEL yooj) | *c.* a form of dance |
| 7. encore | (ON kor) | *d.* list of food that may be ordered at a restaurant |
| 8. menu | (MEN yoo) | |
| 9. rendezvous | (RON day voo) | *e.* skilled cook; chief of kitchen |
| 10. souvenir | (SOO va neer) | |

*f.* something kept or given as a remembrance of someone, a place, or an event

*g.* flood; heavy rainfall

*h.* meeting by arrangement at certain time or place

*i.* audience's request to hear or see something again

*j.* rubbish; ruins; remains of something destroyed

## QUESTING FOR UNDERSTANDING

1. Some readers tend to remember only that Roland didn't want to seem like a fool for sounding a call for help. Now, in fairness to Roland, state two or more other reasons he gave for not calling for help. Then tell what you think this reveals about him.

2. Many readers find Ganelon a very interesting character.
   a. Tell what kind of man he was and support your views by making references to the story.
   b. Describe the threats he said Charlemagne had made against Marsilies. Be specific.
   c. Tell what finally happened to Ganelon, and explain why this was a strange turnabout or twist of fate.

# El Cid and the Cowardly Brothers

The *Poem of the Cid,* written in 1140, concerns Rodrigo Diaz, also known as El Cid Campeador (the Lord Champion) who was born in 1043. After leaving his hometown and family-owned mill, he became a great warrior. His fame and wealth grew as he fought the Moors.

The Moors were Arab and Berber conquerors who occupied parts of Spain from 711 to 1492. The word "Moors" also refers to the people of Morocco in northern Africa.

In El Cid's day, Spain was divided into a number of kingdoms. In the epic, El Cid's king twice exiled (sent away) the warrior because he wrongfully believed El Cid had not served him faithfully. While away, the banished Cid decided not to cut his beard as a sign of his love for his king. And even when he was permitted to return, he continued to wear his famous beard which he claimed no man had ever dared to tug or dishonor.

Some events in the epic are based on historical fact, and some are fictitious. In this tale we see the last part of an unusual court trial taking place on horseback.

## Major Characters

**El Cid**  military leader, ruler of Valencia, Spain

**Dona Elvira and Dona Sol** daughters of El Cid

**Diego and Fernando**  husbands of Dona Elvira and Dona Sol

**Felix Munoz**  nephew of El Cid

**Alfonso**  king of Castile

## Vocabulary Preview

**haughty**  overly proud of oneself, and scornful of others
The *haughty* guest spoke to hardly anyone at the gathering.

**spendthrift**  someone who wastes money; wasteful
The *spendthrift* had no money left for the week's groceries.

**booty**  plunder; things taken from an enemy in wartime
All the *booty* was shared by the victors of the battle.

**mocking**  making fun of
The unhappy man believed that people were *mocking* him.

**vanquished**  defeated; conquered
The unprepared troops were quickly *vanquished.*

# I.  A Terrible Deed

The wavy-haired youths hated their teenaged brides. After having wasted their own personal fortunes, the slim brothers had married the lovely daughters of a very rich man. But Diego and Fernando were unhappy because they believed that their wives weren't good enough for the sons of Count Gonzalo of Carrion.

Their young brides were Dona Elvira and Dona Sol. These dark-eyed beauties were the daughters of Rodrigo Diaz, El Cid, the great champion who had crushed many of the invaders who'd dared to trouble the land now called Spain.

Now on a sunny morning in Valencia, El Cid's great city, Diego and Fernando were waiting in a great hall in their father-in-law's palace. Some of the other nobles there were speaking in whispers as they waited for El Cid to awaken from a short nap. However, the spendthrift and haughty brothers stood silent and apart from everyone else, staring out an open window. They sneered as they watched a worker in the courtyard throwing chunks of meat to El Cid's pet, a huge golden lion. The snarling beast was leaping wildly, crashing against the bars of its cage.

After a while, the brothers looked around and stared at their sleeping father-in-law. He was stretched out on a couch, with his hands resting on his great beard. His beard was very long for he had vowed not to cut it as a sign of loving loyalty to Alfonso, King of Leon and Castile.

A short time later, a terrible roar filled the air. "It's the beast!" shouted a wide-eyed noble, pointing across the room. The immense lion was standing on the ledge of an open window. Its great teeth were flashing like daggers in the sunlight!

Trembling from head to foot, Fernando threw himself to the ground and quickly crawled under El Cid's couch. His brother, equally terrified, went racing through a door into the next room. There he crouched low in a corner behind a dripping winepress. All the other men stood their ground. They wrapped their cloaks around their arms, drew their swords, and stood ready to defend their sleeping lord.

At that moment, awakened by all the noise, El Cid sat up. Seeing what was happening, he quickly rose to his feet and signaled for the men to stand quite still.

"Hold!" commanded El Cid as the beast came bounding toward him. "Hold!" he shouted again, and the creature stopped short in its tracks. Then the courageous man walked boldly up to the panting

animal and gently stroked its golden mane. After that he led the calmed beast back to its cage in the courtyard.

When El Cid returned, he found the nobles hiding their smiles at the behavior of the cowardly brothers. But then the men burst into roars of laughter when Diego walked in with his pants stained purple by the wine drippings. However, El Cid didn't laugh at all. Instead, he raised his hand and said, "Be silent, good sirs!" Indeed, the noble lord didn't care to hear anyone laughing at other people's misfortunes.

Soon El Cid called his men over to study some colorful maps spread out on a long table, and began speaking about matters concerning Valencia and other places in the land. But Diego and Fernando only pretended to show any interest. Filled with hatred and anger, they wrongly blamed El Cid along with his nobles for their shame.

"Revenge will be ours," whispered Diego to his brother. "We have only to wait for the right moment!"

Some months later, Valencia was attacked by an army of Moors led by a fierce and turbaned king from Morocco. El Cid led his men into battle, and before long the Moors were defeated. It was a marvelous victory for El Cid and his forces. Great wealth was taken from the defeated army in the form of fine horses, sturdy weapons, and much silver and gold. El Cid gave his men a generous share of the booty, and he sent many magnificent steeds as a gift to King Alfonso.

Believing that his sons-in-law had behaved bravely in battle, for one oɪ them showed a captured steed, El Cid praised the youths. "It fills my heart with joy that you rode against my enemies for me!"

Diego and Fernando thanked him and hurried away. There were frowns on their faces, for they wrongly believed that El Cid was mocking them. And they still believed this when, later on, he gave precious battle swords to each of them. To one he gave the weapon called Colada, and to the other he gave the one called Tizonia. Of course, the youths accepted the gifts, although they knew that many nobles were secretly joking about their true behavior in battle. And all this made the youths even more determined to seek revenge for their great shame.

The young lords of Carrion let some time slip by, and then called on El Cid with some unpleasant news. "We plan to return to our estates in distant Carrion," said Diego with a wicked twinkle in his eye. "And, of course, we shall take our dear wives with us!"

This surprising turn of events troubled El Cid and his wife, Dona Jimena. They didn't care to see their daughters leave the safety of their walled city. But they were good parents, and they knew that it was the custom for wives to follow their husbands. So on the morning that their daughters left for Carrion, the sad parents hid their tears as the girls kissed them again and again.

El Cid sent many servants and guards along with the travelers. He also sent his nephew, Felix Munoz, to keep a special eye on his daughters.

The journey was a tiring one, so the group of fifty people had to stop and rest from time to time. One night they set up camp near a bubbling stream in a green oak forest. Everyone had a fine time eating, drinking, and singing merry songs. And everyone slept well around the roaring fires that kept the wild animals away.

In the morning, the brothers sat up slowly. Yawning and stretching, they pretended to be very tired. "My brother and I will rest here for a while longer," said Diego. "You people ride on ahead. We and our wives will catch up with you." Smiling slyly, he turned away as the puzzled group got ready and then rode off through the trees.

The brothers waited a while to be sure that the others were too far away to hear anything. Then, jumping to their feet, the brothers threw off their capes and rushed forward. Laughing wickedly, they set about beating their helpless wives. And though the young women cried for mercy, the cruel men kept striking them until the girls fell senseless to the ground.

"Now let's leave them here!" grinned the cowardly Diego. "They won't last long. These woods are filled with wild and hungry beasts!"

Pleased with themselves, the brothers rode off. As they traveled through the woods, they laughed and talked aloud about their deed. "Now we have our revenge for the shame we suffered because of the lion." said Fernando. "And we are also free of our marriages! We should never have taken El Cid's daughters as our brides. They are not our equals; we never should have married beneath our station in life. Now let the wolves and other wild beasts make short work of them!"

Diego nodded happily. "We can always say that they took a wrong turn and became lost in the woods," he said. "Come on, now! Let's ride home to a better life in Carrion!"

Still speaking, they rode past someone who was hiding behind some trees near the road. It was Felix Munoz, El Cid's nephew, and he had heard enough to make his blood run cold. The clever youth then followed the tracks left by the cowardly brothers' horses. Soon he found his cousins lying unconscious in the grass. Calling their names, he helped them to recover their senses and sit up. He used his new hat to bring them water, and then helped them to their feet. After that, he seated them on his horse and led the steed by the reins.

"Rest easy, sweet cousins," he said. "Rest easy. You'll soon be quite safe and well." And the young ladies, trembling and sobbing, thanked their kind cousin over and over again.

When El Cid heard about the foul deed that had been committed, he was enraged. Quickly he sent word to King Alfonso to inform him of how the young lords of Carrion had dishonored him and his daughters. And he pointed out that the young lords had also dishonored their king, for it was Alfonso who had arranged the marriages at the request of the young lords of Carrion.

Without delay, the insulted and furious king issued his orders. "Send word that Diego and Fernando are to appear in my court at Toledo," he commanded angrily. "El Cid's honor shall be restored!"

Of course, the two brothers and their family were shocked to learn about the royal command. However, they had no choice but to see that Alfonso was obeyed.

# II.  Battling for Justice

On the day of the trial, El Cid sat on a chair of carved ivory, a seat of honor near the king's throne. From there, El Cid could see the two defendants sitting at a wooden table, smiling and chatting as though they were sure all would go well for them.

The crowded courtroom had become very noisy, so the king raised his hand for silence. Then he turned to El Cid, who had just finished murmuring a prayer. "Make known your demands for justice," said the king.

El Cid stroked his beard and nodded. "I would like my precious battle swords returned to me," he said quietly.

Turning, the king spoke briefly with the judges seated nearby. "So be it," he said at last. "The swords must be returned at once."

Diego smiled. "This is a small price to pay," he whispered to his brother. "We're getting off easy."

Stroking his beard again, El Cid stared at the cowardly brothers with a fierce look. "Step by step, my daughters shall be avenged," he said in a deep voice that sent chills running down the spines of the defendants. And Diego's smile disappeared as El Cid went on.

"Take this sword, my nephew," said El Cid as he turned to a bright-eyed young man called Pedro Bermudez. "Now it will have a more worthy master." Then he turned to a young and light-haired noble called Martin Antolinez. "May this sword bring you honor," he said as he gave him the other weapon.

King Alfonso nodded his approval and then asked El Cid to go on with his demands. Bowing, El Cid said, "I gave these men three thousand silver marks before they left Valencia," he said. "They are no longer my sons-in-law, so I want all that treasure returned to me."

Hearing this, the brothers turned pale. "We gave back the swords. That should be enough to end all this," said Diego. However, the king just shook his head slowly from side to side.

"But we haven't a single coin left," declared Fernando. "How can we repay what we don't have?"

Leaning forward in his seat, a silver-haired judge pointed a finger at the youths. "If you have no money, then you must pay in other goods," he said. "You must give up all your swift war horses, your packhorses, your mules, your fine swords and other things of value. If this doesn't bring in enough, you must borrow from others to raise the needed sum!"

Fernando's mouth dropped open, and Diego hung his head at

the thought of having to borrow from his friends. Then, after all the arrangements for paying back El Cid had been taken care of, the youths stared at the frowning champion as he began speaking.

"My king, now let my main complaint be heard by the court. For I will not see these young lords escape without a challenge!" he said with force. "Young lords of Carrion, tell me when I ever harmed you in any way, and I will beg your pardon here in court. Didn't I give you my dear daughters, along with riches and honor? Why, then, did you beat them so cruelly and leave them alone in the woods filled with wild beasts?"

Fernando jumped to his feet at these words. "We are of high birth! As lords of Carrion we should have married daughters of kings or emperors!" he shouted. "We did right in leaving them. We have lost no honor!"

Trembling with rage beneath his long red cloak, El Cid turned to Pedro. "You ever-silent man, speak up!" he commanded. "Speak up for your blood cousins. For if I reply to Fernando's words, you will lose your chance to bear arms against him!"

Pedro stepped forward with his hand clutching Colada. "You lie about being a man of honor," he declared. "Don't you remember how you fled when a Moor was riding after you on the battlefield? I struck him down and gave you his steed so you could say you had slain an enemy! Well, I'll keep your secret no longer, honorable sir!"

Gasps of surprise and ripples of laughter could be heard throughout the courtroom as Pedro went on. "And surely you remember how you hid under El Cid's couch when his pet lion escaped from its cage! Now dare to oppose me, and with my sword I'll prove the truth of all I've said."

Stunned by Pedro's words, Diego leaped to his feet. "We are lords of the purest blood!" he shouted. "I say we did right in leaving wives who were not worthy of us. I'll fight anyone who challenges my claim!"

Unable to control his anger any longer, light-haired Martin rose to his feet with Tizonia in his grip. "You false coward!" he cried. "Don't you remember how you ran to hide behind a winepress when El Cid's lion escaped? Your pants were stained purple from top to bottom!"

Once again, gasps of surprise and peals of laughter sounded throughout the courtroom. And just as Alfonso raised his hand for silence, a tall and burly man named Ansur came stumbling toward El Cid. He was the young lords' oldest brother, and he was sputtering with rage as he said, "What is all this foolishness? Tell El Cid to go away and tend his mills as he used to do when he was a boy. This man should be grinding flour and collecting his money. Whoever led such a man to think about arranging weddings for his daughters with my highborn brothers?"

Almost before Ansur finished making his thoughtless remarks, one of El Cid's well-built vassals was on his feet. "Shut your foul mouth," said Muno, waving his hand before his face. "You gulp down breakfast before praying, and your breath disgusts everyone you greet! I say you are an evil man and a traitor, false to all men! Come on, now, and I'll make you admit you're everything I say you are!"

Suddenly, King Alfonso's fist came slamming down on the arm-rest of his throne. "Silence!" he commanded. "Those who have been defying each other will meet in combat. The winners will gain great honor. Be ready for the duel when the sun rises tomorrow!"

At this, Diego and Fernando begged the king for a favor. They said that since they had given up all their horses and weapons to repay El Cid, they would need some time to get ready. Bowing low, they asked that the contest take place in Carrion at some later date. After some thought, the frowning king agreed to this, and the great trial at Toledo came to an end.

On the morning of the trial by combat, the young lords' friends and relatives began arriving early. They stood crowded together in groups a safe distance from the boundary lines marked on the field of battle by the king's judges. The king told those who were to fight that anyone who crossed a boundary line would be considered beaten.

Then El Cid's three knights spoke in secret to the king. They were quite concerned over the appearance of so many armed supporters of the young lords. So before the contest began, Alfonso had some special words for the two brothers. "If you try anything wrong today, I'll make you pay for it. There will be no place for you to hide from me!" And upon hearing this, Diego and Fernando were filled with gloom as they rode over to their places at one end of the huge field.

When all was ready, Alfonso raised his hand as the signal to begin. Soon a rumbling sound like that of distant thunder was heard. It became louder and louder as Diego, Fernando, and Ansur went racing forward to meet the advancing Pedro, Martin, and Muno. The men had shields against their chests, and their heads were bowed very low as they charged forward with their lances aimed straight ahead.

Pedro and Fernando were the first to clash in battle. Fernando's lance broke in two places as it struck Pedro's shield. However, Pedro's lance pierced Fernando's shield and struck him in the chest, drawing blood. After that, the straps on Fernando's horse gave way, and the shocked lord fell into the red dust with a loud thud. And when he saw Pedro advancing on him with the mighty Tizonia, he cried out, "No more! No more! I am vanquished!"

In the meantime, Diego and Martin struck at each other with such great force that both their lances broke. Quickly then, Martin raised Colada and the whole field seemed to light up in its bright glow. With a swift movement, Martin cut away the upper part of Diego's helmet. The top of the helmet flew away, along with a bit of flesh and much of Diego's wavy hair.

Sure that he was about to die, Diego pulled the reins to wheel his horse around. But Martin was too fast for him and struck him with his sword. However, he hit him not with the edge, but with the flat side of the weapon.

"Help!" shrieked Diego. "Protect me, my king!" Then he turned his horse aside to avoid yet another stroke of the sword, and rode over a boundary line. At once, the judges declared the young lord vanquished in battle.

The last two contestants, Ansur and Muno, kept striking at each other's shields with one mighty blow after another. Before long, Ansur's lance pierced Muno's shield and cut into his armor, but failed even to scratch the warrior's flesh. In turn, Muno's lance tore through Ansur's shield, pierced his chest, and sent him flying from his saddle. And when Muno approached the bleeding man with lance in hand, Ansur cried out, "Strike no more! The field is yours. You have won!"

When word of the great victory reached El Cid in Valencia, he was overjoyed. "Once again my family has its honor!" he proclaimed with tears in his eyes. And though he was happy that day, his joy and his honor were to grow even greater. For with the approval of King Alfonso, El Cid's daughters married princes and, in time, became queens of Aragon and Navarre. And through the years many of El Cid's descendants sat upon the thrones of Spain.

# QUESTING FOR INFORMATION

## A. Getting the Main Idea and Facts

Write the letter of the answer that best completes each statement.

1. This story is mainly about a man's desire to regain _____.
   a. three thousand silver marks
   b. his family's honor
   c. two precious swords

2. As a sign of _____, El Cid refused to cut his long beard.
   a. loyalty to his king
   b. love for Valencia
   c. concern for his betrayed daughters

3. An army led by _____ attacked Valencia and was vanquished.
   a. Count Gonzalo
   b. the King of Navarre
   c. a turbaned king from Morocco

4. The young lords hoped that _____ would find their wives.
   a. Felix Munoz
   b. the Moors
   c. wild beasts

5. Alfonso ordered that the brothers were to appear in his court at _____.
   a. Carrion
   b. Toledo
   c. Morocco

## B. Going Beyond the Facts

Write the letter of the answer that best completes each statement.

1. We may infer that, in El Cid's time, young ladies from noble families usually married _____.
   a. men whom they knew and loved
   b. men chosen for them
   c. men only from their own kingdom

2. Probably, Pedro and other vassals didn't tell El Cid about the young lords' true behavior in battle because they _____.
   a. didn't want to upset him
   b. were all paid to keep silent
   c. feared the young lords' anger

3. Of the three events mentioned below, statement _____ describes the one that happened last.
    a. El Cid said he didn't want the lords to escape without a challenge.
    b. El Cid learned that the lords would have to repay him with goods and borrowed money.
    c. El Cid requested that his battle swords be returned to him.
4. We may assume that Pedro, Martin, and Muno felt _____ after hearing what the king said to the brothers just before the duel at Carrion.
    a. confused    b. worried    c. relieved
5. We may conclude that Diego and Fernando probably felt _____ when El Cid's daughters became queens.
    a. amused    b. honored    c. shocked

## QUESTING FOR MEANINGS

Write the letter of the word that best completes each statement.
a. spendthrift    b. booty    c. vanquished
d. mocking    e. haughty

1. Much valuable _____ was gathered from the deserted army tents.
2. The children were told that _____ others is very unkind.
3. In time, she _____ her fear of meeting new people.
4. He is a great _____ who is always borrowing money.
5. The members of that family are so _____ that they ignore most of their neighbors.

## QUESTING FOR UNDERSTANDING

1. Discuss more than one reason why King Alfonso would care to see El Cid receive justice and the young lords punished.
2. It's said that El Cid was a man of strong feeling and action. Support this by giving examples from the story to illustrate the following:
    a. his kindness concerning someone's misfortune
    b. his generosity toward others
    c. his respect for his king
    d. his love of family
    e. his concern for personal honor.

# QUESTING FOR ENRICHMENT

A. English contains some words borrowed or derived from Spanish. Some of these are listed below in column A. Match these words with their meanings in column B.

**A**

1. alligator
2. bronco
3. cargo
4. corral
5. indigo
6. mosquito
7. patio
8. siesta
9. sombrero
10. tornado

**B**

a. load of goods carried by a vehicle
b. inner yard open to sky; paved outdoor area for dining or relaxing
c. wild or partly tamed horse in Western U.S.
d. flying insect, the female of which stings
e. large, flesh-eating lizardlike animal
f. blue dye from certain plant or coal tar; deep violet-blue color
g. whirlwind; violent windstorm
h. pen for holding or capturing cattle, horses, or other animals
i. high-crowned, wide-brimmed straw or felt hat
j. afternoon rest or nap

B. As you probably recall, the years marked B.C. are those before the birth of Christ. The years after are marked A.D. (Anno Domini). Study the example of a time line below. Then read the sentences and select the letter of the response which makes each sentence correct.

| | Trojan War | Homer writes Iliad | Virgil writes Aeneid | Beo-wulf written | El Cid born | Arm-strong walked on moon |
|---|---|---|---|---|---|---|
| | 1100 BC | 850 BC | 29-19 BC | AD 725 | AD 1043 | AD 1969 |
| 2000 B.C. | 1500 B.C. | 1000 B.C. | 500 B.C. | ← • → A.D. 500 | A.D. 1000 | A.D. 1500   A.D. 2000 |

1. The years marked B.C. occurred (a. before, b. after) those marked A.D.
2. The *Iliad* was written (a. before, b. after) the *Aeneid*.
3. The birth of El Cid occurred (a. before, b. after) the Trojan War.
4. *Beowulf* was written (a. before, b. after) the birth of El Cid.
5. Men landed on the moon (a. before, b. after) Homer lived.

# El Cid and the Night of the Ghostly Rider

Robert Southey, the English poet and writer, produced a fine translation of the ancient and famous *Chronicle of the Cid.* His version, published in 1808, is a blend of works from various sources, including the great *Poem of the Cid.*

Over the years there have been many retellings of a stirring tale, not a part of the actual *Poem of the Cid,* from the greatly admired *Chronicle.* The tale is one that helps bring the stories about El Cid's epic adventures to a close, and for that reason it is presented here. It concerns an attack on Valencia, El Cid's walled city.

The story that follows is set in 1099, and is based on the version in Southey's translation. In this tale, we see why the people of Valencia show no fear at the sight of a ghostly rider on a moonlit night.

## Major Characters

**El Cid**  ruler of Valencia
**Dona Jimena**  wife of El Cid
**Bucar**  foreign king, enemy of El Cid

**Alfonso**  king of Castile, ally of El Cid
**Gil Diaz**  close friend of El Cid

## Vocabulary Preview

**gravely**  seriously; solemnly
The courageous fireman was *gravely* injured.
Judge Smith spoke *gravely* about the harm caused by careless drivers.

**allies**  people or countries united for a special purpose
The United States and Britain were *allies* in more than one war.

**monastery**  a place where nuns or monks work and live by themselves
The tourists visited a very old *monastery* in France.

**preserved**  kept from change or harm
Freezing *preserved* the food for a long time.

**accompanied**  went along with
Maria *accompanied* her mother on the shopping trip.

**W**eird shadows danced on the gray stone walls. The huge bedroom was dim in the light of the flickering and smoky candles. Ghostly pale, El Cid lay on his bed with his long white beard covering his broad chest. The great warrior, now an old man, had been gravely injured. Many people feared that his life was slipping away. Yet every half hour or so, he would do something very strange. He'd open his dark eyes and glance at two gold chests on a nearby table; then he'd snap his eyes shut again.

"How odd," whispered a lanky man to his fellow nobles. "Why should the sight of those locked chests be so important to him?"

Just then El Cid, the lord of Valencia, opened his eyes again. "Dear wife," he sighed to Dona Jimena who was praying at his bedside, "I've just had a dream about our dear son and my good father. They left this world so long ago. Surely, this means that it's almost time for me to join them."

His wife gently stroked his feverish brow. "Oh, my dear," she wept, "what will we do without you to protect us? It's said that King Bucar and his allies are planning to attack our city."

El Cid smiled weakly. "Do not fear, my love," he said. Then he stared at the golden chests, and several nobles in the room shook their heads sadly when he did this. They believed that he was acting strangely because he was about to die.

Dona Jimena dabbed at her eyes and continued to pray for her husband and Valencia. Indeed, the city was soon to be in great danger, for King Bucar and his allies from Morocco were already on ships cutting through the waves toward Spain.

Bucar was standing alone on the deck of the first ship. His long robes puffed out like sails in the wind as he stood thinking to himself, "El Cid has always defeated me! Each time my men saw him, they just broke ranks in terror and ran," he thought. "But soon the great number of men in my army and in the armies of my allies will surely amaze him! There will be no stopping us, and Valencia will be ours at last!"

Back in Valencia, the hour had grown late. Only El Cid's wife and his most trusted friends were watching at his bedside and, at the stroke of midnight, they gasped when he suddenly opened his eyes.

"Listen closely," he whispered hoarsely. His dark eyes glistened as he spoke. "In time I'll tell you my plan to save our people. But for now, just do as I ask. Secretly prepare a special drink for me for each of the next seven days. Mix some of what you find in those chests in a cup of water. No other food or drink must pass my lips!"

The listeners looked at each other with wonder in their eyes. However, they promised to do as El Cid commanded. And in the days that followed they performed the strange ceremony in secret.

On the seventh day, El Cid called his wife and closest friends together. "Now I'll tell you the rest of my scheme to save our people from the invaders," he said. He pointed to the golden chests and whispered his plan. The listeners could hardly believe what they were hearing, yet they promised to follow El Cid's wishes down to the last detail.

Some time later, Valencia was completely surrounded by the forces of King Bucar and thirty-five other kings. Their huge armies were camped some distance away from the high city walls. Thousands of tents covered the fields and hills. Day after day, the invaders attacked the massive walls, but each day they were driven off. Yet Bucar and his men weren't discouraged.

"The men of Valencia just fight us from the tops of the walls," declared Bucar. "They see how great our numbers are. Neither they nor El Cid will dare to come out against us!"

A turbaned general raised his curved sword overhead. It flashed in the firelight. "Now we really don't have to fight at all," he laughed. "Let's just blockade the city. No one will be able to go in or out, and soon the people will begin starving. Before long they'll gladly throw open the city gates for some crusts of bread."

Bucar stroked his dark mustache and danced about. He was delighted with the thought of taking Valencia so easily, so he agreed with his allies to keep the city blockaded.

A long time went by, but the brave people of Valencia refused to give up. The troops in the invading armies were growing weary of waiting. They yearned to go home to their families. "Let's just attack the city and be gone," cried many a soldier. "Surely, the hungry people have grown weak and weary by now."

At last Bucar and the other kings agreed to wait no longer. They decided to prepare for a great assault against the city. For this, they had their men begin building huge war machines to smash the gates and to help men climb the walls. And before long the machines were almost ready.

"Soon we'll be ready for the attack," announced Bucar one evening. "The great city will be ours within a few days!" Then he and the other invaders began feasting, and strains of loud music echoed through the hills.

By midnight the tired and boastful warriors were asleep. Only a few guards were half awake, leaning on their spears. The full moon glowed overhead, making everything silvery pale and ghostly.

The night was strangely silent. Too silent! A guard in the invaders' camp felt a chill creep down his spine. "What's going on?" he mumbled to himself as he peered about into the still night. "What strange thing is in the air?" Then, sleepy and troubled, he closed his eyes and leaned against a tree for a few moments of rest.

In the distance, huge gates to the city began swinging open ever so slowly. A man carrying a banner on a high pole stepped out through the gates and into the moonlight. Five hundred knights came marching out after him. Following these warriors and leading one hundred more, a tall man came riding forth on a magnificent horse. This man held a shining sword in the air, and his bright eyes stared straight ahead at the great camp at the foot of the hills.

The sleepy guard yawned, opened his eyes, and caught sight of the advancing warriors. "That banner! It's El Cid's own banner!" he gasped. "And the man on horseback is El Cid himself!" Then, before he could sound an alarm, the terrified guard turned and ran as El Cid's forces came charging forward.

Shouts of fear and confusion tore through the air as the Moorish invaders came running out of their tents. Horns blared and drums beat as a number of Moors rushed this way and that, trying to beat off their attackers. However, the Moors who stood their ground to fight were very quickly defeated. In the meantime, their fellow warriors turned their backs and went running or riding wildly toward the sea.

When King Bucar and the other kings saw what was happening, they stared in terror and disbelief. For in the uproar and confusion it seemed to the kings that their men were being pursued by thousands of knights in armor bright as moonstruck snow! And the knights' tall commander was holding up what appeared to be a flaming sword.

"El Cid has special powers! He's beaten me again!" screamed Bucar as he turned to flee. Then he pushed his way through his terrified troops to get to his nervously stamping horse.

Bucar and the other escaping invaders went racing over the hills and toward the seashore. They didn't stop to look back once. When they reached the water, they went rushing wildly into the waves. The fearful men were so eager to reach their ships that they began pushing and fighting with one another. Soon the dark waters were filled with thousands of men splashing about. Their cries for help filled the air, and many unlucky men drowned on that terrible night!

When the sun came up, El Cid could be seen leading the people of Valencia toward nearby and friendly Castile, one of the kingdoms in Spain. Men, women, and children followed him with their belongings tied up in great bundles. On and on they walked behind their famous leader who was sitting up tall on his fine steed. And Gil Diaz, El Cid's close friend, walked beside, leading the horse by the reins.

Soon El Cid's beloved people were safe within the borders of Castile. After that, some of his men journeyed with him on the way to a monastery near Burgos. This city was not too distant from Bivar, El Cid's place of birth.

While they were journeying, King Alfonso of Castile and an honor guard rode out to meet the travelers. And when the king saw El Cid, his mouth dropped open. "I know for certain that El Cid left this world some time ago," he said. "How is it that his skin appears so fresh and fair? He looks like a man who has just fallen asleep."

Gil Diaz bowed respectfully to the king. "El Cid was very wise. On each of the seven days before he left us, he drank a special potion. This helped to preserve his inner organs," explained Diaz. "Later on, he was embalmed and we rubbed him with a special mixture to preserve his flesh. He'd kept all the things we'd need in two golden chests near his bed."

The bearded king nodded thoughtfully. "Ah, yes! I have heard that the people of Egypt do this with their kings," he said. "How wise my old friend was to learn of such things!" Then he said no more and accompanied the men on their sad journey.

Upon reaching the monastery, the men gently took El Cid down from his horse. With sorrow in their hearts, they closed his eyes. Then they loosened the boards that had kept his back steady and his arm raised in the air. When all this was done, they carried his body into a church where he was given great honor. And everyone there agreed with Gil Diaz when he declared, "Both in life and in death, El Cid was Spain's noblest hero!"

# QUESTING FOR INFORMATION

## A.  Getting the Main Idea and Facts

Write the letter of the answer that best completes each statement.

1. This story is mainly about how _____.
   a. Armies from Morocco blockaded El Cid's city
   b. Some trusted nobles preserved El Cid's body
   c. A trick saved the people of El Cid's city

2. Some nobles thought their leader was acting strangely because
   _____.
   a. he was about to die
   b. his city was under attack
   c. his wife's tears troubled him

3. While waiting outside the walls of Valencia, Bucar believed that El Cid was _____.
   a. afraid to send out his forces
   b. preparing an attack on his camp
   c. no longer alive

4. El Cid had a force of _____ knights.
   a. one hundred      b. five hundred      c. six hundred

5. Many invaders _____ soon after El Cid appeared.
   a. fled to Castile      b. were drowned      c. attacked the city

## B. Going Beyond the Facts

Write the letter of the answer that best completes each statement.

1. We can tell that El Cid was depending on _____ to help defeat the invaders.
   a. the size of his army
   b. a clever trick
   c. help from King Alfonso
2. We may conclude that because of _____ many invaders perished.
   a. a violent storm     b. damaged ships     c. a great panic
3. Statement _____ describes the event that took place last.
   a. Bucar went riding away in terror
   b. A Spanish king learned El Cid's secret
   c. Gil Diaz led El Cid's horse toward Castile
4. Sentence _____ is a statement of opinion.
   a. El Cid was the greatest of heroes.
   b. El Cid cared about the people of Valencia.
   c. El Cid planned ahead.
5. The words that best describe Gil Diaz's behavior are _____ .
   a. clever and ambitious
   b. prayerful and brave
   c. respectful and loyal

## QUESTING FOR MEANINGS

Write the letter of the word that best completes each statement.
   a. gravely
   b. allies
   c. monastery
   d. preserved
   e. accompanied

1. The young singer _____ himself on a guitar.
2. There was a very large vegetable garden behind the _____ .
3. Many valuable art works are _____ in fine museums.
4. Many people are _____ concerned about the dangers of air pollution.
5. The _____ met to plan their next move against the enemy.

## QUESTING FOR UNDERSTANDING

1. Explain why Bucar and the other kings believed that they saw each of the following:
   a. thousands of El Cid's knights
   b. hosts of men in white armor
   c. a leader with a flashing or fiery sword

Discuss why all of the above helped cause the defeat of the invaders.

2. Some part of the reader's enjoyment of this tale is based on what is called *suspense* (a feeling of uncertainty about events or other matters). Discuss one or more times that the reader was left with a feeling of suspense.

## QUESTING FOR ENRICHMENT

*Preserve* and words derived from it are very important ones in our world today. Use the word that best completes each sentence.

preserve      preserves      preserver
preservation      preservatives

1. _____ are sometimes added to packaged or canned foods.
2. The sailor threw a life _____ to the man in the water.
3. The animals were kept safe in a special _____ .
4. Grandmother made some peach and strawberry _____ .
5. People should always strive for the _____ of what is right and just in society.

# The Lady Knight and the Face in the Mysterious Mirror

*The Faerie Queene,* an epic published in 1596, was written by Edmund Spenser. The land mentioned in the poem represents England and all the lands ruled by Spenser's queen, Elizabeth I. Among Spenser's reasons for writing his epic was his wish to please and glorify Elizabeth. He also wanted to glorify his country, and to give readers some images of truly noble people living wisely and well.

Although he wrote his epic in the late 1500's, he set it in an earlier time. He gave his work a medieval setting, a time when knights were powerful and greatly honored.

One knight in the poem was a maiden called Britomart. (Notice how her name brings the word Britain to mind.) In this tale based on Spenser's work, we see why this young lady was unable to see her face in the mirror she held before her.

## Major Characters

**Britomart** a beautiful girl, disguised as a knight

**Glauce** Britomart's nurse and servant

**Scudamore** a knight

**Amoret** Scudamore's wife

**Busirane** an evil enchanter

**Artegall** known as the Knight of Justice

## Vocabulary Preview

**ebony** hard, heavy, black wood from tropical trees
A beautiful mask of carved and polished *ebony* was on display.

**vile** evil; foul; disgusting
The *vile* thief laughed as he stole the helpless victim's money.

**masqueraders** people in disguise, usually wearing masks and costumes
Many *masqueraders* were competing to win the prize for the most original costume.

**tournament** a contest among mounted knights using lances or swords to win prizes; a series of athletic contests
The knight who won the special *tournament* was given a jeweled sword.

**finesse** (French word for *fineness*) delicacy; refinement; ability to handle situations carefully
There was no *finesse* in the man's behavior.

# I. The Kidnapped Bride

The maiden's golden hair streamed down around her as she slowly walked through her father's treasure room in the huge palace. She was daydreaming, wondering who her husband would be and what he would be like. Humming to herself, she lifted the lid of a chest and discovered a beautiful mirror inside.

Gasping, Britomart almost dropped the glass from her hands. For in the mirror she saw not herself, but the image of a handsome knight. And around the mirror were these words: "Artegall in Achilles' armor, which he won."

From that time on, the love-struck maiden walked about sighing and thinking about the face in the mirror. After this had been going on for some time, her faithful old nurse became worried. So she took her young mistress to see Merlin the Magician, the creator of the mirror.

Merlin smiled to himself when he saw them entering his underground cave. He already knew why they were there, but he let them tell him everything before he spoke.

"Though Artegall doesn't know it, he's the son of a great king," said Merlin. "He was kidnapped as an infant and taken away to Faerie Land. There he has become a great champion, the Knight of Justice."

Britomart's hazel-green eyes shone with excitement as the magician went on. "Find him and bring him back so that he can help fight his country's enemies. Then you shall marry him, Britomart! And among your descendants will be many great people, including a great queen, who will bring safety to our threatened people during her reign. She will be glorious, and will bring glory to our land!"

At once, good Britomart was determined to set out for the sake of her people and to find her true love. Her nurse and servant, Glauce, realized this and gave her mistress some good advice. Britomart listened to her old friend and began practicing to use the weapons of a knight. The tall girl soon found that she was very good at this. Then she secured the gold-trimmed armor and an enchanted lance that had been hanging unused in a church for many years. Finally, dressed as a knight, she set out on her quest.

The maiden's golden hair was tied in a knot under her helmet. Britomart kept the visor of her helmet down over her lovely face. She didn't want people to know that she was a young lady in shining armor. Glauce, her faithful childhood nurse, was disguised as her squire and riding nearby. The sleepy woman's wrinkled face was drooping on the shield she carried for her beloved mistress.

They'd been traveling for a long time now. And more than once the tall and large-limbed maiden had proved to be a worthy knight. She had already done battle and rescued several men who were being treated unjustly. And she had accepted no reward, for she believed in fighting only for honor and not for riches. In truth, her fame was spreading rapidly. Many people were already calling her the Knight of the Ebony Lance.

Now on this sunny afternoon, she and her nurse were riding along under shady trees at the edge of a green forest. Sighing deeply, Britomart raised the visor in her helmet to let the cool air go sweeping across her face.

"Oh, Artegall! Where can you be?" she murmured. For while she was journeying and fighting for justice, she was continuing to search for the man she dearly loved.

Still thinking of Artegall, she kept riding along. A short time later, she spotted a bubbling stream of clear blue water ahead, and began riding toward it. But then she suddenly pulled her white steed to a halt. There was someone sprawled on a nearby stretch of tall grass!

A young knight was lying there with his face on the ground. His helmet and spear lay beside him. But his shield, which bore the image of Cupid, the god of love, lay far off as though it had been hurled away in a fit of despair. And his horse, waiting patiently, stood under a nearby tree.

The sandy-haired knight, who was by no means a weakling, was groaning and sobbing as though his heart would break. "Oh, my sweet bride!" he cried. "My Amoret, stolen from me on our wedding day! Locked away in a castle! And I can find no way to save you!"

Britomart's heart was filled with pity for the sorrowful man. Pulling her visor down over her face, she rode closer to him. "Gentle knight! Perhaps I can help you," she called.

Sir Scudamore slowly turned toward Britomart and looked up. Resting on his elbow, he shook his head and sobbed his reply. "No one can help me, Sir Knight! No one can fight against evil Busirane's terrible power. Surely, that man is now using magic spells to force Amoret to forget about me! And, alas, there's no safe way to break into his mighty castle!"

Britomart raised her lance and said, "You mustn't give up. As worthy knights, we must do whatever we can to rescue that maiden. I mean to save her, or to die trying!"

"No! No!" cried Scudamore, jumping to his feet. "You'll surely be killed. It's better that I die of grieving rather than let you waste your life!"

Britomart shook her head. "You're wrong, my friend," she said. "A life isn't lost or wasted if it brings endless fame!" Then she persuaded Scudamore to gather his weapons and lead her to the enchanter's castle.

When they reached the dismal place, even the brave Britomart gasped at the danger that lay before them. Blocking the gate to the castle was a stretch of leaping and roaring flames! They thrashed about wildly like angry serpents! Clouds of thick smoke, stinking of sulphur, filled the air! It was all so terrible that Britomart and her companions were forced to draw back, coughing and choking.

Britomart waited a while to catch her breath. Then she left her horse and went racing forward. Scudamore and Glauce were shocked by her action.

"Come back! Come back!" screamed Glauce.

"You'll never get through!" cried Scudamore. "It's hopeless!"

But Britomart refused to listen to their pleas, and continued running hard. She raised her huge shield before her and held her breath. Then she went rushing into the flames, swinging her great sword from side to side. The weapon made a sound like the roaring wind as it went cutting through the air with mighty sweeps! Right and left it flew, fanning the flames aside. And like a bolt of lightning cutting through the clouds, Britomart passed safely through the flames and smoke.

Seeing this, Scudamore was filled with new courage. He went dashing forward with his shield before him, and with his sword held high. But the intense heat and bitter smoke again forced him to turn back. And when he reached safe ground, he threw himself down and began banging his head on the earth.

In the meantime, Britomart caught her breath and stood ready to do battle with the enchanter's guards. But to her great surprise no one rushed out to challenge her. Where were Busirane's evil helpers? Were they all elsewhere because they believed that no one could ever get through the flames?

It was all very strange. And even stranger was the fact that Britomart was able to roam freely through the castle searching for Amoret. Neither Busirane nor any of his people were anywhere to be seen.

So on and on the young knight searched for the missing damsel. In time, she reached the only remaining rooms in the castle. Upon entering the first of these chambers, she was greatly surprised by its beauty. It was richly decorated with colorful tapestries, and with draperies gleaming with gold and silver threads.

The next room was even more richly decorated. There, Britomart saw an immense iron door at the far end of the vast chamber. She could see that it would take more than a strong shoulder or heavy sword to break it down.

The wise maiden decided to wait and watch for a while. However, no one appeared, and evening shadows soon began filling the room. Yet Britomart decided to remain just where she was. And though her eyes began growing heavy, she refused to fall asleep. She stood tired but awake, hiding behind a golden statue. She was determined to stand ready for her next move, whatever that might have to be.

Before long, the room was entirely dark. All was very still and silent for a while. Then all of a sudden the shrill blast of a trumpet tore through the air! A terrible storm of howling winds arose! Dreadful thunder and flashes of lightning filled the room. And an earthquake rocked the chamber as though the earth were being torn apart at its foundations!

Britomart was stunned by all this disorder, but she remained in her secret hiding place. She was determined to find and rescue Amoret at any cost.

Suddenly, a violent whirlwind appeared out of nowhere and went spinning wildly across the room. Then it crashed into the thick iron door, causing it to fly open! At once, a richly costumed man stepped out of the brightly lit room. He looked like an actor ready to appear in a play. And he began waving a leafy branch that seemed to be a signal for some kind of show or celebration to begin.

The wide-eyed Britomart watched from behind the golden statue as countless costumed marchers came parading out of the enchanter's inner room. Some of the masqueraders emerged singing loudly and cheerfully, filling the air with noisy merriment.

Among the marchers was a beautiful but sad-faced lady. Pale as ivory, she seemed like a ghost called up from the land of the dead by an evil spell. She was being led by two wicked-looking men.

After a while, the circling marchers began reentering the room with the huge iron door. And just as the last of them went through the door, Britomart leaped out from her hiding place. She went rushing toward the door, but a great blast of roaring wind slammed it shut in her face!

"Oh, no! Now I'll have to wait until it opens again," grumbled Britomart. "But I'll be ready when it does! The vile enchanter is surely just beyond that door!"

The determined maiden spent the next day exploring the castle.

She stood ready the next night when the doors suddenly flew open again. Expecting to do battle with many, she stepped bravely into the room. However, her mouth fell open in surprise when she saw only two people there. The huge crowd had vanished! Where had the marchers gone? Was there a secret way out of the room? Had Britomart imagined the weird celebration? Surely the enchanter's castle was a place of strange happenings!

Now only Amoret and Busirane were in the room. The stocky, dark-bearded man was sitting with his back to the door, enjoying the cool air rushing in as he worked. He was bent over a huge book in which he was making strange marks in blood. He had already tried a thousand charms to make Amoret fall in love with him and forget about Sir Scudamore. But not one of the charms could change Amoret's steadfast heart. And now the pale and troubled maiden stood helpless, bound to a post with heavy chains.

Hearing footsteps, Busirane turned and spotted Britomart! He jumped up, knocking over his pile of books. Then he pulled out a dagger and went lunging toward Amoret! But Britomart was too fast for him! She grabbed the crazed man's arm and tugged him back.

Wild with rage, Busirane then struck wildly at Britomart. And when she saw that he'd drawn some drops of her blood, she struck back with her mighty sword! She hit him so hard that he crashed half-dead to the floor. Her next stroke would have finished him, but Amoret's cry saved the man.

"Don't slay him, Sir Knight!" she pleaded. "Only he knows the charms and spells that can restore my health and calm my troubled heart!"

Nodding, Britomart stood over the fallen enchanter. She raised her sword and held it over his head. "If you care to live, you'll do as I say! Restore Amoret's health and peace of mind!" she commanded fiercely. "And do it now!"

Busirane began sweating. "Yes! Yes, Sir Knight!" he said with a trembling voice. "Just as you wish! Just as you wish!" Then he began going through his books. He kept turning pages quickly, and chanting strange verses aloud. And from time to time he glanced up nervously at Britomart's flashing sword.

Before long, a rosy glow returned to Amoret's face. Her dark eyes began sparkling. Her body was free of all weakness and pain, and her mind was clear as sunlit air. Smiling happily, she thanked Britomart again and again for her help. Then she watched with joy as her rescuer bound shamefaced Busirane to the post with his own chains. And Amoret's joy grew even greater when she heard that Sir Scudamore was waiting outside the castle. For of all the people in the world, she loved him best.

Soon the young women were hurrying through the castle. Britomart was surprised to see that the beauty of the richly decorated rooms was no more. The rooms were bare and crumbling. Their beauty had been false, and all their former glory was decayed.

Britomart was also surprised when she saw that there was no roaring fire at the castle gate. In truth, when Busirane's power was broken, the fire became like a burnt-out torch. So now the young women were able to run over the ashes to the green grass ahead.

But, alas, the maidens found only Britomart's horse standing there. Sir Scudamore and Glauce were nowhere around. They had gone off in haste and terror to seek more help.

Amoret wept bitterly with disappointment. Then she just waited through the night with Britomart. And when no one came looking for them the next day, the two maidens rode off together to face whatever dangers might lie ahead.

# II.  Strange Meetings

Britomart and Amoret had been searching for Sir Scudamore and Glauce for many days. During that time, the young ladies had become great friends. As they rode along or sat by their campfire, they sometimes discussed their hopes and fears. And they often encouraged each other just as all good friends do in time of trouble.

In the meantime, Sir Scudamore and Glauce were searching for them. Of course, faithful Glauce kept the secret that she and her mistress were women.

As the searchers traveled through the woods one day, they ran into a small group of riders. Two of them were foolish knights who were false friends to each other. They were accompanying two ladies who weren't the harmless creatures they seemed to be.

One woman was named Ate. She was a stringy-haired hag who was a very devil on earth. She hated to see people happy and enjoying heaven's many blessings. It was her greatest wish to cause discord in the world. She enjoyed nothing more than causing mischief and ruin for worthy knights and other good people.

Her companion was Duessa. She was a witch who had changed herself to appear like a lovely young woman. And after some words with Sir Scudamore, Duessa began stirring up more trouble for him.

"Gentle knight, why do you worry yourself about Amoret?" she asked. "Perhaps she's chosen to love another knight."

Scudamore began trembling at these words. Then Ate giggled hoarsely and said, "Oh, you foolish knights who worry and fight over women! And I laugh especially at you, Sir Scudamore. You might as well know right now that the woman you love already loves another man! You're wasting your time searching for her!"

Gasping, Scudamore gripped the handle of his sword. "Why do you taunt me with such a terrible lie?" he shouted. "How can you say such things about my dear wife?"

Ate pointed a bony finger at the red-faced man. "Because I saw her with my very own eyes," she snapped. "Now what do you say to that?" Then, twisting the ends of her stringy hair, she rode off with the grinning knights and evil Duessa.

For a while, Scudamore sat speechless with shock. Then he suddenly turned to the wide-eyed Glauce. "So, that's why they weren't waiting at the castle! And we thought they had set out to find us!" he roared.

"May ugly shame follow your master forever! He is a false traitor! And you are the false creature who serves him! Now be prepared to share the punishment for his crime!"

Filled with rage, Scudamore drew his sword as the aged Glauce almost died with fear. "Let me explain everything! There's a lot you don't understand!" she cried. Then she bravely started trying to set matters straight.

But Scudamore raised his sword. He was so furious that he refused to listen to her attempts to clear things up. Three times he raised his sword to strike the trembling squire, but each time he held back from doing so. Finally, he just warned the old squire not to keep trying to defend the missing knight.

Glauce, afraid for her life, promised to hold her tongue from that moment on. And she just rode quietly behind the enraged man who was now more determined than ever to find Britomart and Amoret.

Elsewhere, the two young women continued their search. One afternoon during their travels they arrived at a large clearing where a tournament was being held. Many knights were there. Each was hoping to show that he was the most skilled at arms. The contest was already in its third and last day.

The knight who was doing best was a tall man who was feeling very pleased with himself. He had overthrown many fierce and powerful challengers. And he was very surprised when he saw a strange looking new challenger come riding on to the field of battle.

Everyone stared in wonder at the new arrival's unusual appearance. His helmet and armor were completely hidden under wild weeds and woody moss. His horse was covered with small branches of oak leaves. And there was a strange sign on the knight's huge shield. It read, "Savageness without finesse!"

"Look at that sign," said one of the women who had been watching the tournament. "He certainly does look like a savage without refined or delicate ways!" At this, many people broke into laughter and began calling him the Savage Knight.

Behind his visor, the knight smiled. It was Artegall! He was so well disguised that no one realized that he was the famous and mighty Knight of Justice. He was there to enjoy practicing his skill at arms. Also, he was hoping to win the admiration and heart of the most beautiful young lady there.

Turning, he pointed his lance and went charging at the nearest knight. With one stroke he sent the powerful man tumbling from his horse. Then he kept on battling, unhorsing each challenger who came riding out against him. And after he broke his lance, he used his sword to vanquish all the others who dared to challenge him.

Smiling, Artegall looked around. He felt sure that he would be declared the winner of the tournament. But then, in the golden glow of the evening sun, another knight came riding out of the crowd. It was none other than Britomart! Like the others, she was eager to test her skill against that of the Savage Knight.

Speeding ahead, she pointed the ebony lance toward Artegall's helmet. A loud crash filled the air and Artegall fell back. He went sliding down over his horse's tail, and hit the ground with a great thud! His body was so sore that he didn't even think about getting up for a long time.

After that, he watched as another knight, and then many more, tried to beat Britomart. But like Artegall, each of them soon went flying off his horse. And so it was no wonder that the Knight of the Ebony Lance was declared the third-day winner. This also made her the winner of the entire tournament.

People who'd been watching the contest hoped to see the face of the victor. However, Britomart wouldn't lift her visor. And when she was offered a prize, she refused to accept it. Quickly then, she galloped away with the smiling Amoret seated behind her. They were anxious to get some sleep and then continue their search for Amoret's true love.

Many days went by, and still the searchers had no luck. Sometimes they stopped to rest under shady trees for a while. It was during one of these times that Britomart dozed off. Amoret didn't feel sleepy, so she decided to walk around a bit. But the poor girl didn't realize that she should never have set out alone. In no time at all, she couldn't find her way back to Britomart. And the more she rushed about in panic, the greater the distance grew between her and her sleeping friend.

When Britomart awoke, she stretched and looked around. Horrified, she saw that Amoret was nowhere in sight. She jumped to her feet and shouted for Amoret. Hearing no reply, she mounted her horse and went riding through the forest. "Amoret! Answer me!" she kept shouting as she searched near and far. But when the stars began to appear, she had to give up for the day.

"Oh, my dear friend," she wept. "Where can you be?" Then filled with sorrow and fear, she tried to get some rest. And she began her search again as soon as the sun came up the next morning.

Many days went by, but the searcher had no luck. In the meantime, Sir Scudamore just kept riding from place to place as he kept looking for Britomart. The frightened and silent Glauce followed not far behind him. At one point, they ran into a knight who was riding alone through the woods. It was Artegall, now dressed in gleaming armor. He didn't give the other travelers his name. Instead, he just introduced himself as the Savage Knight.

"Where are you going?" Sir Scudamore asked the magnificent looking rider. "Has the queen sent you out on a special quest?"

"No," answered Artegall. "Right now I'm on a mission of my own. A certain knight brought me great shame at a tournament, and I am seeking to pay him back. The Knight of the Ebony Lance shall lie in the dust at my feet!"

Scudamore straightened up in his saddle. He'd realized at once that they were both searching for the same person.

"The man you seek is also the man I am seeking," said Scudamore. "He stole my bride from me, and must pay for this foul deed! Now let us ride together, Sir Knight, to seek our foe. I pledge to help you when we run into him!"

Artegall agreed to this and began riding along with Scudamore. Soon they emerged from the forest and began crossing a grassy plain. Glauce, still holding her tongue, rode behind them.

Suddenly, Sir Scudamore pointed straight ahead. There was a knight in the distance. It was the troubled Britomart! She was riding slowly, thinking about her lost friends and about the face in the mysterious mirror.

"Look! The Knight of the Ebony Lance! At last I shall have my revenge!" cried Scudamore. "Oh, good Savage Knight, I now ask one favor of you. Please let me fight him first, for he harmed me first!" And when Artegall nodded, Scudamore went racing ahead.

Britomart spotted the knight riding toward her. She was shocked to see that he was charging forward with his lance ready to strike! So she bent forward on her horse. Then tightly gripping her ebony spear, she went racing ahead like a violent wind!

Her powerful lance struck Sir Scudamore so hard that both he and his horse went crashing to the ground. And there the knight lay groaning, too stunned to get up.

Watching all this, Artegall grew angrier than ever. He glanced at the steel tip of his lance, and grinned. "It will soon be all over for him," he muttered. Then he pulled his visor down over his face and went galloping across the plain. Soon he was very close to Britomart.

"It's all over for you!" he shouted as he took aim with his lance. And seconds later, he found himself flying out of his saddle. Britomart had unhorsed him again!

Furious, he jumped up from the ground and drew his sword. Like a hound lunging at a deer, he leaped toward the approaching rider. His blade just missed her! But she fell to the ground anyway when her wounded horse suddenly reared up on its hind legs!

Swift as lightning, Britomart stood up and drew her sword. Then she began fighting furiously with Artegall. Her sword strokes were so mighty that Artegall was forced to move further and further backward. And though he bore a slight chest wound, he bravely continued to fight.

Then, when he saw Britomart hesitate for a moment to catch her breath, he charged at her. His many sword strokes fell thick as a shower of hail! Yet Britomart stood her ground.

Their swords clashed and clanged! To and fro each of them went, sometimes pursuing and sometimes being pursued. But then, as chance would have it, Artegall's sword struck Britomart's visor and tore it from her helmet!

Jumping back, Artegall gasped. "An angel!" he cried upon seeing his opponent's face. It was framed in her helmet by wisps of her golden hair.

Overcome by her beauty, Artegall dropped his sword and fell upon one knee as he continued to stare. But by doing this, he left himself open to defeat. So Britomart rushed forward and stood over him.

"Get up and surrender, or die!" she said with flashing sword in hand. And when he rose and begged her pardon, she took off her helmet. Her golden hair, loosed from its knot, streamed down around her. It was as bright as summer sunshine!

Both Artegall and Scudamore just stood there, amazed at her beauty. And Scudamore was horrified to think that he had sought to slay this angelic creature because of a vile troublemaker.

Moments later, the joyful Glauce rode up to Britomart, who was delighted to see her old friend. Then Glauce said, "By your love for me, my dear, grant these knights a truce! All can be explained."

Britomart yielded to this request, and the knights began taking off their helmets. Seconds later, Britomart's mouth dropped open, and the sword fell from her hand. "Am I imagining things?" she thought. "Can this be Artegall, or is it someone who could be his twin?"

Then Scudamore broke into her thoughts. He explained how he had been tricked. After that, he told how he had met the Savage Knight, who was now revealed as Artegall! And as soon as Britomart heard that name, her heart leaped up.

Glauce then told all she knew to help clear things up. And Britomart explained to the sorrowful Scudamore how Amoret had become lost. "But don't worry," she added. "I'll go on seeking until she's found."

Sir Scudamore thanked her, and prayed in his heart for his young wife's safety. However, he needn't have worried, for a great knight called Arthur of Britain would soon find and reunite Amoret with her loving husband. But for now, Sir Scudamore could only stand and watch the smiling Britomart and Artegall.

In time, their destinies would be fulfilled. They would go on to perform great deeds as knights. At one point, Britomart would rescue Artegall from a cruel enemy's prison. Then Artegall would go on to defend his country successfully. After that, the happy couple would marry. And among their many great descendants would be the famous Queen Elizabeth I, who would save her people from foreign enemies and bring glory to Britain.

But now, on the day that Britomart and Artegall first gazed lovingly into each other's eyes, they just stood talking quietly. And not many days after that, Artegall begged the smiling maiden to promise that she would become his wife. Of course, her answer was yes. And she said it gladly to the young man whose face to her was no longer just an image in a mysterious mirror.

# QUESTING FOR INFORMATION

## A. Getting the Main Idea and Facts

Write the letter of the answer that best completes each statement.

1. Britomart's goodness and determination helped her succeed on a quest which she had undertaken mainly to _____ .
   a. gain riches and other rewards for her bravery and achievements
   b. develop more skill as a knight and to win endless fame
   c. be helpful to the people of her land and to find her true love

2. It was _____ who suggested that Britomart begin practicing to use knight's weapons.
   a. Merlin     b. Glauce     c. The Savage Knight

3. Britomart cut through the flames and smoke like a _____ .
   a. leaping hound     b. whirlwind     c. bolt of lightning

4. Glauce could have solved a serious problem if _____ had allowed her to speak after they had met Ate.
   a. Busirane     b.. Scudamore     c. Merlin

5. Although it was just fantasy invented by Spenser, it was said that _____ would be one of Britomart and Artegall's descendants.
   a. Elizabeth I     b. Arthur of Britain     c. Duessa

## B. Going Beyond the Facts

Write the letter of the answer that best completes each statement.

1. We may infer that Merlin was _____ that Britomart had peered into the mysterious mirror.
   a. annoyed     b. pleased     c. sorry

2. We may conclude that Scudamore banged his head on the earth outside the castle because he _____ .
   a. felt defeated
   b. feared to face the enchanter
   c. had slipped

3. It seems correct to say that Artegall's disguise and the sign on his shield showed that he _____ .
   a. was a savage
   b. didn't trust other knights
   c. had a sense of humor

4. Probably, the enraged Scudamore didn't strike Glauce with his sword in the woods because _____ .
   a. of his sense of honor
   b.. she was a woman
   c. of his fear of Britomart

5. It would seem safe to say that Glauce was _____ .
   a. sneaky and suspicious
   b. intelligent and loyal
   c. lazy and cowardly

## QUESTING FOR MEANINGS

Write the letter of the word that best completes each sentence on the next page.
   a. tournament     b. vile     c. ebony
   d. finesse     e. masqueraders

1. The beautiful furniture was made of _____ .
2. We enjoyed seeing the jolly _____ marching in the holiday parade.
3. With great _____ , the woman solved the argument between her two neighbors.
4. The tennis _____ was exciting to watch.
5. The _____ remark offended everyone who heard it.

## QUESTING FOR UNDERSTANDING

1. One of the things that Spenser wanted to bring out in his poem was the value of sincere friendship. First, briefly discuss some qualities of a true friend. Then discuss examples of how Britomart and Amoret showed that they were real friends. After that, do the same for Britomart and Glauce.

2. The story of Britomart brings to mind the fact that there have been many great women questers and achievers. Discuss the quests and achievements of two or more of the women listed below. Then you might care to name and discuss other women achievers of the past or present. (The person you name might be someone like a caring community leader you know of, or some other woman you truly feel ranks as a woman of achievement.)

*Some names to consider:* Jane Addams, Susan B. Anthony, Clara Barton, Marie Curie, Amelia Earhart, Indira Gandhi, Helen Keller, Sacagawea, Sojourner Truth, Harriet Tubman

## QUESTING FOR ENRICHMENT

Edmund Spenser wrote his famous epic in the late 1500's. It was a time when the English language was still in its early stages of what we call modern English.

The spellings of many words that Spenser used had not been settled on in those days. The italicized words in the sentences below appear just as the poet spelled them in his poem. See if you can give today's spelling for each of them.

1. Yesterday, a knight in shining *armorie clombe* the hill to the castle.
2. We heard the *sowne* of a trombone and a *trompe*.
3. The ship's *capitayn* lost the *kaies* to his cabin.
4. She had sharp *eyen* and was able to *thrid* the needle.
5. He was *affeared* to hear tales about ghosts and *sprites*.

# The Rivals and the Clever Maiden of the North

*The Kalevala* is the national epic poem of Finland. It deals with humans, semidivine beings, and supernatural forces. It was created from collected stories, poems, and songs of the Finnish people. Some of the selections were already many centuries old when Dr. Elias Lönnrot, a physician, set out to collect and shape the material into a work for all to enjoy. He published his final version of the work, which he called *The Kalevala,* in 1849.

Kalevala means "the land of the sons of Kaleva." He was a hero from the ancient myths of the Finnish people.

The tale that follows, which might be called a love story, is based on an episode from the epic. In this tale we see why a fish head is the most important gift a young man gives to his future mother-in-law.

## Major Characters

**Ilmarinen**  the blacksmith
**Louhi**  mistress of North Farm

**Louhi's beautiful daughter**
**The old magician**

## Vocabulary Preview

**sauna**  a steam bath made by pouring water over hot stones
Paul felt refreshed after taking his very first *sauna.*

**rivals**  people competing with each other to gain the same thing
My cousins are *rivals* for the same position on the team.

**pact**  a bargain or treaty between countries or people
The leaders of the countries signed a *pact* ending the war.

**dazzle**  to confuse or blind for a while with very bright light
Sunlight on ocean water can sometimes *dazzle* people at the beach.

**viper**  a poisonous snake
The copperhead, like the rattlesnake, is a *viper.*

**"O**h, if I could only hold her in my arms," moaned the sandy-haired blacksmith. As usual, Ilmarinen was thinking about the maiden he loved. Then he sighed and went on working at his forge in Kalevala.

Sheets of flame from the forge swirled up toward the clouds. Streams of sweat rolled down the smith's powerful arms. He was known as the eternal smith, for it was said that he'd forged the heavens and had hammered out the skies.

He had also forged the Sampo, a large mill with a beautiful many-colored lid. It had been extremely difficult to make, and was the kind of machine that people throughout the ages have dreamed about. The mill churned out grain from one side, and salt from another side. And from its third side it churned out gold!

The smith had made the Sampo for old Louhi, mistress of a farm in the damp and gloomy country to the north. In exchange for the Sampo, the witch had promised to let the smith marry her lovely daughter. But the blue-eyed maiden had wept when it was time to leave with him.

"If you take me away, who will make the birds sing here? Who will make the meadows turn green?" she'd cried. "Oh, I'm needed here! I'm not ready to leave and be married."

So the patient smith had gone back alone to Kalevala. Three years had passed since that day. But the smith couldn't drive the maiden's sweet face from his mind. Even now as he worked, the yellow sparks from his forge made him think about the golden streaks in her sky-blue eyes.

As he worked on, his sister came running up to him. Annikki was drying her hands on her apron. She had just been doing the laundry at the water's edge.

"What will you make for me if I tell you something important?" she laughed. "The old magician has just sailed off in a ship with sails of red and blue. It has gold and silver trimmings on the mast, and the boat is spilling over with treasure!"

The smith shrugged his shoulders. "But what's all this to me?" he asked.

"He's on his way to North Farm!" the girl answered. "He hopes to win the heart of the maiden you love!"

The smith's mouth fell open. Then working faster than the wind, he forged copper belts, gold earrings, and other fine things. These he gave to his sister before rushing off to have a sauna and to dress in fine clothing. After that, he had his horse hitched to a sleigh with steel runners. And he prayed to Ukko, the Thunderer, for a powdery snowfall to speed the sleigh along.

Soon the smith was racing along in his sleigh decorated with silver bells. In time, he found himself zooming along the blue water's edge. There he caught sight of the old magician's boat. It seemed to be flying over the sparkling water.

"Ho, old friend!" called the smith. "I, too, am going to see the maiden in the North Country!"

An angry look shot out from the old magician's eyes. The elderly yet still handsome man began frowning. This troubled the smith, for he knew that the magician was related to the Wind god and had special powers. Indeed, the magician was a great singer whose songs could shake the earth, cause the heavens to storm, and make many other wondrous things happen.

So the worried smith called out to him. "Let's make a friendly pact now, mighty singer! Let's agree not to take the girl away against her will!"

Frowning, the magician began scratching his short beard. He really didn't like the idea of a pact very much. However, in time he looked up and shouted, "Very well! A girl really should go with the man she chooses!"

The rivals then kept speeding along until they were in sight of the maiden's home in the cold and dismal North Country. And when Louhi's gray dog spotted them in the distance, it began barking wildly.

"What's old flop-ears barking about now?" grumbled the master of North Farm. Puffing on his pipe, the old man shuffled to the door and looked out. "There are two men on their way here," he said.

The mistress of North Farm, dark-robed Louhi, heard this and quickly put a log on the fire. "If blood streams from the burning log, these men bring war to our land," she said. However, she soon began smiling as she saw honey oozing from the burning log.

"Ah-ha!" exclaimed Louhi. "These men come in peace, seeking a sweet wife!" Then she and her daughter hurried to the doorway and looked out. They watched as the magician sang his boat to the nearby shore, and as the smith stopped his sleigh near some tall and misty pine trees.

The mistress of North Farm recognized the visitors. She realized that they had come as rivals for her daughter's hand. Quickly then, she ordered her child to fetch a cup of mead. And when the girl returned, Louhi gave her further instructions.

"Give the first drink to the man you choose," said the grinning and ever-greedy woman. "Be smart, my dear, and select the great singer. His boat is heaped with treasure!"

The maiden sighed and lowered her eyes. "I've already made up my mind. I will marry the smith," she said, tossing back her rich brown hair. "I want a husband who is young and strong."

Moments later, the magician reached the doorway. Smiling, he asked, "Lovely maiden, will you come with me and be my wife?" But his smile soon faded away as the young lady shook her head. Then he watched sadly as she greeted the smith and gave him the cup of mead.

Grinding her teeth in anger, Louhi stared at the old magician. She hoped that he'd at least turn the smith's feet to ice. However, the man just smiled a bit sadly. "A bargain is a bargain," he said. "Besides, I should have looked for a wife without a young and handsome man as my rival!"

Not pleased at all, the mistress of North Farm turned toward the smith. She saw him reaching toward her daughter's hand. "Not so fast!" she cried. "Before you marry my child, you must prove yourself worthy. It's not enough that you once made a Sampo for me. Now you must plow every foot of the largest field on my farm. It's the one filled with vipers!" The wrinkled woman then chuckled and hurried away.

The smith turned to the maiden. "A bite from one of those snakes would finish me," he groaned. "How can I ever plow a field filled with those killers?"

The bride-to-be was as clever as she was lovely. She narrowed her eyes, thought for a while, and began to smile. "You're the greatest of all smiths," she declared. "Forge a plow. Make it of gold and silver to catch the light and dazzle the vipers!"

The smith liked her idea and quickly forged a plow. He also made iron shoes, steel leggings, and a metal vest for himself. After that, he hitched his horse to the plow and stood ready to go cutting through the field. At once, thousands of snakes lifted their heads out of the tall grass to see what was going on.

"Hear me, you vipers!" warned the smith. "If you would save yourselves, crawl into the underbrush at the edges of the field. Otherwise, you will be cut down!" Laughing, the smith then went tearing through the ground with the blazing plow.

Dazzled, the snakes leaped and thrashed about wildly in their efforts to escape from harm. And not long after that the field lay completely plowed.

Louhi frowned angrily when she appeared on the scene. She shook a bony finger into the smith's smiling face. "You're not finished yet," she snapped. "Now you must go into the forest of Tuoni, lord of the dead. Bring back Death's bear and the dread wolf. But forge nothing on land to help you!" Then filled with glee she hurried away, certain that the smith would fail.

Once again, the worried man turned to his sweetheart. "All is lost!" he exclaimed. "How can I ever hope to bring back Death's bear and the dread wolf?"

The bride-to-be walked back and forth, lost in thought. After a while, she began smiling again. "Go out onto that flat rock in the foaming waters of the rapids," she said. "There you can forge strong shackles for the creatures' legs, and steel bits for the mouths of the beasts. Then forge bridles of iron to lead the creatures away!"

Again the smith was pleased with her thinking. So out on the flat rock in the water he made the things he needed, and then hurried to the forest of Tuoni.

He prayed as he crept into the dark forest. "Oh, Fog Spirit, hear me," he murmured softly. "Let heavy mists fill the forest. Surround the beasts with dense fog and keep my movements hidden from them."

Barely moments later, a heavy blue mist began rolling through the forest air. The heavy fog prevented Death's great bear from sniffing or seeing the man creeping up on him. With a lunge, the trembling smith snapped the heavy shackles onto the bear's huge legs. And when the beast howled in fury, the smith thrust the steel bit into its gaping jaws.

After that, the smith crawled deeper into the forest. He could just make out two little slits of yellow light through the mist ahead. He knew at once that these were the eyes of the wolf! So the smith went sliding and slipping as quietly as a snake up to the beast. Swift as lightning, the smith snapped the shackles onto the wolf's legs and slipped the steel bit into its snapping jaws! Then, shouting for joy, he dragged the struggling beasts to Louhi's door.

The mistress of North Farm became furious at the sight of the smiling man. Now she was more determined than ever to keep the smith from marrying her daughter.

"You haven't won yet! There's still one more test to go," Louhi croaked hoarsely. "Go and catch the giant pike that swims in Tuoni's dark river. But use no net in doing so!" Then she hurried away with an evil smile on her lips.

The smith was greatly disturbed. He knew that no one had ever returned alive from attempting this task. Even his clever sweetheart looked worried as the couple sat thinking under a misty pine tree. But suddenly the girl's eyes began to sparkle. "You're called the eternal smith!" she said. "So why don't you forge a great bird, a fiery eagle to catch the pike?"

The smith's eyes lit up at once. A fiery eagle! It was a wonderful idea. So the man worked day and night until he forged a giant bird with talons of iron and claws of steel! And when all was ready, the smith leaped onto the bird's broad back. "Fly, my eagle!" he shouted. "Fly to the dark river and capture the giant pike!"

With flashing wings, the eagle soared through the air. Soon it was circling over the dark river. The bird then turned on its side, causing one wing to brush the clouds above and the other to brush the water below. This disturbed the river monster and brought it swimming up from the depths. The huge fish was longer than seven boats placed in a row, and its sharp teeth were as long as rake handles.

The creature came crashing up through the waves. Its wide and dripping jaws snapped at the smith! But the eagle's swift movements saved the man from harm.

The bird's eyes blazed like red-hot coals; its wings blazed like sheets of flame. The eagle then went roaring down through the air with its steel claws opened wide. And like a thunderbolt, it struck the river monster! After that, the eagle pulled the wildly thrashing creature from the waves. It carried the fish to the top of a tall oak tree where it began tearing away at its catch.

"Stop that!" roared the smith. "You mustn't eat the pike. It was caught for Louhi!"

These words angered the eagle as it quickly tore the fish's head from its body and dropped it to the ground. Then, after finishing its meal, the bird shook the smith from its back and went soaring toward the clouds. Its huge wings flashing in the sunlight grew smaller and smaller in the distance, and soon the bird could be seen no more.

Sighing, the smith picked up the giant fish head. He carried it with many a puff and groan to Louhi's house. There he threw it down with a great crash before the surprised woman. "I've brought you a gift," he declared. "From the bones in this head, a beautiful and long-lasting chair can be made for you!"

The mistress of North Farm sighed deeply. There was nothing more she could do to stop the wedding. So, a great marriage feast was held, and it was attended by many guests. Even the old magician was there, and he sang many happy songs.

Of course, the happiest man there was the smith. He knew that soon he'd be on his way home to Kalevala with the clever maiden of the North, the lovely girl with golden streaks in her sky-blue eyes!

## QUESTING FOR INFORMATION

### A. Getting the Main Idea and Facts

Write the letter of the answer that best completes each statement.

1. This story is mainly about how a troubled smith _____ .
   a. made an unusual machine      b. feared a great magician
   c. won his bride

2. It was said that the _____ had been hammered out by the smith.
   a. skies     b. mountains     c. treasure ship

3. During the race to see the maiden, the rivals _____.
   a. argued angrily
   b. made an agreement
   c. refused to speak
4. The smith prayed for a _____ in the Forest of the Dead.
   a. powdery snowfall     b. dense fog     c. gold and silver plow
5. The smith said that a long-lasting chair could be made from
   _____.
   a. tall pine trees
   b. copper and silver
   c. bones from a fish's head

## B. Going Beyond the Facts

Write the letter of the answer that best completes each statement.

1. The magician's behavior toward the smith and the maiden showed that the great singer could be a _____ person.
   a. cruel     b. fair     c. suspicious
2. We may infer that the supernatural beings called on by the smith were _____.
   a. afraid of him
   b. friendly to him
   c. unconcerned about him
3. We may conclude that the maiden _____.
   a. had a mind of her own
   b. always obeyed her mother
   c. didn't like magicians
4. We may infer that Louhi's real purpose for assigning tasks to the smith was to _____.
   a. gain another Sampo
   b. test his determination
   c. destroy him
5. The statement that is an opinion is _____.
   a. The smith would have been unhappy if the maiden had chosen the magician.
   b. The maiden would have been better off if she had chosen the magician.
   c. Louhi would have been pleased if her daughter had chosen the magician.

## QUESTING FOR MEANINGS

Write the letter of the word that best completes each sentence.
a. pact     b. viper     c. sauna     d. dazzle     e. rivals

1. John could hardly see through all the steam in the _____ .
2. The hunter stayed away from the _____ moving in the grass.
3. Mr. Lopez and Mr. Brown were _____ for the same job.
4. We made a _____ to help each other in times of trouble.
5. Did the bright light _____ you for a moment?

## QUESTING FOR UNDERSTANDING

What do the following sayings mean, and how do they apply to the problems of the smith and the maiden?
   a. Where there's a will there's a way.
   b. Necessity is the mother of invention.

## QUESTING FOR ENRICHMENT

Indeed, in literature and in life, people are sometimes compared to animals. Some examples follow: the young woman was as wise as an owl; he eats like a bird; that child is a lamb.

Write the letter for the meaning in column B next to the number for its expression in column A. Write each number with its letter.

| A | B |
|---|---|
| 1. a bull in a china shop | a. person paying no attention to what's happening around him |
| 2. a lamb among wolves | |
| 3. a wolf in sheep's clothing | b. dangerous person who tries to appear harmless |
| 4. an ostrich with its head in the sand | c. clumsy or thoughtless person who causes damage |
| 5. a fish out of water | d. helpless person among dangerous people |
| | e. person not comfortable in new or unfamiliar surroundings |

**From**
# THE EAST

# Gilgamesh, the King Who Discovered His Other Self

*Gilgamesh* is the oldest known epic. It was recorded on clay tablets in the near east in about 2000 B.C., but it told a story set in much earlier times, called prehistory. The epic was composed in the Sumerian language in ancient Mesopotamia. Much of this land is now part of Iraq.

*Gilgamesh* might be called the "grandfather" of many epics because of its age, and because some later epics seem to have borrowed ideas from it. Like King Gilgamesh, some characters in these later epics went on quests, faced great perils, lost someone close, visited the underworld, and dealt with supernatural forces.

King Gilgamesh, the child of a goddess, was called "He Who Saw Everything" because of his experiences during a fantastic journey. In this tale, we see how, in exchange for one of the greatest treasures of all time, Gilgamesh is left with only an old snakeskin.

## Major Characters

**Gilgamesh**   king of Uruk

**Enkidu**   Gilgamesh's look-alike friend and partner

**Shamash**   the sun god

**Humbaba**   guardian of the cedar forests

**The Distant One**   the man to whom the gods had given everlasting life

## Vocabulary Preview

**tyrant**   a dictator; unjust ruler
The *tyrant* didn't allow his people to question his laws.

**oppressed**   burdened or kept down unjustly
Many *oppressed* people came to the New World looking for freedom.

**encounter**   an unexpected meeting; battle
After years of being apart, the two old friends had a surprise *encounter*.
The fierce *encounter* between the angry men was terrible to see.

**scorpion**   a small animal, related to spiders, with a poisonous sting on its tail
Resting under a rock, the *scorpion* escaped the noonday heat.

**endured**   suffered; bore; tolerated
The explorers *endured* many hardships to find the ancient temple.

# I. A Strange Encounter

"**T**he king is a tyrant!" grumbled many people. They were greatly oppressed and terribly weary. Their king kept many of them busy doing things like working long hours serving in his palace or keeping the walls of his city in good condition. The king, handsome and as strong as an ox, seemed to care only about himself and his glory.

He often stood stroking his curly black beard and admiring his very beautiful city. The tall buildings of burnt red brick glowed in the golden sunshine. "The city of Uruk will bring me great glory! Surely my name will live forever!" he would cry with a smile.

But the tired people of Uruk didn't smile at all. Each day they cried aloud to their gods for help. Finally, their tearful prayers touched the hearts of some gods. So it was decided that the goddess Aruru should make a creature that would stand up against the proud tyrant.

Aruru made a clay figure that looked very much like the long-haired king. She dressed the figure in simple clothing and then gave it life. After that, she placed the sleeping creature in a green forest some distance from Uruk.

Soon the newly made look-alike of Gilgamesh began to stir. Enkidu opened his dark eyes and saw many wild animals drinking peacefully at a nearby pool. And he saw some other animals just standing and staring at him.

Enkidu smiled. He could see that they meant him no harm. And before long, he and the animals became close friends, sharing the good things of the forest and watching out for each other.

Everything was going well until the day that a hunter spotted Enkidu. The hunter gasped when he saw the powerful creature tearing apart an animal trap with his bare hands. "The king must hear about this!" cried the hunter as he ran off.

"What's that?" roared the king upon hearing the report. "A man-like creature living in the forest?"

The frowning Gilgamesh then sent for olive-skinned Harim. She was one of the most beautiful women in Uruk. Her dark hair flowed down to her waist, and her brown eyes could melt any man's heart.

"Your beauty will catch the wild man's eye. Go now," said Gilgamesh. "Bring the one who protects the animals back here to me!"

Harim bowed low and then set out to obey the tyrant's demands. On and on she walked under the blazing sun until, almost fainting from the heat, she stepped into the shady forest. Sighing, she sat down to rest on some cool grass, and took a drink from a pool of clear blue water.

Just at that moment, Enkidu walked out through the trees. He stopped in his tracks. Never before had he seen a creature so lovely. Then, without any fear, he walked right up to her and smiled.

Soon Enkidu began spending all of his days with Harim. He liked the sound of her soft voice as she taught him to speak. And he listened with a frown whenever she spoke about the unjust king.

"How can he be so cruel to his fellow creatures?" he declared one day. "I'd change things if I were in Uruk!"

Harim was very pleased when she heard this. So she pleaded with Enkidu to go back with her to see the great city and the tyrant who ruled it. And after Enkidu agreed to make the trip, he began walking toward the animals drinking at the forest pool. He wanted to say farewell to his friends there. But they just backed away from the creature who now walked and talked like any other man. So with great sorrow in his heart, Enkidu turned and left the forest.

Then after a long and tiring trip, he and Harim finally reached the glowing city of burnt red brick. The young man looked up sadly at the weary men working on the mighty walls. And while Enkidu stared up at the workers, people in the lively marketplace began staring at him. Filled with wonder, they whispered to each other and pointed to the look-alike of their king. And just a short time later, the king himself appeared!

"It's Gilgamesh!" said Harim. At once, Enkidu turned and encountered the tyrant, blocking his way. Guards quickly drew their swords and rushed forward. But the king just waved them back.

"I'll take care of this myself!" snarled Gilgamesh. Then he raised his arm and sent his great fist smashing into Enkidu's broad chest. The forest creature staggered back a few feet, but then came rushing ahead. Swinging his elbow forward, he sent it crashing into the king's open jaw!

Shocked and grown angrier than ever, the king of Uruk lunged at Enkidu and fell with him to the ground. Soon the two mighty men were rolling around in the dust. They knocked over food stands, and went crashing into doorposts and walls!

Gilgamesh had never before met an opponent with such great strength! And he stared into Enkidu's face as the fierce encounter went on. Then the amazed king suddenly released his mighty grip on Enkidu and rolled to one side. "Enough!" he shouted, and the fighting ceased. The two men sat up in the swirling dust.

"What's this?" laughed the king. "We seem to be almost equals in both strength and appearance! Why, we're alike as two brothers. Come, my second self! Let us stand together and be friends!"

Enkidu stood up with the king as they brushed the dust from themselves. "If we're to be true friends, there's something you must do," said Enkidu. "Stop oppressing your people. Try to be a more just and caring king."

Gilgamesh's mouth fell open. He looked as if he'd been struck by lightning. No one had ever dared to speak to him like that. For, after all, he was a mighty king and his mother was a goddess. But then a smile broke across his face, and he burst into loud laughter. He stretched out his hand, and in his heart he stored the words of his new friend.

Soon Enkidu and the king became like real brothers. Together they feasted, went riding, and enjoyed life. Things seemed to be going well for them and the people of Uruk. However, their peaceful days were soon to be interrupted.

One morning, Enkidu found Gilgamesh choosing his weapons for a battle. "Humbaba is threatening my people again. That evil one lives on the mountain now giving off smoke and flame," said the king. "The fire and ashes will destroy my people. Shamash, god of the sun, has told me to battle Humbaba! I will destroy that evil one, and my name will live forever!"

Enkidu was pleased that Gilgamesh was anxious to help his people. Yet he looked troubled when Gilgamesh asked him to join in the fight.

"I have a strange feeling," sighed Enkidu. "I fear that something terrible will happen to one of us if we do this together." However, he couldn't let his best friend face grave danger alone. So he joined Gilgamesh and rode with him to the edge of the distant cedar forest. Beyond the forest they could see the smoky mountain.

Enlil, the god who dealt out good and evil to mortals, had made Humbaba the guardian of his cedar forests. And there Gilgamesh and Enkidu found a gate blocking the road ahead of them. Reaching out, Enkidu pushed the gate open. As he did this, a terrible shock went racing through his body! His arm fell numb to his side.

"Evil forces protect this place!" groaned Enkidu.

Gilgamesh grew furious. Rushing forward, he began chopping wildly at the cedar trees that stood in his way.

"Who dares cut down the sacred cedars?" a voice thundered through the trees. Humbaba's face, gray as ashes and hard as stone, appeared above the treetops. Then Humbaba suddenly flashed out a long arm of fire at the men.

They quickly leaped back from the flames. Gilgamesh, wild with anger, called out to his favorite god. "Oh, great Shamash," he shouted. "Protect my friend and me!" Then all at once, a tremendous storm hit the mountain. The earth shook mightily! Trees were torn up by their roots! And Humbaba howled in terror, for the power of Shamash was very great.

"Spare me, noble Gilgamesh!" Humbaba cried. "For I'm just a servant doing my work. Spare me, and I will call you master from this day on!"

Gilgamesh began to feel pity for the creature. But Enkidu warned him that Humbaba was not to be trusted. So the two men rushed forward with fierce yells and killed Humbaba, the evil one of the mountain.

Upon hearing the news, the people of Uruk rejoiced. And the green-eyed goddess called Ishtar also rejoiced. For she'd watched the battle from afar and had fallen in love with the mighty Gilgamesh.

Ishtar rushed down to Gilgamesh, smiled prettily, and asked him to marry her. But he just laughed and said, "You've had too many husbands already!"

Ishtar's eyes flashed wildly! She'd never felt more insulted. So she rushed back into the sky and complained to Anu, the chief god. "Father! Gilgamesh has insulted a goddess!" she screamed. "He must be punished. Send down the Bull of Heaven!"

Anu shuddered at this demand. He didn't want to send out the horrible beast. However, he couldn't stand his daughter's awful shrieking. So he finally shouted, "Open the gates!" and turned his eyes away.

Moments later, the people of Uruk heard a horrible noise. They looked up and saw the Bull of Heaven storming down through the air. Clouds of smoke streamed from its nostrils! The earth shook from the noise of its thundering hooves!

"We're lost! We're lost!" the people howled as they ran to hide. Only Gilgamesh and Enkidu didn't run. They went out and stood waiting in the open fields outside the city.

The raging bull spotted them and made a sharp turn. Lowering its head, it came charging forward at full speed. The monster's huge horns were aimed straight at Gilgamesh. But the king swiftly jumped aside and grabbed the bull's tail as the beast raced by. And Enkidu leaped up and grabbed the beast's sharp horns!

At once, the monster threw back its head to shake off the earth creature. And while it shook its head wildly from side to side, Gilgamesh leaped forward with his sword in hand. Moments later, the slain beast crashed to the ground, causing the land to shake for miles around.

Once again, the people of Uruk had been saved by a caring king and his friend. They sang the praises of both men. And they prayed that all would go well for these protectors of the people.

But before long, Enkidu became seriously ill. The gods were punishing him for his part in killing the Bull of Heaven. Of course, when Gilgamesh heard about this he went rushing to his friend's bedside.

Enkidu smiled up weakly at him. "I have had a dream," he told the king. "I learned that one of us must perish for slaying the Bull of Heaven. It is I who must go. Truly, I will be sad to leave you. Yet I rejoice that you, the son of a great goddess, will remain with your people. Surely you will continue to be a great king, and you will win an everlasting name. And now, my friend, I must leave you. So all life must end some day."

Weeping mightily, the heartbroken king knelt beside his friend who breathed no more. Then with a heavy heart the king rose and slowly walked away. And Gilgamesh knew that he'd never forget his friend who had helped him to find his better and nobler self.

# II. The Search

Gilgamesh wrapped himself in a lion-skin. In this way he showed his great sorrow for his lost friend. And in the days that followed, he grew ever more sorrowful and troubled. He kept thinking about Enkidu's last words: "So all life must end some day." These words troubled him greatly.

A chill ran down the king's spine whenever he thought about perishing. But then his eyes lit up one morning as he remembered something important. There was a man, an immortal man, who might be able to help him! So Gilgamesh quickly decided to set out on a long and dangerous quest.

He was determined to see the man to whom the gods had given everlasting life. "The Distant One in the underworld must help me. Surely he'll share the secret of immortality with me," he told himself. "I have only to find him!"

Gilgamesh's journey took him across burning deserts. It took him up the rocky sides of steep mountains. Yet he never thought once of turning back, not even on the cloudy peaks of Mount Mashu. A lesser man would have become dizzy and pale with fright from the great heights. And a lesser man would have trembled in terror at the sight of the strange-looking creatures who guarded the entrance to a huge cave.

These giant creatures, half man and half scorpion, recognized Gilgamesh as the great king of Uruk. Impressed with his bravery, they listened as he told the reason for his quest. Then the chief Scorpion-Man stepped aside and let Gilgamesh enter the cave. It led to the tunnels which would take him down to the other side of the gigantic mountain.

Soon after that, Gilgamesh was struggling and feeling his way through tunnels that never seemed to end. Some were cold, dark, and windy. Others were steaming hot. But on and on he pushed for hour after hour until, at last, he saw a faint light ahead.

Then bruised and breathing hard, he went stumbling out of the last dark tunnel into a garden blazing with light. It was the most beautiful place he'd ever seen. Colorful and sweet-smelling flowers bloomed everywhere. Bright jewels flashed like stars caught in the trees. And crystal blue water bubbled along in curving streams.

"Surely this must be the garden of the gods!" cried Gilgamesh. And at that moment, he saw a great golden light above him. It was Shamash, the sun god, in his splendid robes.

At once, Gilgamesh told Shamash, his favorite god, the reason for his quest. But the god gave him no promise of help. In fact, he said that it was useless for Gilgamesh to go on searching for immortality.

However, the lord of Uruk refused to believe this. "Just tell me how to get to the Distant One," he pleaded. "I'm sure he can help me."

Shamash began moving slowly across the sky. "Go forward in the direction in which you are facing," said the god. "Find the maiden making wine. She will give you more advice."

Gladly then did Gilgamesh hurry forward. Before long, he caught sight of a maiden making wine in bowls outside her little house. But she drew back when she saw the wild-looking man with sunburnt skin and uncombed hair. However, she soon began feeling pity for him. For Gilgamesh told her about the lost Enkidu, and about his own great fear of perishing.

Shaking her head, the maiden smiled kindly. "Forget about trying to become immortal," she said. "Dance and rejoice each day. Make the most of the gifts of life!"

But Gilgamesh politely refused to be turned back. So the patient maiden just sighed and led him away. She took him to a boat near the bank of a far-off river, and told him to wait there for the boatman.

Gilgamesh paced back and forth, waiting for the man to arrive. Finally, the impatient king grew very angry. In a fit of rage, he reached into the boat and seized two stone tablets that were lying there. Then he sent them smashing down on the rocks along the shore.

"What's this?" someone shouted. It was the stooped and wrinkled boatman who was just getting back with some needed supplies. "What terrible thing have you done? You've destroyed the sacred stones! Their power carried me across the river and kept me safe from the waters of death!"

Gilgamesh gasped. He realized that he could reach the Distant One only by crossing this river. Then he told the boatman who he was, and why he was there.

"Your great impatience has delayed your journey," said the boatman. "Now if you want to get across this river, you must do as I say. Go into the woods, and cut down a hundred and twenty poles. Be sure they're long enough to touch the river bottom. You will use each pole just once as you push the boat across. But you must be sure your hands don't touch the water!"

And so Gilgamesh had to work hard for hour after hour until he had the needed number of poles. Then he stepped into the vessel with the boatman. For a while the sails on the boat carried them along. But after that Gilgamesh had to use the poles, pushing each one down into the water and then letting it go. And he was a very tired man when the boat finally reached the opposite shore.

Gilgamesh stepped onto the land and followed the boatman to the Distant One's home. The immortal one, ancient but unwrinkled, opened the door and was surprised to see the visitor from the upper world. Then he invited him to sit and rest near the warm oven in which loaves of bread were baking.

Gilgamesh thanked the Distant One and his dark-haired wife, and took a seat. He sighed deeply, enjoying the warmth from the oven and the delicious aroma of baking bread.

Pleased and relaxed, Gilgamesh went on speaking. "I am King Gilgamesh, and my mother is a goddess," he said. "I've come to you for help. I tremble at the thought of perishing, and want to learn the secret of everlasting life!"

The immortal one just laughed quietly. "Do you think a house is built to last forever? Does each season last forever?" he asked. "Return to your city. Live out all your years, and enjoy each one."

But Gilgamesh refused to be turned away. "I've endured great hardships to reach you," he said. "Please share your secret with me. Tell me how you became immortal!"

Leaning back, the Distant One sighed deeply. "Very well. Listen carefully," he said. "Many ages ago, the gods decided to destroy mankind because people had become so unruly. My wife and I had always been quiet people who honored the gods, so one of them helped us to save ourselves and our family from a great flood that covered the earth. When the waters went down and we left our boat, we found we were the only survivors. Then the gods held a special meeting and decided to make my wife and me immortal."

Gilgamesh nodded and smiled upon hearing this story. "So the gods made you immortal," he said. "Perhaps they'll do the same for me. I've traveled far and have suffered much in my quest. If the gods could be called to a special meeting about me, they might decide to grant my wish!"

The Distant One just smiled at this. "You want someone to ask the gods to hold a special meeting about you?" he asked. "You hope to become immortal, but I can see that even now you're having trouble keeping your eyes open. Immortals never sleep!"

Gilgamesh sat up at once. "I'm not falling asleep," said the exhausted man.

Again the Distant One just smiled. "Then let's see if you can pass a test. I ask you to stay awake for six days and seven nights," he said. "Can you do this?"

Gilgamesh took a very deep breath. "That's no challenge," he said with a grin. "Of course, I can pass such a test." However, even as he spoke, his eyelids grew heavier and heavier. Before long, he was fast asleep.

The Distant One had his wife bake a loaf of bread for each day that Gilgamesh slept. And when Gilgamesh finally woke up, the Distant One pointed to the loaves of bread that had been baked for the sleeping man. Most of the seven loaves were already stale.

Gilgamesh had failed the test. With his head bowed, he slowly rose to his feet. His sad appearance touched the heart of the Distant One's wife. So she pushed back her long dark hair and hurried over to whisper to her husband.

"Gilgamesh has endured much suffering! Let's give him something. Let him take away one of the hidden flowers, the flowers that give youth to the old!" she pleaded. At first the Distant One refused. But he gave in at last because his wife wouldn't take no for an answer. Grumbling a bit, he told Gilgamesh about the flowers growing at the bottom of a nearby sea, and sent him to get one.

Filled with new hope, Gilgamesh tied stones to his feet and plunged into the sea. He sank rapidly to the bottom. And when he found a flower, he cut the stones from his feet and rose quickly to the surface. Shouting for joy, he held high the wonderful treasure.

"Thank you! Thank you!" he shouted to the Distant One and his smiling wife. "I'll share this with the old people of Uruk. Their happiness will be great!"

Later that day, Gilgamesh left the gloomy land. He crossed over the perilous river. Then he pushed on and on, went past the mountains, and finally stopped to rest at the edge of a green forest.

Exhausted and thirsty, he sank to his knees near a bubbling stream. Carefully he placed the flower on the ground, and then turned for a long drink of cool water. When he turned back again, he was shocked to see something moving swiftly through the grass.

"Oh, no!" he shouted in horror. A snake wearing new skin was dragging the flower down into a hole in the earth! The snake had thrown off its old skin as it escaped with the great prize. The creature had gained the gift of having an ever-youthful appearance!

Stunned, Gilgamesh sat still for a very long time. Sighing deeply, he then rose to his feet. "I see now that it was not meant for me to bring this gift to my people," he said at last.

After that, the tired man walked on and on. Finally, he caught sight of Uruk in the distance. And as he got closer to his city, he lifted his head proudly.

The city had a golden red glow in the late afternoon sunlight. It looked like a bright crown lost in a green meadow.

"Ha!" shouted Gilgamesh. "Surely I will be remembered for my city of great walls and high towers! Uruk will give me an everlasting name!" Then he hurried through the gates of his city so filled with the noise and the wonders of life!

# QUESTING FOR INFORMATION

## A. Getting the Main Idea and Facts

Write the letter of the answer that best completes each statement.

1. Part II of this story is mainly about how a king _____.
   a. oppressed his people
   b. failed a special test
   c. tried to overcome death

2. Enkidu said he had to perish because _____ had been slain.
   a. Humbaba    b. the Bull of Heaven    c. Shamash

3. Gilgamesh's journey across the perilous waters was delayed because of his _____.
   a. sleepiness    b. cowardice    c. impatience

4. The Distant One asked Gilgamesh to _____.
   a. take a test
   b. meet with the gods
   c. smash some stones

5. The flower of eternal youth was stolen by _____.
   a. the chief Scorpion-Man
   b. a snake in the grass
   c. the wine-making maiden

## B. Going Beyond the Facts

Write the letter of the answer that best completes each statement.

1. When Enkidu went to bid farewell to his forest friends, they were probably _____ of him.
   a. proud    b. suspicious    c. jealous

2. It seems correct to conclude that Gilgamesh went to stop Humbaba's actions, which really reflected problems caused by _____ .
   a. volcanic eruptions
   b. great floods
   c. violent thunderstorms

3. We can tell that the Distant One's wife could be _____ .
   a. merry and amusing
   b. kind and determined
   c. selfish and lazy

4. Of the following, _____ is what Gilgamesh wanted most.
   a. to have Enkidu brought from the forest
   b. to be remembered forever
   c. to own the jewels caught in the trees

5. Statement _____ is an expression of opinion.
   a. Gilgamesh suffered great hardships during his quest.
   b. Gilgamesh changed as a result of dealing with Enkidu.
   c. Gilgamesh deserved to be given everlasting life.

## QUESTING FOR MEANINGS

Write the letter of the word that best completes each sentence below.
   a. oppressed
   b. tyrant
   c. scorpion
   d. endured
   e. encounter

1. The travelers hoped they wouldn't _____ serious problems along the way.
2. Voting was not permitted in the land ruled by the _____ .
3. The _____ Pilgrims left the Old World to seek religious freedom.
4. The food of the _____ consists mostly of insects.
5. Juan _____ months of training to be ready to play on the team.

## QUESTING FOR UNDERSTANDING

1. Discuss the double meaning of the story's title.
2. At first, Gilgamesh was a very self-centered person. Show by referring to events from the story that in time he became a better king and a more compassionate (caring) person.

## QUESTING FOR ENRICHMENT

Four of the five adjectives in each column have something in common. Find the adjective that doesn't belong, and be ready to tell why it doesn't belong.

| A | B | C |
|---|---|---|
| brutal | dangerous | nervous |
| cruel | perilous | uneasy |
| kind | risky | relaxed |
| mean | safe | restless |
| ruthless | harmful | troubled |

| D | E | F |
|---|---|---|
| frightened | exhausted | mighty |
| afraid | weary | forceful |
| alarmed | tired | weak |
| scared | rested | powerful |
| fearless | fatigued | strong |

# Sohrab and Rustem

"Sohrab and Rustem" is only one tale to be found in the *Book of Kings* (the *Shah-Nemah*), a very long work. It contains a number of epics about the ancient kings (shahs) of Persia, the country now called Iran. The epics also tell about famous heroes such as the mighty Rustem.

Though started by others, the *Book of Kings* was completed by the poet called Firdausi in 1010. In this tale we see how a man's great victory is really his greatest defeat.

## Major Characters

**Sohrab**   powerful young warrior

**Rustem**   famous warrior of Iran and Sohrab's father

**Princess Tahmineh**   Sohrab's mother

**Shah Kavus**   Emperor of Iran

**Emperor of Turan**   foe of Shah Kavus and Rustem

## Vocabulary Preview

**onyx**   one of the quartz stones used as a semiprecious gem
The man couldn't decide whether to have a black or a red *onyx* set in the ring.

**purposes**   reasons or intentions
Ralph's *purposes* for earning and saving money are good ones.

**parched**   thirsty; dried out or dehydrated
Because their throats were *parched*, the travelers stopped for some cool water.

**opponent**   a rival; foe; enemy
Grandfather grinned when his *opponent* at checkers made a careless move.

**honorable**   deserving honor; noble; honest; upright
My cousin performed an *honorable* act by returning the lost wallet to its owner.

# I. Amazing News

Sohrab was a powerful youth. By his tenth year there was no man who could match him in any contest of strength. Before long he could outride and outfight any man in the land. Yet the very tall youth was well liked because of his friendly ways and ever cheerful smile. In fact, Sohrab's name meant *full of smiles*. However, on this sunny morning, Sohrab's face was filled with gloom. Silent and alone, he just went striding along on his mighty legs. And even powerful men leaped aside to let him pass.

Soon the youth arrived at his huge home, pushed open the heavy gates, and hurried into the walled garden. There he found his mother sitting at the edge of a sunlit fountain. She was the Princess Tahmineh, daughter of the king of Samangan, a small country near the border of the great nation called Turan.

The dark-haired lady was dreamily running a hand through the clear blue waters. Catching sight of her son's reflection in the water, she looked up in surprise. "Sohrab! Why are you here?" she said. "Why aren't you out enjoying yourself with other young people on this fine morning?"

Smoothing back his mass of black hair, Sohrab leaned forward. "Mother, we must speak. The time for truth has come," he said in a firm voice. "No longer can I wait for answers. This day you must reveal my father's name to me, and you must tell me why you've kept it a secret for so long."

The princess gasped, and quickly rose to her feet as Sohrab went on. "Why am I so different from other youths? Why am I so much stronger and taller? And why am I so skilled in arms?" he asked. "Has it something to do with my father's identity? Oh, Mother, you must tell me all! You must put my troubled mind to rest!"

For a few moments, Tahmineh remained silent. Then her eyes began gleaming as she spoke. "Many years ago, the emperor of Turan wanted to rule Iran, our neighboring country. He tried to seize the shah's throne when it became empty, but he was defeated by Rustem, the greatest warrior in Iran.

"A new shah was then placed on the throne. Since that day, the emperor of Turan has hated the noble Rustem," said the princess. "It is the same Rustem who is your father!"

Sohrab stepped back, astonished at her words. Could it really be true? Was he really the son of the world-famous champion? The excited youth was about to speak, but he remained silent as his mother put her finger to her lips.

"Listen well," said the princess as she looked about to be certain that they were alone. "I knew how much the emperor hated Rustem, the only man I've ever loved. So Rustem and I were secretly married, and when you were born I kept your father's name to myself. For I feared the angry emperor might seek to harm the son of his great foe!"

Tahmineh looked into Sohrab's dark eyes, and saw them glowing with pride and wonder. "Rustem returned to Iran before you were born," she said. "He had to defend his country against other invaders. Even now he's there, helping the shah. And even though Shah Kavus doesn't give him proper honor, your father stays there. He remains faithful to his land."

Clenching his mighty fists, the youth threw back his broad shoulders. "The shah should honor noble Rustem!" he declared. "My father has served his country well!" Then, catching his breath, he asked, "In truth, Mother, does my noble father know about me?"

A troubled look appeared on Tahmineh's lovely face. "Yes, my son. I sent him secret word when you were born," she said. Then tears began welling up in her eyes. "He quickly sent back rich presents of rubies and bags of gold. And I have here with me another gift, one that he left you before you were born."

From around her neck, the princess lifted a golden chain. Hanging from the chain was a beautifully carved piece of onyx. Tahmineh's fingers trembled as she placed the jewel into Sohrab's hand.

"Before Rustem left, he handed me this jewel," she said. "He told me that if we had a daughter, she was to wear it in her hair. But if we had a son, he was to wear it around his arm."

The youth stared at the stone and his face was full of smiles again. Then he asked eagerly, "Does my father know about my strength? Does he know about my great skill with weapons?"

At once, the princess shook her head. The black ringlets covering her forehead quivered as she trembled from head to foot. "No, no!" she wept. "He believes you're still a child playing at games! I've kept the truth from Rustem, for surely he'd have sent for you if word about your great powers had reached his ears. Oh, Sohrab, my heart would then have been torn with grief!"

Sohrab's chest swelled with pride as he began pacing back and forth, thinking hard. A daring plan was beginning to form in his mind. Finally, he felt that it was time to speak.

"Mother, I mean to raise an army and march against Shah Kavus," he said. "Even the emperor of Turan would be pleased to hear of this, for he and the shah have been enemies for many years now."

At this, Tahmineh cried, "But you're just a youth! Would you dare to make war against your father's nation?"

"Yes, Mother," Sohrab replied. "But don't be unhappy. Surely your heart will be gladdened when you hear my plan. I'll fight to defeat the ungrateful shah. When he falls, I'll see to it that Rustem wears the crown and sits on the throne of Iran! And you shall be his queen!

"Then my father and I will march against the emperor of Turan. He will no longer oppress the people of Samangan or any other nation, and I will wear his crown!"

Upon hearing this, the princess bowed her head and stared sadly into the pool of blue water. She knew that now there was nothing that could hold back the young lion.

True to his word, Sohrab began preparing for battle. He gathered many of the nobles and warriors of Samangan into his army. His grandfather, the king, gave him countless weapons and whatever else he asked for. His mother supplied him with a huge and magnificent horse, one of the offspring of Rakush, Rustem's own famous steed. She also arranged for her brother to go along with Sohrab so that he could point out Rustem to him.

While all this was going on, the emperor of Turan grew more and more delighted. He called Human, one of his most trusted officers, to his meeting hall for a secret talk. "Some time ago, my spies told me that Sohrab is Rustem's son. I've kept this knowledge to myself, waiting for a time when I could use it for my own purposes," he said with a sly grin. "Now I have another chance to seize Iran for myself. So I want you to gather an army from Turan and present yourself to Sohrab. Tell him that I send my friendship and help. And promise him that I myself will gladly place the crown of Iran on his head."

Human's eyes gleamed wickedly as the emperor went on. "I want you to make sure that Rustem and Sohrab don't recognize each other as father and son! Then the young lion may slay the aging champion for us. After that, we'll rid ourselves of Sohrab while he sleeps. And Iran will be mine at last!"

When Sohrab saw the many men sent to him by the emperor, he rejoiced. Now he was surer than ever that victory would be his. So with banners flying and drums beating, Sohrab led his great army forward.

Day after day, Sohrab's forces marched deeper and deeper into Iran, striking down anyone who dared to stand in their way. In time they captured a gleaming white castle that looked down on a nearby stretch of flat land. Sohrab had his men pitch their colorful tents near the castle and then settle down to wait for the expected approach of the Persian army.

Before long, the shah's huge army arrived and camped on the hills on the other side of the plain. However, the army didn't attack Sohrab's forces. Instead, the shah's generals gathered together in a large tent to discuss their problems. "News has reached us that the new champion from Turan has already caused great destruction in our land!" growled one bearded man. "This young Turk must be stopped! Our men grow more fearful of him by the hour."

A burly officer stood up, smacking the dust from his cloak. "Fortune smiles on us tonight," he laughed. "Great Rustem has joined us. Shah Kavus has sent him here to help us. At this very moment, the mighty warrior is settling into his tent. He'll rid us of this young lion!"

On the next night, Rustem disguised himself as a Turk and crept into Sohrab's camp where the men were feasting and singing in the light of their campfires. Rustem wanted to see the great champion who was leading this army. Then, standing in the shadows, he gasped as he caught sight of the youth. He saw that Sohrab was as tall as a cypress tree, and that his arms were huge and strong.

Just then, Princess Tahmineh's brother walked past the place where Rustem was hiding. "Who's there?" said Sohrab's uncle. "Come into the light where I can see you better." But before he could say anything more, he was struck down by the mighty Rustem and fell lifeless to the ground. And when his body was discovered, his nephew was filled with grief and rage.

## II.  Face to Face

Early the next day, Sohrab had a captured Iranian warrior dragged before him. "Look out over the tents across the plains," said Sohrab, "and tell me which of them belongs to the famous Rustem!" At once, the warrior was filled with worry. He didn't want to point out Rustem's tent because he feared that the aging champion might be slain by this powerful young dragon. He didn't want his army to lose its greatest fighter.

"How can I point out the tent of someone who isn't there?" answered the tall warrior. "Rustem is off fighting elsewhere for the shah."

Upon hearing this, Sohrab struck down the young man, leaped upon his horse, and rode fearlessly right up to the edge of the Iranians' camp. There, with a voice like thunder, he challenged the shah or any of his men to come out to face him. "I'll make you pay for taking my uncle's life!" he roared.

There was great confusion in the camp, and no one rushed out to accept the challenge. Then some nobles hurried over to Rustem's tent and helped him to buckle on his armor, while others saddled his mighty horse. A short time later, he went riding forth proudly. His horse named Rakush, which means lightning, carried him swiftly right up to Sohrab.

Throwing back his leopard-skin cloak, Rustem called out, "This is a rocky place. Let's ride to smoother ground!" And so the two warriors went galloping close to the center of the wide plain separating the two armies.

Frowning with determination, Sohrab turned and made ready for battle. However, Rustem raised his hand to stop him from charging forward. He had been studying Sohrab and began to have feelings of concern for the brave and fine-looking youth. "Something tells me to have pity on you," he called out as he stroked his dark beard which already contained a few white hairs. "Truly, I wish you no harm. I don't want to strike that noble head from your young body!"

This brief speech and Rustem's deep voice touched Sohrab's

heart. "Your words move me," he said. "Let me ask you something. Can it be that you are the famous Rustem?"

"No!" answered Rustem at once. "I am just an ordinary soldier in the shah's army." Of course, this was not true. Rustem was saying this just to make Sohrab think that there were even more powerful warriors back in the camp of the Iranians.

Now there was nothing left for Sohrab and Rustem to do but fight. So first they rode a little apart, and then whirled about. Holding lances and swords, they came charging forward. Their weapons crashed one upon the other time and time again. Sparks filled the air! And so great was the warriors' strength that soon their lances were splintered and their swords were hacked like saws.

The armies were watching all this from the edges of the plains. The next thing they saw was a fierce battle with clubs. Round and round the huge clubs went, whistling in the dusty air. Again and again they went smashing down on the warriors' shields and coats of mail. In time, the clubs lay broken on the ground, and the armies saw the two heroes wrestling mightily in clouds of dust.

Some time later, the two fighters were parched with thirst, so they stopped to drink and to rest a while. It was during this time that Rustem groaned, "This young dragon is wearing me down. His courage drains the hope from my heart!"

Soon the two warriors were on horseback again, shooting arrows at each other. The many arrows went racing by like flocks of attacking eagles! Yet neither hero was injured, for armor, shields, and swift movements protected each of them. Finally, the enraged fighters shouldered their bows and went riding wildly toward each other in the growing darkness.

Rustem reached out, hoping to yank the young Turk from his horse. But Sohrab's broken club came crashing down on Rustem's arm as the riders went racing by, and Rustem groaned aloud in pain. Soon after that, the warriors fought each other no more and rode away. However, their great contest was to continue with the rising of the sun.

That night the champions didn't get much rest at all. The aging Rustem kept wondering if he could defeat the young lion. And Sohrab was troubled about the identity of his marvelous opponent. He turned to Human, the officer sent to him by the emperor of Turan. "The Persian's shoulders and arms are much like mine. His chest and legs are equal to my own. Can it be that this aged man is Rustem?" said the youth. "Oh, my mind is sorely troubled."

The dark-eyed Human smiled and scratched his beard. "No, that man isn't Rustem," he said. "I saw the great Rustem many years ago. He looks nothing like your opponent." And at these words, Sohrab nodded sadly and then closed his eyes to try to get some sleep.

Rustem was up early the next morning. He quickly prepared himself and rode out in the golden light to await the young champion on the plains.

Before long, Sohrab appeared in full armor and swinging a club. But upon seeing Rustem, he lowered the weapon and the youth's face was full of smiles. "How did you spend the night?" he called, as though speaking to a friend. "I spent many hours thinking about this conflict between us. Come, let us put aside our weapons! Let's make a pact of peace for, in truth, I mean you no harm."

"Noble youth!" answered Rustem. "You can't trick me! Save your gentle words. Make ready for battle, and let Heaven decide which of us will fall!" Then Rustem leaped down from his horse. And Sohrab, with a mournful sigh, did the same.

Standing face to face, the two heroes suddenly sprang forward and began fighting like enraged lions! Each was a mighty wrestler, and found it hard to bring down the other. Sweating and aching with pain, they fought through the whole day. Indeed, the battle raged on right up to the setting of the sun. And just as the last light of day disappeared, Sohrab went crashing into Rustem like a wild bull. Seconds later, Rustem was pinned to the earth!

Great sadness filled Sohrab's heart as he raised his dagger overhead. But at that same moment the clever Rustem thought of a trick. "Stop!" he shouted. "This is not the custom in this land. It's not honorable to destroy a man after throwing him down for the first time! Here a true warrior gives his opponent a second chance!"

Sohrab was a gallant youth. At once, he released Rustem and the Persian champion quickly jumped to his feet. Then, because night had fallen, they fought no more and rode back to their camps. Their terrible contest was to be continued the next day.

Early the next morning, Rustem washed himself in the cool water of a running brook, and then prayed aloud. He begged his god to give him even greater strength. Then with his heart filled with fear he went out to the field of battle to await Sohrab.

Before long, Sohrab came rushing onto the field like an enraged elephant. "You escaped from me last night," he roared with a voice like thunder. "And now you dare to face me again! Have you no fear for your life?"

Rustem made no answer but lunged forward at once, and soon the two heroes were engaged in a fierce struggle. Clouds of dust swirled up around them as they stamped about, wrestling on their feet. Then, in a swift and surprise move, Rustem seized Sohrab's belt, hurled him to the ground, and lunged at him with his sword. Stunned, the dying youth lay helpless upon his back.

Gasping, Sohrab lifted his dark eyes to the blue dome of sky. "People will joke and laugh about the shortness of my life and of how I was thrown into the dust," he groaned. "All my troubles were for nothing, for I have not seen my father. I yearned to meet him face to face. Useless now is the token I brought to prove myself his true son!"

Rustem's heart was deeply touched, and he knelt beside Sohrab as the youth went on. "All is over for me. Fate has brought me low," he said. "Yet I pity you, mighty stranger! For when my father hears of this deed, he'll seek you out. You won't escape him! He'll find you even if you were to become like a fish lost among all the fish in the ocean. He'll find you even if you were to become like a star hidden among all the stars in the sky. There is no hope! No matter where you hide, my father will find you. For you have slain the son of mighty Rustem!"

When Rustem heard these terrible words, he dropped his sword and fell back. The air became dark in his eyes and he sank to the earth. When he opened his eyes again, he reached out for Sohrab. "Can this really be happening?" he sobbed. "Oh, brave lad, I am Rustem!"

Upon hearing this, Sohrab was filled with misery. "If you are my father, then your stubborn heart has slain your son!" he cried. "I appealed to you to tell me your name. Now we meet too late!"

Rustem continued sobbing as Sohrab went on. "Around my arm is a chain with a stone fastened to it," he groaned. "It is my father's own gift to me. By this token he would know that I am truly his son."

With trembling hands, Rustem lifted the youth's sleeve and beheld the onyx flashing in the sunlight. "Oh, Sohrab! My own son!" he cried aloud. "What have I done?" Weeping bitterly, the unhappy man tore at his clothes and covered his head with dust.

"Do not weep, for surely it was meant to be this way," said Sohrab. Then he grasped Rustem's arm as he went on. "Father, I beg you to do something for me. Show me your love by not letting the shah destroy my men. They didn't come as his enemies, but only to please me. Let them return home in safety."

Nodding, Rustem promised that this would be done. Then he

held his son in his arms as the youth continued to speak. "I came here like the thunder, and I vanish like the wind," he murmured. "But perhaps, Father, we may meet again in the world above."

And so it came to pass that after the sun had set that day, Sohrab perished on the darkened plain. And when Rustem returned to his own people, he built a great fire. Into the roaring blaze, he hurled his tent, his saddle, and all his armor. Then, with a heavy heart, he watched the leaping flames in silence as his pride crumbled into ashes.

# QUESTING FOR INFORMATION

## A. Getting the Main Idea and Facts

Write the letter of the answer that best completes each statement.

1. This story is mainly about _____.
   a. a woman's great efforts to protect her child
   b. a warrior's fateful trick on his son
   c. a youth's tragic search for his father

2. Sohrab's name meant _____.
   a. young lion      b. filled with smiles      c. champion

3. Tahmineh arranged for her _____ to accompany Sohrab to Iran.
   a. brother      b. uncle      c. father

4. Sohrab carried _____ to show that he was Rustem's son.
   a. a ruby      b. a letter      c. an onyx

5. Sohrab suspected that the aging warrior was Rustem because of his _____.
   a. face      b. armor      c. build

## B. Going Beyond the Facts

Write the letter of the answer that best completes each statement.

1. Each of these words except _____ describes Rustem's behavior at some point in the story.
   a. crafty      b. humorous      c. fearful

2. We may assume that after Sohrab's death Rustem sent word to the army of Turan to _____ .
   a. go back home
   b. get ready for battle
   c. join the shah's forces

3. We may infer that _____ would be pleased to hear about Sohrab's fall and about Rustem's broken spirit.
   a. The Shah of Iran
   b. the Emperor of Turan
   c. the King of Samangan

4. It would seem that Rustem burned some things in order to _____ .
   a. send signals to his army
   b. turn from war and killing
   c. make himself warm and comfortable

5. Of the following statements, _____ is an opinion.
   a. Sohrab was a powerful warrior.
   b. Sohrab was concerned about his remaining troops.
   c. Sohrab was foolish to go to Iran.

## QUESTING FOR MEANINGS

Write the letter of the word that best completes each statement below.
   a. onyx
   b. purposes
   c. parched
   d. opponent
   e. honorable

1. The runner came in two seconds before her closest _____ in the race.
2. Jane added a fine _____ to her collection of quartz pieces.
3. It is never _____ to ignore doing one's share of the work.
4. The committee made a list of the many fine _____ for which the club's money might be used.
5. Because of the lack of rain, the land remained _____ all year.

## QUESTING FOR UNDERSTANDING

1. Briefly discuss how each of the following helped bring about the tragedy in this story.
   a. the lies and fears of Rustem
   b. Human's lie
   c. the ambition and trickery of the emperor of Turan

2. Explain the meaning of Sohrab's line: "I came here like the thunder, and I vanish like the wind."

## QUESTING FOR ENRICHMENT

Modern English contains some words borrowed or derived from languages from the Middle and Far East. For example, *coffee* and *sofa* are from Arabic, *tea* from Chinese, and *pajamas* from Hindi (one of the languages spoken in India). Below are more words from some of the many languages spoken in the Middle and Far East.

Write the letter for the meaning in column B next to the number for its word and source in column A. Write each number with its letter on your paper.

Then do the same for columns C and D on page 173.

| A | B |
|---|---|
| 1. angora (from Turkish) | *a.* place for selling, usually filled with stalls and shops |
| 2. bazaar (from Persian) | |
| 3. bungalow (from Hindi) | |
| 4. caravan (from Persian) | *b.* type of loose robe or dressing gown |
| 5. kimono (from Japanese) | |
| | *c.* hair from special breeds of rabbits or goats; a kind of yarn for knitting |
| | *d.* type of small house with one story |
| | *e.* procession of travelers journeying together for safety in desert or elsewhere |

## C

1. algebra (from Arabic)
2. shish kebab (from Armenian)
3. jubilee (from Hebrew)
4. sari (from Hindi)
5. tycoon (Japanese from Chinese)

## D

a. special anniversary or celebration of same
b. kind of arithmetic in which letters represent some numbers
c. top leader; powerful businessman
d. pieces of meat and vegetables cooked on a skewer (long wood or metal pin)
e. draped garment or dress with many yards of lightweight material

# Chuko Liang and the Hundred Thousand Arrows

After the fall of the united Han Empire in A.D. 221, China was divided into three regions. The Wei kingdom was in the north, the Shu kingdom in the southwest, and the Wu kingdom in the southeast. In the mid 1400's, Lo Kuan Chung wrote an epic novel called *A Tale of Three Kingdoms* telling how kingdom fought kingdom to see which emperor would rule all China. The novel also tells about the adventures of heroes like Chuko Liang, a Shu scholar and military leader. (In some translations he is called K'ung Ming.)

The story below is based on an episode from the famous book. In this tale we see how deadly arrows shot at Chuko actually save his life.

## Major Characters

**Chuko Liang**   a scholar and general

**Lu Su**   a sea captain and Chuko's friend

**Chou Yu**   Chuko's military commander

**Tsao Tsao**   the enemy commander

## Vocabulary Preview

**reputation**   a good or bad name; a person's value as judged by others
   Mrs. Jones has a fine *reputation* as a helpful teacher.

**awnings**   coverings of canvas or other material overhanging doors, windows, and other spaces
   New *awnings* were hung over the store windows to keep out the sun.

**strategy**   planning or directing military or other actions
   The general's *strategy* for winning the battle was successful.

**porcupine**   an animal covered with long, sharp spines called quills
   The *porcupine* is found mainly in heavily wooded regions.

**forecast**   to predict; prophesy; tell what is to come
   The weatherman *forecasts* sunshine for the weekend.

"It may be a trap! Be careful," warned Lu Su. "You know the commander frowns upon your great reputation. I fear that he means to put you to shame, my friend!"

Chuko Liang smiled at this. "That's a chance I'll have to take. He's called all his officers to a meeting, so I can't refuse to be there." Grinning, Chuko Liang stroked his thin dark beard as he walked into the great tent.

The heavy commander, fierce in his armor, glared at Chuko Liang. "As I was saying," he growled, "we'll soon be facing General Tsao Tsao. His mighty army is camped across the Yangtze River, and his warships are ready for action. We must discuss our choice of weapons to use against his forces."

Upon hearing this, Chuko Liang began stroking his beard again. The slim man's dark eyes began gleaming brightly. The other officers turned to look at him, for they greatly admired and respected him. In silence, they waited for the master of strategy to speak.

Chuko Liang bowed politely to the commander. "My lord, we must use bows and arrows," he said.

Chou Yu stared at the young scholar and general. "That's just what I thought," he snapped. "At least one hundred thousand are needed. Will you see that all the arrows are provided soon, young master? I'm putting you in charge of this task."

Again Chuko Liang bowed. "Gladly," he replied. "When will you need the arrows?"

Grinning slyly, the commander clasped his hands behind his back. "In ten days," he answered. "Do you think you can have so many ready by then?"

Twisting the ends of his beard, Chuko Liang stood thinking for a few moments. "But surely Tsao Tsao's army will attack us in less than ten days," he said. "We'll be destroyed if we wait so long."

The commander leaned across the pile of maps on his table. "Then just how soon can you deliver the needed arms to me?" he snarled.

"Within three days," Chuko Liang answered quietly.

The commander slammed both fists down on the maps before him. "Don't make jokes!" he roared. "This is a serious matter!"

Chuko Liang pulled himself up to his full height. "But I am serious," he responded. "I'll deliver one hundred thousand arrows in three days. However, if I should fail to keep my word, you may punish me according to the rules of the army."

Now the commander smiled happily and began patting the sword at his side. Sure that Chuko Liang must fail at this task, Chou Yu gladly agreed with the bargain.

Later that day, Chuko Liang was walking through the long lines of tents in the sprawling camp. Lu Su, short and stocky, walked beside his friend. Lu Su's eyes were dark with worry. "What have you done?" he moaned. "How can you keep such a promise? Don't you know the commander expects you to fail?"

But Chuko Liang was too busy thinking to be worried. "I have a plan in mind," he said, "and you must help me, my worthy friend." Then Chuko Liang pointed to the many ships in the harbor as he went on. "You're in charge of many ships. I want you to lend me twenty boats with thick awnings, and a crew for each boat. Also, see that a thousand bales of straw are delivered to the harbor by tomorrow morning."

Lu Su said nothing. He'd learned long ago to trust Chuko Liang's ideas, no matter how strange they seemed to be. So the sea captain nodded and hurried off to do his friend's bidding.

The next evening, Lu Su hurried down to the misty shore. Chuko Liang, standing on the top deck of the first ship, spied his friend and waved him aboard. Shortly after that, their ship began leading the others through the darkening green waters. Linked by thick ropes, the ships followed one after the other. They looked like ducklings swimming in single file.

That night the ships were not far from the north side of the broad river. Chuko Liang's vessels bobbed gently in the water. They were just a few hundred yards away from Tsao Tsao's camp, but the ships couldn't be seen by Tsao Tsao's forces because a very thick fog lay over the river. Not even the men on Tsao Tsao's nearby warships could see the string of Chuko Liang's boats riding the gently rolling waves.

Chuko ordered his men to take cover under the thick awnings on their ships. He commanded them to stand ready with their huge war drums and great gongs. Then, at the stroke of midnight, he began to shout with force. "Now!" he roared. "Make noise! More noise than you've ever made before!"

At once, the crews on the ships began beating wildly on their war drums and striking their huge gongs! The noise went crashing over the waves like earsplitting thunder. The terrible sounds boomed through the air in the enemy camp, and Tsao Tsao's lamp rattled and shook on his bedside table.

Tsao Tsao leaped up and rushed out of his tent. "Chou Yu's

forces are out there. They're trying to draw us into a trap," he bellowed. "But we won't go out into the fog. We won't be trapped!" Then the angry man ordered five thousand archers to line the shores and shoot arrows in the direction of the noise.

Soon five thousand more archers were sent to join the others at the shore. Their swift arrows went whistling through the fog. In time there were so many arrows flying that they looked like a silvery waterfall as they arched down toward Chuko Liang's vessels. But the arrows did no harm. They just struck the great bales of straw lining the decks and padding the hulls of the ships.

The rain of arrows went on for more than an hour. Before long the ships looked like giant porcupines covered with quills. This greatly satisfied Chuko Liang, so he shouted orders for the string of ships to begin moving back across the river. And as the vessels turned away, Chuko Liang grinned and reminded his men to say thank you to Tsao Tsao for his generous gift. The men began shaking with laughter. "Thank you for the gift of arrows," they shouted to Tsao Tsao through the thinning fog.

It was dawn when the ships reached the south shore and, before long, the fog was entirely gone. Smiling, Lu Su stood next to Chuko

Liang. "This is truly wonderful!" exclaimed Lu Su, staring at the many arrows. "But how could you know that there would be a dense fog over the river last night? Do you have powers of magic?"

Chuko Liang smiled at his amazed companion. "Powers of magic? No, my friend," he laughed. "But I do possess a special power, the secret of which I'll gladly share only with you."

The young general tapped his own forehead two or three times. "The secret power is in here," he said. "A general must know more than just how to lead his men. He must think ahead about many things, even the weather. And so I studied hard and learned long ago how to forecast the weather. It was easy for me to know that a thick fog would roll in last night. That's why I could promise to deliver the arrows within three days."

Lu Su nodded and smiled broadly. He was still smiling when the commander and some of his officers arrived at the shore. Chou Yu's dark eyes seemed to open as wide as his mouth as he stood there staring hard. Stacks upon stacks of arrows lined the shore!

Finally, Chou Yu turned to his officers. "This is truly amazing! Chuko Liang has kept his word," he declared. "I think the time has come for me to admit to his greatness as a master of strategy!"

Turning then to Chuko Liang, he made a slight bow and smiled. "Long will this day be remembered," he announced for all to hear. "It will be called the day of Chuko Liang and the hundred thousand arrows!"

## QUESTING FOR INFORMATION

### A. Getting the Main Idea and Facts

Write the letter of the answer that best completes each statement.

1. This story is mainly about how a _____ .
   a. dense fog covered the Yangtze River
   b. knowledge of weather forecasting was helpful
   c. clever man gained needed supplies
2. Chuko Liang promised to deliver the needed arrows _____ .
   a. overnight      b. within ten days      c. within three days
3. The person who suggested that Chuko Liang should be punished if he failed was _____ .
   a. Chuko Liang      b. Chou Yu      c. Lu Su

4. Tsao Tsao believed his enemies were trying to _____.
   a. gather all his arrows
   b. lead his forces into a trap
   c. attack his camp
5. Chou Yu finally admitted to Chuko Liang's greatness as a _____.
   a. master of strategy    b. sea captain    c. forecaster of weather

## B. Going Beyond the Facts

Write the letter of the answer that best completes each statement.

1. We may infer from events at the beginning of the story that the commander _____.
   a. wished to reward Chuko Liang
   b. was jealous of Chuko Liang
   c. feared Chuko Liang's anger
2. The word that best describes Lu Su's behavior toward Chuko Liang is _____.
   a. suspicious    b. selfish    c. loyal
3. We may conclude that Chuko Liang had his men make lots of noise in order to _____.
   a. attract the flow of arrows
   b. build up his men's courage
   c. get the enemy forces to retreat
4. After Chuko Liang's raid, Tsao Tsao probably did not attack Chou Yu's army immediately because he _____.
   a. had lost many men
   b. feared Chuko Liang's special powers
   c. needed more weapons
5. It seems correct to conclude that Chuko Liang was a _____.
   a. magician    b. crafty person    c. nervous man

## QUESTING FOR MEANINGS

Write the letter of the word that best completes each statement below.

a. awning    b. porcupine    c. forecast
d. reputation    e. strategy

1. The raised quills of the _____ made it look like a huge pincushion.
2. We were glad to hear the reporter _____ good weather for Saturday.
3. An _____ over the front door kept the top steps free from snow.
4. One clever _____ after another helped the team win the big game.
5. Our town mayor has a fine _____ as an honest and hardworking person.

## QUESTING FOR UNDERSTANDING

1. Give examples which show that Chuko Liang carefully thought ahead concerning the safety of his men and ships.
2. Give examples which show that Chuko Liang probably thought ahead to what Tsao Tsao would think and do.

## QUESTING FOR ENRICHMENT

Four of the five verbs in each column have something in common. Find the verb that doesn't belong, and be ready to tell why it doesn't belong.

| A | B | C | D | E |
|---|---|---|---|---|
| forecast | cheered | growled | commanded | dashed |
| predict | laughed | snarled | ordered | hurried |
| foretell | chuckled | smiled | demanded | crept |
| recall | giggled | snapped | obeyed | ran |
| foresee | wept | grumbled | directed | rushed |

# The Strange Weapons of Chuko Liang

In A.D. 221, China was divided into the Shu, Wei, and Wu kingdoms after the fall of the united Han Empire. For many years following, these kingdoms fought each other to see which emperor would sit on the "dragon throne" and rule over all of China. *A Tale of Three Kingdoms,* an epic novel written in the mid 1400's by Lo Kuan Chung, tells about this conflict and about the adventures of heroes like Chuko Liang, a Shu military leader.

In today's story, based on an episode from the famous novel, we see why Chuko decides to wear a thin robe instead of thick armor to face nearby enemies.

## Major Characters

**Chuko Liang**  a scholar and general (Shu kingdom)

**Kuan and Chang**  Chuko Liang's captains

**Ssuma Yi**  the enemy commander (Wei kingdom)

## Vocabulary Preview

**lute**  a stringed instrument with pear-shaped body and bent, long neck
The *lute* is played by picking at its many strings.

**penalty**  the punishment for an offense
The judge ordered a *penalty* of fifty dollars for speeding.

**authority**  the power and right to control
Badges are the symbol of the *authority* of police officers.

**risk**  to take a chance of being harmed or taking a loss
People *risk* their lives when they cross against traffic lights.

**swaggered**  strutted or walked about in a bold, proud way
The winner of the election *swaggered* across the platform.

The news was very bad. Huge armies of the emperor of the Wei kingdom were sweeping over cities in the Shu kingdom. The immense armies, led by the fierce General Ssuma Yi, were scoring victory after victory.

Upon hearing of their advance, Chuko Liang halted the march of his small army of Shu warriors. He called over two of his bravest captains, Kuan and Chang. After giving them secret orders, he sent them off with fewer than two thousand men. Then he proceeded to the city of Hsi, also called West City. And there he remained, gathering supplies and waiting for news of Ssuma Yi's next move.

It was not long before two of Chuko's scouts came racing along the winding road to the city. Their horses were kicking up clouds of dust.

"We're dead men already! All is lost!" cried a thin scout to his partner.

The second scout just smiled. "Then you don't know our great leader very well," he laughed. "Chuko Liang will know what to do. Somehow he'll save us. The great Wei army will be stopped!" Then he said no more. He and his partner just galloped wildly ahead until they rode through the gates of the city.

Leaping from their horses, they went bounding up the steps of the young general's headquarters. Chuko and his officers were leaning over a large map spread out on a table. Looking up, Chuko saw the dust-covered scouts. "What news do you bring? Give us your report," called the slim but muscular man.

The frightened scout brushed the hair out of his eyes. "Oh, great one," he gulped. "We are lost! The fierce Wei armies are approaching. Ssuma Yi has more than a hundred thousand men at his command. Within a few hours they'll be at the city gates!"

Chuko Liang frowned upon hearing this news. Then he dashed outside and climbed to a high section of the city wall. As he stared into the distance he could see the two armies advancing along separate roads. Great clouds of dust were being kicked up by the men as they marched along. The long clouds of reddish dust looked like great dragons winding their way toward the city.

After a few moments of watching, Chuko hurried back to speak to his troubled officers. Smiling broadly, he then sent a soldier to fetch some things for him.

In no time at all, the man was back. He was carrying some sticks of incense, a lute, and a colorful robe which Chuko sometimes wore when he was relaxing. "Ah, now I have my weapons," exclaimed Chuko Liang. "With these I mean to face the Wei armies!"

Brushing the hair out of his eyes, the frightened scout stared at the general. "Those are your weapons?" he gasped.

"Yes, and so is this," said Chuko, tapping his forehead. "Now you and all the other troops left in the city must do as I command!" Suddenly, Chuko Liang's smile was gone. His voice was harsh and forceful. The men shuddered, for they knew that when this kind man spoke in this way he was someone to be feared and obeyed.

"There must be no trace of our army left in the city. Have our men come down from the lookout towers. Take down all the flags and banners," ordered Chuko. "Then hide yourselves, and make no noise. Indeed, no one is to move or make a sound, under penalty of death!"

Soon everyone went rushing out of the room, except for a few men. Chuko Liang had ordered them to remain behind. "You are to exchange your uniforms for the clothes of workmen," he said. "When you've done that, open the front gates of the city. And leave them open! Stay there and begin brushing up the leaves and twigs. Work very slowly, and show no fear!"

The men looked at each other in amazement. However, they soon rushed off to do as they'd been told. Then Chuko put on his long robe. He picked up the lute and incense sticks, and with two young boys climbed to the highest section of the city wall. One youth carried Chuko's sword for all to see, and the other carried Chuko's wand of authority.

Chuko lit some sticks of incense and placed them in cracks along the wall. After that he grinned and began playing his lute. Smiling, softly, he watched the smoke from the incense go curling toward the pale blue sky. But from the corner of his eye, he was watching something else. His sharp eyes could see the two Wei scouts peering up at him from behind some nearby trees.

"How can this be? The gates are wide open, and some workmen are quietly brushing up twigs and leaves," said one of the scouts.

The second scout nodded. "And that man relaxing in his robe on the wall is the famous Chuko Liang!" he said. "But where are his men? Look, there are no army flags or banners flying anywhere. The whole Shu army must be gone! Let's ride back and give Ssuma Yi this happy news!"

However, when the scouts gave the stout general their report, he just laughed aloud. "Don't you realize that we're dealing with a great master of strategy? Surely, he has some trick in mind. Wait here, you fools! I'll ride out to check things for myself!"

The general went riding forth on his gray charger. He rode hard until he was only a short distance from the city. Then slowly moving a little closer to the wall, he looked up at Chuko and carefully studied the quiet scene. "It's all so peaceful," he thought to himself. "Too peaceful!"

After that, he rode back to his camp. And he laughed as he spoke to his officers there. "Chuko Liang must think I'm a great fool," he said. "He expects me to lead my men into a trap! Surely, he has many troops hiding within and outside the city. Who knows how big the army waiting to ambush us may be?"

All the general's officers, except for his second son, smiled as Ssuma Yi went on. "But we won't fall into Chuko Liang's trap," declared the general. "I'll lead my men far to the north! Away from the ambush!"

Ssuma Yi's warrior son clutched angrily at his sword. "But how can you be sure that a Shu army is waiting to attack us at the city?" he cried.

The youth's father laughed and clapped his hands together. "Because there are still people living in the city. And Chuko Liang would never leave them unprotected! He would never risk the safety of his people!" he shouted. "So it's certain he has an ambush planned. But this time I have outsmarted the famous master of strategy!" Grinning happily, the general swaggered from his tent and soon began leading his armies toward the high hills of the north.

From afar, Chuko watched the moving masses of dust. The Wei armies were moving down the two roads on their way northward. The gray clouds of dust kicked up by the long lines of men looked like serpents winding their way toward the distant hills.

Then Chuko turned and looked down into the city. Suddenly he burst into laughter and began dancing about on the high wall. "Come out, my noble troops! You and the people of the city have been saved! The city has been spared!" he shouted. And with joy in his heart he watched as people carefully came walking out into the streets and began looking around.

"All is well!" people began shouting. "Chuko Liang has saved us!"

Then one of Chuko's officers called up to him. "Master, how did you manage to get two great armies to leave just by showing yourself?"

At this, Chuko grinned broadly. "I knew that Ssuma Yi would ride up to check on things for himself, for he's a very cautious man. He watched me pretending to relax with none of my soldiers in sight. I knew that he would quickly suspect that I was trying to trick him, because he knows I would never leave my people open to danger," he said. "So the great Wei general turned his armies away. Now we have more time to gather supplies and move everyone away from here to a safer place!"

However, there was one person who still had some doubts about their safety. Brushing the hair out of his eyes, the thin scout shouted up to Chuko. "But what if Ssuma Yi decides to return tomorrow, before we've had a chance to get very far! His forces are still far greater than ours!"

Chuko smiled slyly and leaned forward. "Don't worry so much, my young friend," he replied. "Ssuma Yi's forces will be kept busy for a long while by my brave captains, Kuan and Chang. A few days ago I sent them and their men to wait in the hills to give trouble to Ssuma Yi's passing armies!"

People's mouths fell open at Chuko's words. For a long moment there was complete silence in the city. But then, like a sudden burst of firecrackers, loud cheers exploded through the evening air.

The cheering continued as Chuko climbed down from the wall. And as he hurried through the happy crowds, he laughed to himself as he thought about the incense, the lute, and his long robe. For, indeed, they were the strangest weapons ever used by the famous master of strategy!

## QUESTING FOR INFORMATION

### A.  Getting the Main Idea and Facts

Write the letter of the answer that best completes each statement.

1.  The headline which best brings out the main idea of this story is _____ .
    a.  Wei Armies Advance on City
    b.  City Saved by Clever Plan
    c.  Troops Disappear from Troubled City
2.  Chuko Liang sent two brave _____ to wait in the hills for Ssuma Yi's armies.
    a.  scouts      b.  generals      c.  captains
3.  Chuko Liang had all _____ removed from sight.
    a.  lookout towers
    b.  flags and banners
    c.  street sweepers
4.  Ssuma Yi's report was challenged by his _____ .
    a.  officers      b.  son      c.  scouts
5.  Chuko Liang's weapons included each of the following except _____ .
    a.  firecrackers      b.  a lute      c.  sticks of incense

### B.  Going Beyond the Facts

Write the letter of the answer that best completes each statement.

1.  We may infer that Chuko Liang had his sword and wand of authority brought up on the wall so that he would _____ .
    a.  be obeyed by the youths
    b.  feel more important
    c.  be more easily recognized
2.  Ssuma Yi's scouts probably thought that the city _____ .
    a.  was deserted
    b.  held hidden troops
    c.  could easily be taken
3.  Chuko Liang must have realized that Ssuma Yi was probably wondering about _____ .
    a.  the size of the Shu army
    b.  where to get fresh supplies
    c.  the men brushing up leaves and twigs

4. The word _____ best describes Ssuma Yi's reaction toward Chuko's behavior on the wall.
   a. furious     b. suspicious     c. cowardly
5. We may conclude that Ssuma Yi must have felt _____ as he quickly led his forces northward.
   a. ashamed of his action
   b. worried about being ambushed in the hills
   c. very pleased with himself

## QUESTING FOR MEANINGS

Write the letter of the word that best completes each statement below.

a. lute
b. authority
c. penalty
d. risk
e. swaggered

1. The police charged the reckless driver a heavy _____ for speeding.
2. People shouldn't _____ their safety by touching fallen wires.
3. The bully _____ until he reached the principal's office.
4. A judge gave the detectives the _____ to search the house.
5. The guest artist played a _____ and other rare instruments for us.

## QUESTING FOR UNDERSTANDING

1. Chuko Liang was an intelligent and thoughtful man. Give examples which show that he was:
   a. a fast thinker     b. a man who carefully thought ahead.
2. Chuko Liang could have saved himself and his remaining troops by leaving the city and its people. However, he chose to remain there. What does this tell us about him as a *man* and as a *military leader?*

# QUESTING FOR ENRICHMENT

Write the letter for the word in column B next to its antonym in column A. Write each number with its letter on your paper.
Then do the same for columns C and D.

|  **A** | **B** |
|---|---|
| 1. *forceful* voice | a. advancing |
| 2. *retreating* army | b. strange |
| 3. *cautious* driver | c. weak |
| 4. *familiar* voice | d. small |
| 5. *immense* lake | e. careless |

|  **C** | **D** |
|---|---|
| 1. *tame* creature | a. mild |
| 2. *famous* actor | b. fierce |
| 3. *nervous* officers | c. unknown |
| 4. *youthful* scout | d. relaxed |
| 5. *harsh* climate | e. elderly |

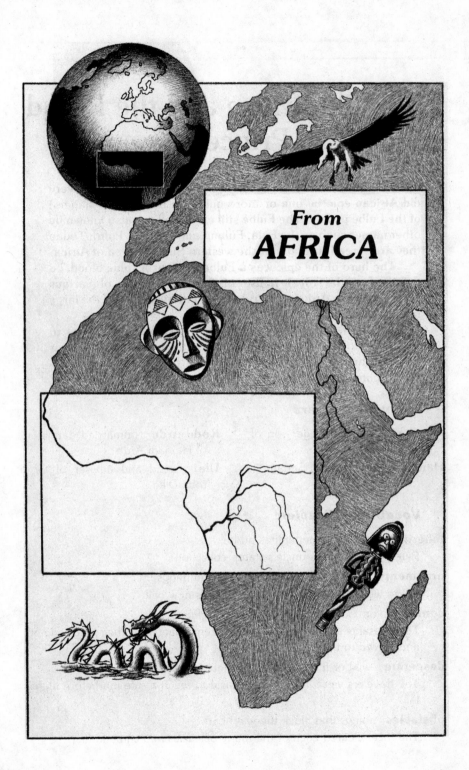

# From
# AFRICA

# The Wild Prince and the Proud Princess

The story that follows is based on *The Blue Blood,* a very old African epic by one or more unknown bards (poet-singers) of the Fulbe people. The Fulbe still exist, and are also known by other names such as the Fula, Fulani, and Pullo (or Pulu). Today they are spread throughout the western Sudanic area of Africa.

The hero of the epic was a Fulbe. He was a "blue blood," a member of the royal house of Ardo. Members of various branches of the Ardo House ruled over different parts of the large land area called Massina.

Goroba-Dike, the young blue blood, set out on a quest to find a solution to a personal problem. In today's tale we discover how two human ears kept in his wallet help make his special dream come true.

## Major Characters

**Goroba-Dike**  a younger son of a king of Massina

**Hamadi Ardo**  king of Sariam

**Kode Ardo**  unmarried daughter of Hamadi Ardo

**Ulal**  friend and adviser of Goroba-Dike

## Vocabulary Preview

**inherit**  to receive something as an heir
Peter will *inherit* his uncle's stamp collection.

**ornaments**  decorations to add beauty; trimmings
There were pretty *ornaments* on Maria's new belt.

**common**  ordinary, and sometimes not refined
The peasants and other *common* citizens cheered as their king rode by and waved to them.

**desperate**  wild or frantic because of fear or suffering
The travelers were in *desperate* haste to reach a safe inn before nightfall.

**obstacles**  things that block the way; barriers
The racer cleared each of the many *obstacles* and came in first.

# I. Contest of the Silver Ring

Hide! Hide!" shouted both young and old whenever the wild young man went riding into one of the Bammana villages in Massina. They were terribly afraid of Goroba-Dike and what he would do next. For he often did strange and cruel things like forcing a poor blacksmith to make some fine metal weapons without using a forge.

The wild young man was of the blood of the Fulbe House of Ardo. Members of this family had been ruling over Massina for five hundred years. However, the young blue blood was not a happy person.

"I'm just a younger son in my family," he would often grumble to himself. "As a younger prince, I'll have no land to inherit. My father's kingdom will never be mine. It just isn't fair!"

One morning, as the well-built young man sat feeling sorry for himself in his family's fine home, he was approached by a man called Ulal. The tall man was a bard, a wise singer, and he worked for Goroba-Dike. The people of the villages had secretly given Ulal a pot full of gold. They wanted him to tell Goroba-Dike that his wildness was doing the country harm, and that neither he nor they had anything to gain from his terrible behavior.

"Hear me, my prince," said Ulal to the young man who sat staring at the floor. "You shouldn't take your bitterness out on the people. They haven't caused you any harm. It's not their fault that you can't inherit any land here."

Goroba-Dike looked up as the wise man went on. "Massina is huge, so why remain here? Why don't you turn your attention to the Pulu, who are also your people, and travel to the city of Sariam? There you may gain a kingdom for yourself!"

The thought filled the prince with new hope. "Good! Let's not waste any more time," he said, jumping to his feet. "Let's start off today!"

Soon the two men set out on their long journey. The silver ornaments on their fine reins and saddles sparkled in the sunlight as they rode on through villages and forests. Stopping only for short rests, they kept pushing on until they caught sight of a great city up ahead. However, they didn't go riding into the busy place.

The weary travelers stopped at a peasant's farmhouse outside of Sariam. Quickly then, the anxious youth dressed himself in the peasant's oldest rags as Ulal looked on in wonder.

"I'll go into the city disguised as a beggar," said Goroba-Dike. "I want to look things over for myself. You remain here and take care of our horses and belongings."

A short time later, the prince stopped at a blacksmith's shop in the city. "I am a Pulu," he said. "I'm a poor man's son and down on my luck. If you'll feed me, I'll gladly work for you."

Wiping the sweat from his brow, the smith nodded in agreement. And soon the prince began working with a will at the bellows. Then, after laboring for a while, he looked up and asked, "To whom does this great city belong?"

"To King Hamadi Ardo, a twig of the Ardo tree," answered the smith. "He is very rich, and has three daughters. Two of them are married to fine warriors."

"What about the other daughter?" asked the youth.

"Oh, her name is Kode Ardo," said the smith. "That princess is the proudest Fulbe maiden in all Massina! She wears a silver ring, and says she will marry only the man who can wear the ring on his little finger. For she says that it will fit only a true Fulbe, a man with delicate bones and tender fingers."

The next morning, as on other mornings, fine young Fulbe warriors stood in front of Hamadi Ardo's great house. Filled with hope, they watched as Princess Kode Ardo came out of the house and moved among them. She was a beautiful maiden with dark and flashing eyes. And though she was small, she carried herself like a proud queen.

Kode Ardo drew off her ring and passed it around to see if it would fit any of the young warriors there. One man couldn't even get it over his fingertip. Another man got the ring down only to the first joint. A third man, sweating and straining, got it only as far as his second joint. Finally, the ring was passed back to the princess who put her nose into the air and walked back into the great house.

The following morning the contest took place again. And once more there was no one among all the Fulbe warriors, from far and near, who could slip the ring onto his finger. This bothered King Hamadi Ardo, for his patience was at an end. Turning to his daughter, the white-haired king said, "This can't go on. Now you must marry the best man at hand!"

Hearing this, the smith who had given Goroba-Dike a job stepped forward. "There's a young man working for me. His clothes aren't exactly clean and he comes from outside the city. He says he's a Pulu," said the smith, "and one can see he's a Fulbe."

King Hamadi nodded and ordered that the young stranger be

brought to him. Quickly then, the smith hurried to his shop and told Goroba-Dike that the king wanted to see him at once.

"But I'm all dirty. Look at my clothes," said the young man. However, he gave in when the smith kept insisting that the king was to be obeyed. So looking like a filthy beggar he went to stand before the king in the square.

Hamadi Ardo studied the strong young man's noble bearing for a while. Then he asked, "Are you a Fulbe?" And to this, Goroba-Dike nodded.

"Tell me your name," said the king.

"That I will not reveal," answered the young man.

Nodding, Hamadi Ardo accepted this response and went on. He took the ring from his trembling daughter and said, "Try to slip this ring on your little finger." Goroba-Dike did as he was asked, and to everyone's surprise the ring fitted perfectly!

"Wonderful," exclaimed the king. "Now you must marry my daughter!"

"No! No!" cried the princess. "I won't marry such an ugly, dirty man! He's just a common man from the country!"

But Hamadi Ardo silenced her at once. "It was your own will that caused this. You have brought this upon yourself," he said. "Now you will marry this man!"

And so it was that the wild young blue blood joined the royal family of Sariam. Goroba-Dike was quite pleased, but his new wife was not. And though he knew the princess was unhappy about marrying him, he continued to hide the fact that he was really a blue blood. For his own special reasons, he felt it was not yet time to let the truth be known.

# II. The Strange Bargain

Soon after the wedding, terrible news reached the king and his family in the king's great meeting hall. Invaders, the Burdama people, were thundering through the land and stealing all the fine cattle of Sariam. At once, two of the king's sons-in-law snatched their weapons and dashed outside to gather their men to fight off the Burdama. However, Goroba-Dike just lay idle in a corner of the meeting hall.

Frowning, the king turned to his new son-in-law. "What's this?" he exclaimed bitterly. "Why don't you take a horse and go riding off with the others?"

Goroba-Dike just shook his head. "Climb on a horse? I've never been on a horse before," he said. "Give me a donkey. I can stay on a donkey."

A short time later, the king, the princess, and others stood watching as Goroba-Dike went riding off on a donkey. But instead of riding after the warriors, he rode off in the other direction. The sight of this caused Kode Ardo to begin weeping aloud. "Oh, Father," she cried, "what misery you have brought upon me!"

Before long, the prince arrived at the peasant's farmhouse. There he jumped down from the donkey and called to Ulal. "I've married the king's daughter, the proudest maiden in Massina," he said. "But you can't join me in the city just yet. Now I must leave at once, for the Burdama invaders are stealing our cattle. Hurry now with my clothes and weapons, and saddle my horse!"

In almost no time at all, Goroba-Dike went racing across the country and came riding out of the forest. Soon he overtook Hamadi Ardo's men and began riding along at a little distance from them. He looked magnificent in his fine clothing and headdress. The silver ornaments on his reins and saddle sparkled in the bright sunshine.

His brothers-in-law and other warriors spotted him and wondered who he could be. Then one man exclaimed, "That must be Djinar, the powerful spirit! Let's win him over to our side, and we'll be victorious!"

The king's sons-in-law then sent some men riding over to question the marvelous-looking creature. Goroba-Dike listened to these men and said, "Yes, I am Djinar, and I will help you. But first we must agree on my payment. I want each of your leaders, the king's sons-in-law, to send me one of his ears!"

"What?" gasped one man. "But that's impossible! What would people say?"

Goroba-Dike pulled himself up tall on his splendid horse. "Your leaders may say they were hurt in battle. That would give them honor."

After that, the men rode back and delivered the message to their shocked leaders. At first, the king's sons-in-law refused to take part in the strange bargain, but in time they changed their minds. They knew that they needed help to defeat the Burdama.

With the two ears in his large wallet, Goroba-Dike rode over and placed himself at the head of Hamadi Ardo's army. Looking back, he shouted, "You must not tell anyone that Djinar helped you!" Then he went charging forward, and great clouds of dust rose in the air as the army came riding after him.

Shouting fiercely, Goroba-Dike struck at the surprised Burdama. His strength seemed like that of a hundred men and soon the invaders began to flee in terror. And the prince continued to strike down one Burdama after another and to take their fine horses.

After the battle, Goroba-Dike rounded up the cattle and all the horses he had won from the enemy. These he turned over to his brothers-in-law, and then galloped away through the trees.

The king was delighted with the gift of so many splendid animals. "Never has a man ever had such brave and generous sons-in-law," he declared. "And each of you has lost an ear in doing battle to serve me! You are both great heroes! But now, tell me, where is my other son-in-law? Did he ever find you and join in the battle?"

Everyone standing in the square laughed at this. "He rode off in the wrong direction this morning," said a young and well-built warrior. "And we haven't seen him since then!"

A little while later, Goroba-Dike came riding back into the city on his donkey. Once again he looked shabby in his torn and dirty rags. And as he passed the blacksmith's shop, the smith ran out and shouted, "Stay away from my doorstep! You're no warrior!"

"Leave me alone," answered Goroba-Dike. "I've told you that I am just a poor man's son!" Then he struck the donkey and put it into a gallop. Moments later, he went riding up to the crowd gathered in the square. Once again, the crowd burst into laughter, and they didn't stop even when the princess began sobbing.

That evening, Goroba-Dike sat quietly in a corner as the young warriors told about their brave deeds in battle. "I was the first to charge against the enemy," bragged one man. "I captured the horses," claimed another. And the two sons-in-law told over and over again how they had been hurt in the heat of battle.

Except for the princess, the people of Sariam were feeling very happy. However, their joy was soon to be ended. For early the next day the Burdama were back, attacking the city in great numbers. All the warriors quickly began preparing for battle, but Goroba-Dike went out and swung himself up on his donkey. Then he went hurrying out of the city.

Upon reaching the farm, he leaped from the donkey and shouted for his bard. "Quickly, quickly," he commanded, "get my things and saddle my horse. The Burdama have returned." And before long, the young man was once again on his way to do battle for the people of Sariam.

In the meantime, the Burdama had surrounded the city. One large group was charging through the streets on their way to the king's home. Seeing this, Goroba-Dike broke through their ranks and sent many men flying from their saddles. Then he put his spurs to his horse and raced ahead. He kept his horse leaping over obstacle after obstacle until he arrived at the king's great courtyard. Goroba-Dike was shocked and greatly angered to see two men trying to carry off his wife.

"Help me!" screamed the princess. "My cowardly husband has fled! Help me! Save me from the Burdama!"

Furious, Goroba-Dike struck down the first man with a spear. But as he did this, another man thrust a spear into Goroba-Dike's thigh. And the princess gasped in horror when she saw this happen. "You're wounded!" she cried as she rushed forward. Forgetting all about her own safety and appearance, she tore off half her gown and wrapped the cloth around Goroba-Dike's bleeding leg. He just turned his head and smiled as she did this, because she didn't recognize him.

After that, he spurred his horse once more and went racing into the thick of battle. He fought furiously, scattering his foes in every direction. He kept running men through and hurling them to the ground. The Burdama were filled with terror and began rushing out of the city in desperate flight with Hamadi Ardo's army in pursuit.

Later on, Goroba-Dike turned and rode off to the farmhouse. There he put on his rags again, got onto his donkey, and began riding back to join the king and the others. Then as he passed the blacksmith's shop, the smith came running out.

"There's a dog on the street," shouted the smith. "Get a move on, dog! And stay away from my house, you coward!"

This caused the smith's thin wife to come running out. "Be quiet," she warned the smith. "Stop your fool talk. That man is a Fulbe, and no one should ever insult a Fulbe!"

"Hold your tongue, woman!" roared the smith. "That man ran away just when he was needed!"

Goroba-Dike was furious, but he didn't strike out at the smith. Instead, he just called out: "What did you expect from me? Ever since I've been here I've always said I was just a poor man's son!" Then he put his whip to the donkey and soon reached the great square at a gallop. There the king was standing and speaking to his warriors about the day's events. Kode Ardo was there too, and when she saw her husband come riding up so calmly she began to cry. "Oh, Father," she wept, "why have you made my life so miserable? I'll have nothing more to do with that shabby creature! That worthless coward!"

Goroba-Dike just shrugged his shoulders at her words and went to sit in a shady corner of the square. From there he listened to the bragging of the warriors. One said, "I drove back a large group of the Burdama by myself." Another man said, "You should have seen me scatter the Burdama!" A third man said, "It was I who chased off the main body of the Burdama army!"

Then a grinning man called out to Kode Ardo. "Where was your brave husband while all this was going on?"

"Oh, let me be!" sobbed the unhappy woman. "I am filled with sorrow and shame!" Then she ran to hide herself in her room.

That night the princess couldn't fall asleep. She kept tossing and turning, and at midnight she looked over to her husband's bed on the other side of the room. She saw that Goroba-Dike was asleep, and that his rags had fallen from his body. Then she spotted the bandage wrapped around his thigh. The bandage was part of the gown she had torn to bind the brave stranger's wound!

Kode Ardo rose and hurried over to her sleeping husband. Shaking him, she asked, "Where did you get that bandage?"

The sleepy man mumbled, "Just think it over."

Trembling, Kode Ardo shook him again. "Who are you?" she said. "Tell me who you are!"

Sitting up, Goroba-Dike replied, "A king's son. But don't repeat what I've told you to anyone for the time being. I have my reasons for this. Now, my dear one, warm up some tree-butter and dress my wound with it." And the princess, filled with joy, did as he asked.

Before anyone else was up the next morning, the prince rode his donkey back to the peasant's farmhouse. There he changed into his splendid clothes and ordered Ulal to ride back to the city with him.

By the time they arrived in the city, the king was standing outside in the great square before his home. He and the other people there were busy speaking about the recent victory over the Burdama. However, the princess said nothing and just stood there smiling to herself.

Soon Goroba-Dike and Ulal came riding up to the crowd as everyone turned to stare. Then the bard drove the hitching pegs into the earth, and everyone gazed in admiration at the silver hitching pegs and the magnificently dressed strangers.

Goroba-Dike greeted the princess. She smiled and hurried over to stand beside her husband. Then he turned to the surprised people and began speaking. "I am Goroba-Dike, and this is my wife. I am the son of a great king, and I am the one who drove away the Burdama to save your cattle and your city!"

Hamadi Ardo shook his head. "That I do not believe. My son-in-law couldn't ride a horse," he said. "I have only seen him riding a donkey!"

Goroba-Dike smiled broadly. "If you don't believe me, ask those who were at the battle. They'll tell you that I am the one who helped them."

The warriors standing nearby took a good look at the stranger's face and clothes. "Yes, it's true," said one man, and all the other warriors except Goroba-Dike's brothers-in-law agreed with him.

"We can't be certain," insisted one of the king's sons-in-law.

"That's right," agreed the other son-in-law. "We can't be certain about it at all."

Again, Goroba-Dike smiled broadly. "Perhaps you really don't recognize me," he said. "But you may recognize these!" Then he put his hand into his wallet and pulled out the ears for all to see.

The king gasped at this, and turned to see if his sons-in-law had something more to say. However, the two men remained silent and went hurrying off with their heads bowed low.

Amazed at the turn of events, the king knelt before Goroba-Dike.

"Forgive me for not believing you," he said. "You have proven yourself worthy, so take my kingdom from my hands! I know that you will rule it wisely!"

"Well, then," said Goroba-Dike, "since I am the new king, I would like to give my first command now. It is my order that the smith who insulted me be given fifty strokes with a stick. A stick with knots in it!" And of course the order of the popular new king of Sariam was swiftly carried out.

## QUESTING FOR INFORMATION

### A. Getting the Main Idea and Facts

Write the letter of the answer that best completes each statement.

1. This story is mainly about how _____.
   a. the Burdama invaders were defeated
   b. a clever man gained a kingdom
   c. a princess held an unusual contest
2. Because he couldn't _____, Goroba-Dike behaved wildly.
   a. find a wife      b. inherit land      c. reveal his identity
3. The warriors battling the Burdama believed that Goroba-Dike was a _____.
   a. blue blood      b. wise bard      c. powerful spirit
4. The princess wept because of her _____.
   a. husband's behavior      b. torn gown      c. father's lost cattle
5. Kode Ardo bravely supplied the marvelous stranger with a _____.
   a. weapon      b. drink      c. bandage

### B. Going Beyond the Facts

Write the letter of the answer that best completes each statement.

1. We may conclude that Goroba-Dike's father planned to leave his land to his _____ son.
   a. strongest      b. wisest      c. oldest

2. The words "ambitious" and "_____" seem best to describe Goroba-Dike.
   a. humble    b. crafty    c. cowardly
3. We may say that Goroba-Dike _____ his brothers-in-law.
   a. outsmarted    b. rewarded    c. admired
4. Later on, Goroba-Dike probably _____.
   a. gave Ulal half his kingdom
   b. claimed all the Bammana villages
   c. made peace with his brothers-in-law
5. The humor in this story depends on the reader's knowing some things that the people from _____ didn't know for a while.
   a. Burdama    b. Sariam    c. Bammana villages

## QUESTING FOR MEANINGS

Write the letter of the word that best completes each statement.
a. common    b. desperate    c. inherit
d. obstacles    e. ornaments

1. Vases, little statues, and other household_____ were on sale.
2. From whom did Rita _____ her lovely brown eyes?
3. The young man overcame many _____ and became a great success in his chosen field.
4. This is _____ glass, not a diamond.
5. The thief's _____ leap to escape the police didn't help him.

## QUESTING FOR UNDERSTANDING

1. Identify the characters who made the following statements, and to whom they were made. Then tell what makes each statement so amusing to the reader of the story.

   "I've never been on a horse before. . . . I can stay on a donkey."
   "My cowardly husband has fled! Help me!"
   "Never has a man ever had such brave and generous sons-in-law!"

2. Discuss two or more specific reasons Hamadi Ardo had for being truly grateful to the young man to whom he gave his kingdom. Then discuss his other possible reason or reasons for giving the kingdom to Goroba-Dike and not to one of the other sons-in-law.

## QUESTING FOR ENRICHMENT

Write the numbers 1 to 10. Then from each group of words below, select the *one* word that can be used as a heading or title for the four remaining words in the group. For example, *animals* is the answer for group 1. Why?

| 1 | 2 | 3 | 4 | 5 |
|---|---|---|---|---|
| donkeys | prince | blacksmiths | ornaments | villages |
| horses | princess | peasants | jewelry | cities |
| animals | king | warriors | ribbons | towns |
| cattle | royalty | farmers | vases | places |
| camels | queen | people | statues | nations |

| 6 | 7 | 8 | 9 | 10 |
|---|---|---|---|---|
| sorrow | spears | rings | daughter | silver |
| shame | weapons | bracelets | mother | gold |
| admiration | swords | jewelry | family | copper |
| joy | knives | necklaces | son | metal |
| feelings | arrows | earrings | father | iron |

# Brother and Sister Face the Dragon-Bird

The *Mwindo Epic,* a product of the Nyanga people of Africa, is very old. Versions of it were taken down by Professor Daniel B. Biebuyck for his book, *Hero and Chief.*

In his book, the professor points out that to the Nyanga a great ruler was a wise and settled man. He didn't go off seeking adventure, but remained available to give his people good counsel. Also, it was believed that he had special gifts and powers. In this respect, he was like the divine kings to be found in other cultures.

The following retelling, based on selected material from *Mwindo Epic II,* is set in the forest region of eastern Zaire. In it we meet Mwindo. As a chief's son, he had within him the destiny to become a great chief. However, as the tale shows, he wasn't quite ready for such glory.

As in many other wonderful epics from different parts of the world, the *Mwindo Epic* concerns a gifted human hero, supernatural forces, and travels to other worlds. In this tale we see why a hero leaves his people and hurries away to a safer world.

## Major Characters

**Mwindo** son of Chief Shemwindo

**Nyamitondo** Mwindo's sister

**Shemwindo** father of Mwindo and Nyamitondo

**Lightning** a god

## Vocabulary Preview

**quarreling** arguing; disputing
Some players were *quarreling* with the umpire.

**harmony** order; getting along well with others
People in that neighborhood live in peace and *harmony*.

**cultivate** to prepare land for crops; help minds to grow
A gardener will *cultivate* the soil before planting.

**symbol** a word, sign, person, or object that stands for something else
Uncle Sam is a well-known *symbol* for the United States.

**nature** a person's character; ways in which a person thinks, feels, and acts
Farmer Smith has a generous *nature*.

From HERO AND CHIEF by Daniel B. Biebuyck. Published by the University of California Press © 1978 The Regents of the University of California.

# I.  A Strange Discovery

**A** kingly ruler lived in Tubondo, the main village in his chiefdom. Shemwindo had two wives, each of whom lived in her own house. To each of his wives he had proclaimed, "I want no male children. Present no sons to me!" And later on, when Shemwindo learned that a wife had given birth to two children, he was filled with bitterness because one of the infants was a boy!

The boy, Mwindo, was indeed a very unusual child. First of all, he was born holding a shoulder bag containing a rope, medicine, an axe, and other useful items. And even more amazing was that these and the other objects in the bag of good fortune could act on their own to help Mwindo.

Also, the child was born holding a conga-scepter, a wand made from a cow's tail. But this was no ordinary scepter, for it held special powers concerning life and death.

Of course, people who saw the child didn't realize the great powers of the objects he possessed. But they did realize that Mwindo was a very special being, for he was born walking and talking! In fact, the infant had already been seen carrying firewood and gathering vegetables for his mother.

Yet in spite of the marvels surrounding the infant, Shemwindo refused to accept the child. Could it be that the boy's unusual birth and powers made Shemwindo fear that his son might soon dare to challenge his authority?

Filled with anger, Shemwindo sent for his counselors and issued stern orders. "Keep the girl, but throw the boy into a pit!" he commanded. "I wish to hear no more about him!" And, of course, the counselors bowed to the word of their master.

That night, Shemwindo dismissed the princes and other men from the meeting he'd been having with them on matters concerning the chiefdom. For the chief, like his subjects, valued order and harmony. Indeed, they all felt that quarreling was bad for the land.

Shemwindo then ate well, sent his servants away, and settled down for some rest. Turning in his sleep later that night, he opened his eyes a bit and spotted something in front of him near the hearth. With a cry of amazement, he sat up with his eyes opened wide. His shout awakened the sleeping child, who sat up and began yawning and stretching.

"What's this?" exclaimed Shemwindo. "A child thrown into a pit has risen again! Nothing like this has ever been seen before!"

Then he watched in wonder as the child stood up, smiling proudly. "Hello, Father! I am the one people call *Little-one-just-born-he-walked!*" said the boy somewhat boastfully. "I am Mwindo! Some men hurled me into a pit and covered me over. I didn't like that at all, so I managed to save myself! And here I am!"

Soon it was dawn and the chief's servants appeared. After that, word quickly spread that Mwindo was alive and in the home of his father. People from the village came rushing to the house, and there they devoured the heroic child with their eyes.

Pleased, Shemwindo allowed them to gaze on the beauty of the child for a while, and then called for silence. "This child, Mwindo, has shown great strength and courage. He has done a thing never seen before!" said the chief. "This young hero shall not be turned away. He shall live here among us!" And so it was that Mwindo had a home, and was soon enjoying life along with his sister.

Neither Mwindo nor his sister, Nyamitondo, was very tall, yet each was quite strong and healthy. Mwindo, bright-eyed and full of energy, enjoyed wandering about in search of adventure. The cheerful hero was also a fine singer, and his songs had special power. In addition, the gifted child had the ability to foretell things that were yet to happen.

Nyamitondo was both very clever and quite lovely. The slim girl had dark and flashing eyes. Her winning ways and merry smile captured the hearts of everyone, so it was no wonder that the god called Lightning was pleased when Shemwindo gave him the charming maiden to be his wife. And before long, she was living with her husband in the world above the earth. However, she kept in touch with her family, and came down to visit from time to time.

Upon one occasion, she came down and taught her brother how to cultivate banana trees. The grove was to be a present for their mother. Brother and sister worked hard, and within a short time the trees were growing beautifully.

As they were tending the trees one morning, Mwindo let out a cry of surprise. "Look at this egg in the underbrush. It's huge, and like no other I've ever seen!"

The excited young people gently lifted the egg and carried it back to the village. There they placed it in a hen's nest. From that moment on, Mwindo made certain that no harm came to the egg. And day after day, he waited anxiously for it to hatch.

On a warm afternoon a few weeks later, the giant egg suddenly began rocking back and forth. Then, with a loud crack, the shell split

open. Out leaped a bird larger than any of the chief's hunting dogs! The villagers who saw it jumped back at the sight of the creature. "Ugh! It looks like a dragon! A little dragon with wings!" exclaimed one man. "Drive it away from here, Mwindo!"

Mwindo just laughed at this and began feeding the clumsy bird. Each day after that he threw bananas, potatoes, and chunks of meat to his strange pet. And within a month, the bird was huge. In fact, it was so large that it began flapping its wings and walking about in search of its own food.

One morning, a group of worried people went hurrying to Mwindo's house to speak to the youth. "That creature must be stopped," declared a white-haired man. "It's eating all the chickens in the village and must be destroyed!"

Mwindo just stepped forward with his fists clenched and his eyes aflame. "Whoever slays that bird will be slain by me," he warned. And upon hearing this, the people turned and sadly went back to their homes.

A few days later, the group of villagers was on its way back to Mwindo's home. "Mwindo shows no respect for us!" grumbled one man. "He cares more about that bird and about seeking adventure than he cares for us!"

Arriving at Mwindo's home, the group renewed the quarrel with the youth. "Your wild animal goes on killing," declared a young man with a booming voice. "It grows larger by the day! We've asked you to destroy it, but you have refused. The creature has devoured all our chickens. Now it is eating all our goats. You must stop this thing of evil before it begins attacking people!" Then the villagers just stared at Mwindo in silence until he turned his face and went quietly back inside.

The troubled youth couldn't find a way to stop the beast. So to hide his sense of shame and to escape being pointed at, he hurried to the entrance of the village. There he hurried over to the foot of a tall tree his father had planted. Crawling into a hollow space in the trunk, he began singing and ascending toward the clouds with the tree. He was hoping that Lightning would be able to give him the right kinds of weapons to stop the terrible winged monster.

## II.  A Dangerous Plan

As Mwindo continued on his journey toward the clouds, he kept singing about the trouble in Tubondo. Before long, his sister caught the sound of his voice, and she was there to meet him when the tree touched down on a riverbank downstream from her village.

"I heard your song," said Nyamitondo. "Could things be as bad as all that?"

"Yes," answered Mwindo with shame and sorrow in his voice. "I fear that even now the dragon-bird may be devouring all the people of Tubondo!"

Greatly troubled, Nyamitondo brought her brother to Lightning's special place in the world above the earth. Lightning, a mighty smith, was busy at his forge. But he was glad to see Mwindo, and immediately put aside his own work to help his brother-in-law.

"You need iron tools to fight the beast," said the god. Swiftly then he set about forging special weapons, and great streaks of lightning lit up the place where he worked.

When all the weapons were ready, Lightning smiled and handed them to his wife. Then he explained a clever plan to be used in the fight against the dragon-bird. The young people listened wide-eyed to the dangerous scheme and nodded gravely.

After that, they thanked Lightning and hurried away in the hope that they would not be too late to help their people. And as they traveled earthward, the lovely Nyamitondo glowed like a radiant star.

When at last they reached the earth, they found no one in the village. The only creature there was the dragon-bird, which really was Kirimu, the evil dragon-ogre of the forest! The beast was now truly gigantic, standing taller than any of the nearby trees. Snapping its jaws hungrily, it went swaggering through the village. It was then that the young people realized what had happened. The monster had devoured all the people of Tubondo!

The sharp-eyed creature spied the chief's children, and wheeled about to face them. Then it began beating its wings with great force. But Mwindo and his sister just stood their ground and quickly went over Lightning's scheme. Then, while Mwindo stepped aside as planned, Nyamitondo began walking forward. Straight ahead she marched! Right toward the jaws of the hungry beast!

The bird's eyes burned like flame. Opening its beak as wide as an opening to a cave, the creature charged forward. And then, with a noise like a clap of thunder, the beast snapped its jaws shut and swallowed the girl!

Mwindo gasped at the terrible sight, but he remained to watch as the beast again flapped its wings and began moving forward. But then something very strange occurred. The beast began staggering about on its feet until, quite suddenly, the bird fell. It crashed to the earth like a great boulder, and the light in its eyes went out.

All was still for a few minutes. Then something began moving inside the bird. Moments later, brave Nyamitondo cut her way out near one of the monster's huge wings. Panting for breath, she waved her brother over to her. Then brother and sister sang for joy and cut the bird open, releasing their father and mother. After that, the other villagers began coming out, one at a time, as Mwindo and his sister continued to sing. Their song announced that a young man called the Beautiful-One would emerge from the dragon.

The words of the song proved to be true, for soon a marvelous young man stepped out of the bird's belly. At once, Mwindo and the others understood that the dragon was the first product of the egg, and that the Beautiful-One was the second. Smiling, they realized that he was a symbol of something evil transformed into something good. Then the villagers joined the Beautiful-One in dancing to honor Mwindo and his sister.

Later on, when things in the village were back to normal, Shemwindo called his people together. Shemwindo stood proudly, while his nobles took their places around him. All the other villagers just crowded in silence before their kingly ruler.

"Nyamitondo, you and your brother have shown great courage. You saved us all from a terrible fate!" he exclaimed. "We are truly grateful to your brother, to you, and to your most intelligent husband!" Then the chief presented his daughter with fine gifts which he knew would please Lightning, the god who'd been so helpful. And only seconds later, Lightning himself appeared and swiftly carried away the gifts and his smiling wife, radiant as a star, to the world above the earth.

The people stood wide-eyed, speaking excitedly about the amazing sight they had just witnessed. But when Shemwindo raised his arm, the crowd became silent. Everyone turned, eager to hear his words.

The chief looked straight toward his son as he spoke. "My people, this is my child. This hour I proclaim him a future chief!" he said. "But before he can be enthroned as a full chief, he must make himself worthy. He must bring his nature into balance, and teach himself to bring harmony into the land! And now, my people, I want you to rejoice and dance in his honor!"

Mwindo gasped upon hearing the wonderful news. Then his dark eyes flashed with joy as people began shouting, "Hail to the new chief-to-be!" And Mwindo thought about how *Little-one-just-born-he-walked* was now a man with a great hope. It was the hope of achieving glory as a wise and settled ruler—a true chief whose greatness brings peace and plenty to his land.

## QUESTING FOR INFORMATION

### A. Getting the Main Idea and Facts

Write the letter of the answer that best completes each statement.

1. The main point of this tale is that a young hero _____ .
   a. protected his strange pet
   b. enjoyed searching for adventure
   c. began to change for the better
2. The Nyanga people believed that _____ was not good for the land.
   a. quarreling     b. dancing     c. hunting
3. A god said that _____ were needed to destroy the dragon-bird.
   a. ropes and axes      b. iron tools      c. magical objects

4. The symbol of something evil being transformed into something good was the _____ .
   a. Beautiful-One
   b. conga-scepter
   c. bag of good fortune

5. Shemwindo proclaimed his son a _____ .
   a. chief counselor      b. full chief      c. future chief

## B. Going Beyond the Facts

Write the letter of the answer that best completes each statement.

1. We can tell that Mwindo and his sister _____ their mother.
   a. respected      b. disliked      c. forgot about

2. It seems correct to assume that _____ gave Mwindo some help in his escape from the pit.
   a. counselors      b. magical objects      c. Nyamitondo

3. We may infer that Mwindo felt _____ after the second group of villagers came to speak to him.
   a. guilty      b. amused      c. proud

4. We can tell that Lightning was _____ to help Mwindo.
   a. bribed      b. forced      c. eager

5. For Mwindo to bring his nature into balance, he would probably have to, among other things, gain better control over his _____ .
   a. forestlands and animals
   b. feelings and behavior
   c. father and brother-in-law

# QUESTING FOR MEANINGS

Write the letter of the word that best completes each sentence below.
   a. cultivate      b. symbol      c. harmony
   d. nature      e. quarreling

1. The volunteers worked in perfect _____ and quickly completed the difficult job.

2. Many people seek to _____ their minds by reading fine books.

3. Some foolish _____ between two guests almost ruined the party for everyone.

4. The new neighbor's cheerful _____ soon won her lots of friends.
5. The early light of dawn has long been thought of as a _____ of a fresh beginning.

## QUESTING FOR UNDERSTANDING

1. Describe one or more ways in which Mwindo changed, and tell why such a change or changes could help to make him a good ruler.

2. Nyamitondo was both a fine human being and a heroine to remember. Give examples from the story to show that she was each of the following:

a. a skillful worker     b. a caring family member     c. courageous

## QUESTING FOR ENRICHMENT

A. In the Mwindo story, the Beautiful-One was a special symbol. As you know, a symbol is a sign or token of something that represents or suggests something else. Words or people may also be symbols. For example, $ stands for dollars, O for oxygen, a scepter for authority, a heart for love, the word *dove* for an opponent of war, a road for life, and Robin Hood for a fighter against injustice.

Write the letter for the meaning in column B next to the number for its symbol in column A. Then be ready to discuss the meanings of other symbols you can name.

| A (Symbols) | B (Meanings) |
|---|---|
| 1. stars on U.S. flag | a. peace; goodwill |
| 2. stripes on U.S. flag | b. justice |
| 3. scales | c. good fortune |
| 4. four-leaf clover | d. states |
| 5. skull and crossbones | e. marriage |
| 6. olive branch | f. thirteen original colonies |
| 7. red cross | g. abundance |
| 8. finger band (usually gold) | h. truce; surrender |
| 9. white flag | i. danger; poisonous; pirates |
| 10. cornucopia (horn of plenty) | j. international help organization; medical services |

B.  Go on a *voluntary* quest and write a brief report (a paragraph or more) describing what some key symbols stand for on your city or state flag, or on the flag of another place of special interest to you. Check your school and local library for useful materials. (Tips: Make a list of the symbols, write meanings next to them, and then write a report using complete sentences.) You might care to use one of the following sentences as your topic sentence:

The symbols on the flag of _____ have special meanings.

The flag of _____ contains some interesting symbols.

# Mwindo and the Mysterious Bag of Good Fortune

The *Mwindo Epic* is a product of the Nyanga people of Africa.

As the heroic son of a chief, Mwindo had in him the destiny to become a chief. But because of his sometimes rough or unpolished ways, he wasn't prepared to be enthroned.

Later on, after helping to save his father's people from a terrible beast, he was proclaimed a future chief by his father. However, he was told that before he could be enthroned, he would have to bring his nature into balance.

The following retelling of an episode from the epic is based on material from *Mwindo Epic II*. It is set in the eastern forest region of Zaire. Here we meet Mwindo, not yet a chief, heading his own small village and making use of special gifts.

Like other unusually gifted heroes, such as the Greek hero Achilles, Mwindo is helped or hindered by various gods. (Lightning, a helpful god, is married to Mwindo's sister.) In this tale, so rich in fantasy, we see why a strong young man is suddenly turned into dust!

## Major Characters

**Mwindo**

**Chief Shemwindo** Mwindo's father

**Fire god**

**Kahindo** fire god's daughter

## Vocabulary Preview

**healing** curing; mending
Doctors and nurses are interested in *healing* the sick.

**surpassed** went beyond; was greater than
The young dancer's skill soon *surpassed* that of her teacher.

**garnished** added to decorate a dish of food or to make it tastier
The platter of broiled fish was *garnished* with slices of lemon.

**spectacle** an unusual display or impressive sight
The parade of marchers, bands, and floats was a marvelous *spectacle*.

**pulverized** crushed to powder; destroyed
The turning millstone *pulverized* the grains of wheat into flour.

From HERO AND CHIEF by Daniel B. Biebuyck. Published by the University of California Press © 1978 The Regents of the University of California.

# I. Dropping into Danger

The handsome young man stretched mightily as he rose from his sleep. Feeling rested and content, he walked out into the small village to enjoy the cool morning air. He was in charge of this place, one of the many villages in his father's chiefdom.

Mwindo had good reason to be feeling happy on this fine morning. For just yesterday he had won a great victory. With the help of a magical scepter, he had defeated a chief who was jealous of Mwindo's growing fame, and whose forces had attacked Mwindo's villagers. But now all the people were well and safe, thanks to their young protector and his special powers.

Smiling, Mwindo patted the bag hanging over his shoulder. It was the bag of good fortune with which he had been born. It contained medicine, tools, and other objects that could come to life on their own to help the young man in times of special need. The bag also contained a conga-scepter, a wand made from a cow's tail. This object had many great and mysterious powers.

Mwindo had no idea that he'd soon be needing help from some of the objects in the bag. Indeed, grave dangers awaited him in the very near future. But at this moment he just stood watching his people going about their daily business under a peaceful sky. And he laughed aloud when his two hunting dogs began yelping and playfully leaping up to him.

There was a special tie between Mwindo and his dogs, and to many villagers this seemed to foretell something about Mwindo's future. For between each true chief and his fine hunting dogs there was a mystical tie, a spiritual or mysterious bond of deep trust and understanding.

After a while, Mwindo's thoughts turned to his father, the kingly Shemwindo, whose home was in his main village of Tubondo. Then a faraway look came into Mwindo's eyes. Counselors and other villagers who had gathered around him just stood waiting and watching in silence. They knew that he had the wonderful gift of seeing things they could not see. In truth, he would often foretell things that were yet to happen.

Suddenly, Mwindo turned to his people. "I must travel to the underworld, the land beneath the earth! The time has come for me to meet the gods there, face to face!" he said. "Remain here, all of you. My dogs will stay with you and fight off any outsiders who come to threaten you. Also, my dogs will know where I am, and they will

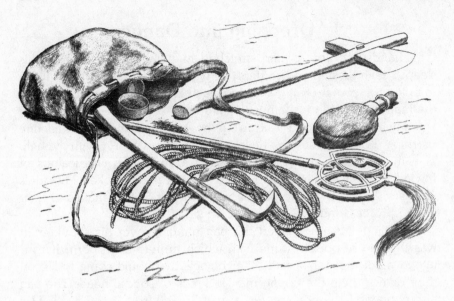

bring me any necessary news. Now don't worry, for I won't be too far away!"

Mwindo's sudden decision surprised the villagers, but they trusted him and held their tongues. Then they watched as he went dashing off into the forest with his bag of good fortune. And Mwindo kept running until he reached a giant fern growing in the thickest part of the forest. At once, he took hold of the plant. Then, with a mighty tug and a pull, he yanked the fern out of the earth.

Plunging into the opening, Mwindo went tumbling down through the darkness until he reached the ground near a wading place in the subterranean world. And there he spotted a young woman sitting on the riverbank.

She was alone and looked quite ill. After a while, she turned and stared in admiration at the handsome young man. Then she called out, "Help me, please! I am suffering terribly!"

Hearing this, Mwindo went rushing over to the unhappy maiden. Using his skills of healing, he did all he could to make her feel well and comfortable. And when she was feeling better, the grateful young beauty smiled sweetly at the stranger.

"Who are you?" she asked softly. "And what are you doing here in the world below the earth?"

Mwindo smiled back at the lovely maiden. "My name is Mwindo," he said, "and I've come to see the god of fire. Can you tell me where to find him?"

The young woman nodded. "Yes, for I am Kahindo, daughter of the god you seek," she answered. "Now let me give you a warning about him, my kind friend. He's a trickster, and he'll try hard to make you look foolish!" Then Kahindo told the youth how to overcome some of the tricks her father might try to play on him at their first meeting.

After that, Mwindo walked into a nearby underground village and climbed up to a huge house on the peak of a steep hill. This was the men's house, the place where the fire god and certain of his villagers spent some time each day.

Pushing open the door, Mwindo stepped into the large room. There he discovered the god of fire sitting with his eyes aglow at the far end of the chamber. Some counselors and other people sat against the walls, staring at the expected visitor.

"I am Mwindo, and I've come to take my father home," said the young man. "Tell me where you've hidden him! I know that he's now here in the world below!"

The god just leaned forward and smiled politely. "Be patient, brave Mwindo. Relax and refresh yourself, my son," he said, holding out a large jar. "Here, dip into this jar and wash yourself."

Mwindo grinned. "No, thank you!" he said. "I don't care to splash my face with your beer!"

The god's eyes opened wide in surprise, yet he was careful to show no anger. Then his face broke into a smile again. "Well, then, since you've come to visit me, there are some things that I'd like you to do for me tomorrow," he said. "Then we'll talk about your father's release. But now you must take time to rest and eat. Sit down here and have some of this banana paste. This pudding has just been cooked, and it is garnished with the most delicious frogs!"

Smiling slyly, Mwindo shook his head as he gazed at the dish. "It would be difficult for me to eat such a meal," he said. "This is especially so since the paste has been garnished with some of your own counselors. The poor things have been transformed into little frogs!"

At this, the frogs sat up, for they were still alive. "We're saved!" they began shouting in human voices. "Oh, young hero, you know many things and have saved us from a terrible fate!"

Once again, the fire god sat quietly, trying not to show his amazement or annoyance. But deep inside he was very angry because Mwindo was showing intelligence that surpassed his own. Now the god was all the more determined to cruelly test the young hero who had come in search of his father. The fire god and his allies were keeping him hidden away in a dark and secret cave.

And so it was that Mwindo, hoping to win back his father, agreed to perform a series of tasks set for him by the fire god. And just before he began the first of the tasks, he was offered a gift by the trickster who was behaving in a very friendly manner.

"Here, take my own belt," said the god. "Place it around your waist, my son. It will serve you well."

Mwindo accepted the belt and thanked the god for it. Then he generously offered the god a gift in return. And the delighted god eagerly accepted the long billhook knife from the bag that Mwindo had over his shoulder.

Now one of the tasks was to plant a new banana grove. This meant that Mwindo was to start from scratch and do the whole difficult job from beginning to end. He was expected to fell trees, cultivate the cleared land for crops, and plant banana trees.

The fire god knew that this was a cruel thing to ask of Mwindo. So he grinned happily and went back to his village after sending the young man into a thick forest. Besides that, he had in mind an evil scheme to use against the busy worker later on in the day.

In the meantime, Mwindo walked into the forest. He looked around at the many closely spaced trees and at the twisting tangles of branches growing everywhere. Finally, he just sighed to himself and said, "Well, here's a real job to be done!"

Alone in the forest, Mwindo continued to look around as he reached into his mysterious bag which, though not very large, could hold many things. He pulled out an ax, and then another, and then another. He kept this up until he had three hundred axes. After that, he pulled out three hundred billhook knives. Then, as though held by invisible hands, the axes began swinging and chopping away at the trees. And the billhook knives, cutting back and forth, began cultivating the cleared land.

Smiling, Mwindo reached into the bag and pulled out one banana plant after another. And he rubbed his hands in delight as he watched what happened next. For the banana plants had begun spinning around, and their roots were twisting themselves into the ground. The banana trees were planting themselves!

Within a few hours the trees were fully grown. Heavy bunches of fine fruit hung from their branches. Mwindo just stared up at them in pleasure and went closer to one of the trees to have a better look. But just at that moment the fire god back in his village began to chant,

"Now, my belt, bend Mwindo! Now, my belt, crush Mwindo!" And at once the belt around Mwindo's waist began growing tighter and tighter.

The belt crushed Mwindo so cruelly that he doubled over in pain and went crashing into the nearby tree. And there he remained without breath, with his body and face pressed against the tree's rough bark. But then the conga-scepter came flying like an arrow out of the mysterious bag and touched Mwindo's lips. His breath returned and he called out loudly to the god who was married to Mwindo's lovely sister.

"Help me, my friend! Help me, Lightning! I am dying!" Mwindo prayed.

The god in the world above the earth heard his brother-in-law's plea. So in a great flash he descended, striking a side of the tree and shaking Mwindo loose. The dazed youth then struggled to his feet, thanked his friend, and began to shout: "Now, my knife, bend my foe! Now, my knife, smash him down!"

And all at once the knife in the fire god's hand began to move. It twisted around suddenly and caused the trickster to go smashing down flat on the ground. And there he lay without breathing, with his face in the earth.

Mwindo hurried over to the village and found the fire god still on the ground. "Why did you endanger me?" Mwindo asked. Then he began beating the god on the head with the scepter. "Wake up, now! Everyone who goes to sleep wakes up again!" said the young man. "Wake up, even though you tried to slay me!"

The fire god sneezed and quickly sat up, glad to have breath again. "Long life! Long life to you, Mwindo!" cried the god. But these were empty words, for even Mwindo's merciful action didn't stop the god from planning more dangerous tricks to try to destroy the young hero.

## II. The Tests Go On

Not long after the time he had been spared, the fire god issued a new challenge to Mwindo. "If you can dance to the drum my people can dance to, and you do not die, then you are a true man! If you live," he said, "I shall give up your father so that you may return home with him."

Mwindo smiled. "What is it that you think your people can do that I can't do?" he asked. "Whatever it is, I'll gladly try it!"

Delighted, the fire god held out his belt. "Here is my gift to take along with you," he said. And once more Mwindo had to accept it and give the trickster the billhook knife in return.

Before long, Mwindo was taken to a pool in the forest. There he saw something that filled him with wonder and surprise. He watched as one of the fire god's people climbed a great tree that was hanging over the pool without touching either of its banks. Then the man leaped and something very strange occurred. He went splashing into the water, and different parts of his body went off in different directions. There was an arm here, a leg there, and so on. But even more amazing was the fact that the man, all in one piece again, soon emerged from the pool.

After that, each of the fire god's people at the pool went up, one at a time. And each of the divers performed the same amazing feat without hesitation or fear.

Soon it was time for Mwindo to try to equal the strange spectacle he had seen. So the brave youth began climbing the tree as everyone watched to see what would happen to him. Then just as Mwindo reached the top of the tree, the fire god back in his village began to chant. "Now, my belt, bend Mwindo! Now, my belt, crush Mwindo!"

And once again the belt began bending Mwindo and crushing the breath of life out of him. With his body pressed against the tree, he lay still and breathless. So once again the conga-scepter acted on its own. It came flying out of the bag of good fortune and touched the hero's eyes, awakening him. Mwindo's breath was restored, and he began calling loudly. "Help me, Lightning! Help me, my friend!"

Lightning heard his brother-in-law's cry and started out at once. In a blazing flash he came cutting down through the earth and into the underworld. But this time he didn't strike a tree. Instead, he struck Mwindo! The young man was instantly pulverized into dust! And like a small cloud of flour, the dust floated down to the dark pool. But only seconds later, even before the watchers had a chance to think, Mwindo emerged from the water. He was all in one piece again, and appeared as strong and as well as ever!

The fire god's people just stood where they were, staring at him in amazement. And they listened in silence as he began to shout.

"Now, my knife, bend my foe!" he cried. "Now, my knife, smash him down!" And again the billhook knife sent the trickster crashing to the earth. Again he lay sprawled on the ground, breathless and with his mouth pressed into the dirt.

Mwindo hurried over to the village and stared down at him. Then he began beating him on the head with the marvelous scepter. "You, wake up! Everyone who goes to sleep wakes up again!" he said. "Wake up, and know that anyone who jokes with Mwindo has a difficult tree to climb!"

Sneezing hard, the fire god sat up. He was fully recovered. "May you always be well, Mwindo!" he cried. "May you always be well!" But of course these were only empty words, for he was still hoping to defeat the young hero.

A short time later, the trickster challenged Mwindo to try to beat another underworld god in a special contest. He promised that if Mwindo beat this powerful god, he would be permitted to carry his father away. Of course, the brave young man didn't back away from this challenge. And once again, with the help of Lightning and of the magical scepter from the bag of good fortune, Mwindo was able to surpass his amazed foes.

Chief Shemwindo, rubbing his eyes, was then released from the dark cave in which he'd been hidden. His joyful son, filled with a sense of triumph, soon began leading him away. Before long, they were climbing up through the hole in the ground where the giant fern had been growing. And as the sky changed to dawn, father and son were approaching Tubondo.

Spotting them on the road, the people of the village rushed out to meet them with joyful music and many gifts. And Shemwindo's dogs leaped happily at the sight of their returned master.

The chief smiled and turned to Mwindo. "My son, you have done well. That is the reason I see my land again!" he said. Then he presented the young hero with some wonderful gifts.

After that, Mwindo returned to his own small village. And as time went by, he earned more fame and gained more knowledge about the ways of ruling well. Then, some time later, he received a command to return to Tubondo.

There he stood beside his father as the kingly ruler addressed his people. "Hear me, for I have important things to say," he declared with his arms raised toward the blue dome of the African sky. "Mwindo has brought his nature into balance, and has taught himself to bring harmony into the land. Today I enthrone my son in the chieftainship. He who brings tribute shall give it to Mwindo. I, his father, shall be second to my son. He shall rule in Tubondo!"

Mwindo had to catch his breath upon hearing these words. And soon he heard the ceremonial drum sounding and spreading the great news. He just stood listening with joy to the wonderful message. Then he thought about the forces of good fortune, and he smiled. For surely the forces of good fortune were still with him.

## QUESTING FOR INFORMATION

### A. Getting the Main Idea and Facts

Write the letter of the answer that best completes each statement.

1. The main point of this story is that a young hero _____ .
   a. earned the honor of being enthroned
   b. showed mercy to a cruel trickster
   c. could often foretell future events

2. Mwindo was given useful advice by _____ in the underworld.
   a. Lightning    b. counselors    c. Kahindo

3. The frogs used to garnish a banana dish were really _____ .
   a. jealous chiefs    b. counselors    c. underworld gods

4. After his first meeting with Mwindo, the fire god felt that Mwindo's intelligence _____ his own.
   a. equaled    b. surpassed    c. was less than

5. The god of fire gave Mwindo a belt as a gift in order to _____ .
   a. honor him    b. wish him luck    c. destroy him

### B. Going Beyond the Facts

Write the letter of the answer that best completes each statement.

1. Probably, the faraway look came into Mwindo's eyes at one point because he was _____ .
   a. realizing that his father was in the underworld
   b. thinking of his victory over a jealous chief
   c. dreaming of his enthronement

2. We may infer that the fire god called Mwindo "my son" because he _____ .
   a. truly admired him
   b. wished for a son like him
   c. hoped to gain his trust

3. A saying that would seem to fit the outcome of the contest between Mwindo and the god of fire is _____
   a. The early bird catches the worm.
   b. He who laughs last, laughs best.
   c. He who hesitates is lost.

4. A word that does *not* describe the fire god's behavior toward Mwindo is _____ .
   a. trustworthy    b. cruel    c. sneaky
5. It seems correct to conclude that _____ was an important custom in the lives of the characters in the epic.
   a. playing tricks on each other
   b. giving gifts
   c. visiting the underworld

## QUESTING FOR MEANINGS

Write the letter of the word that best completes each statement below.
   a. garnished    b. pulverized    c. healing
   d. spectacle    e. surpassed

1. The wrecking machines _____ the old buildings into a mass of rubble.
2. Mushrooms and parsley _____ the steaks served to the guests.
3. Juan _____ his friends in swimming ability.
4. Mrs. Reilly helped in _____ a broken friendship between two of her neighbors.
5. The fierce argument between a coach and an umpire was a sorry _____ at the crowded ballpark.

## QUESTING FOR UNDERSTANDING

1. Professor Biebuyck said that the Nyanga admired Mwindo as "one who surpasses others." With this in mind, do the following:
   a. Discuss some specific ways in which Mwindo surpassed particular characters in the epic. (Include examples from another Mwindo story you may have read concerning his birth and later life.)
   b. Discuss what Mwindo meant when he said that anyone who jokes with him has a hard tree to climb.
2. Like the gods in the Greek and other epics, the gods in the *Mwindo Epic* had some very human traits and feelings. For instance, Lightning was a caring and loyal brother-in-law to Mwindo. Discuss examples which show that the god of fire could be the following:
   a. jealous    b. ungrateful    c. dishonest

# QUESTING FOR ENRICHMENT

A. English contains some words derived from words from various African languages. The word *banjo* (a stringed musical instrument) and the word *gumbo* (type of thick soup) are examples of such words. Other examples appear below in column A. Match them with their meanings in column B. Use the numbers and letters.

| **A** | **B** |
|---|---|
| 1. okra | a. loose-fitting, pullover garment that is usually brightly colored |
| 2. goober | |
| 3. marimba | b. tree that produces nut used in making certain drinks or beverages |
| 4. kola (or cola) | |
| 5. dashiki | c. type of green, sticky vegetable |
| | d. another name for peanut |
| | e. musical instrument, like a xylophone, played by striking it with wooden sticks or hammers |

B. The ancient civilization of Egypt flourished on the African continent between 4000 and 1500 B.C. There were also other flourishing civilizations in Africa long before people from other continents came to its shores. These states had highly organized governments, and contained centers of trade, industry, and learning.

On your paper, see if you can correctly complete the names of great African empires of the past. You will probably be surprised when you discover the "secret" of why the empires are listed in the way they appear below.

*Some Great African Empires of the Past*

1. Gh_____n_____, Songh_____y, Z_____nj
2. B_____nin
3. Ashant_____, Mal_____
4. Zimbabwe-M_____n_____m_____tapa, _____y_____
5. Born_____, Yor_____ba states

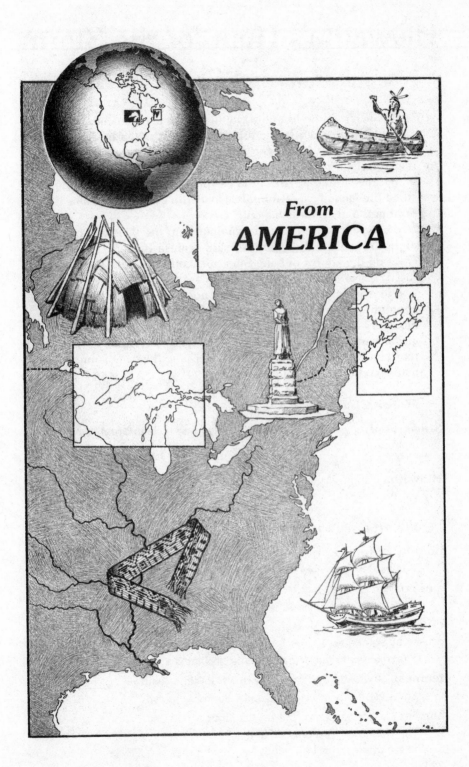

From
**AMERICA**

# Hiawatha's Hunt for the Storm Fool

Legends of the Iroquois Indians tell of a 15th-century chief called Hiawatha who united the five nations of the Iroquois.

*The Song of Hiawatha,* published in 1855, was written by the American poet, Henry Wadsworth Longfellow. It describes many adventures of Hiawatha, a gifted man who even understood the languages of animals. Hiawatha called all animals his brothers, and all birds his chickens.

Longfellow used material mainly from the tales and beliefs of the Iroquois and the Great Lakes Ojibwa Indians. The story is set on the shores of Lake Superior, called Gitchee Gumee or the Big-Sea-Water.

In an early episode from the poem, Hiawatha has been commanded by his father, the immortal West-Wind, to slay all monsters and magicians. In the following tale, Hiawatha struggles against one of the manitos, the spirits or forces of nature that can be good or evil. We shall see how the troublemaker is punished by being made a special chief.

## Major Characters

**Storm Fool** a spirit (manito) in human form; also known as Pau-Puk-Keewis

**Hiawatha** son of the immortal West-Wind

**Iagoo** village storyteller

**Face-in-a-Mist** Iagoo's nephew

## Vocabulary Preview

**nimble** quick-moving; surefooted
We watched the *nimble* mountain goat climb the rocky hillside.

**summit** peak; top; highest point
The climber finally stood proudly on the *summit* of the mountain.

**mischief** foolish or thoughtless conduct that may cause trouble; harm caused by someone
The joker's *mischief* created some problems at the party.

**tempest** a violent and windy storm, sometimes with rain or hail
Ships were driven onto the rocks by the *tempest.*

**harvest** crops gathered; the results of an action
The potato *harvest* was small this year.
The *harvest* of his lazy behavior was the loss of his job.

Some women smiled as the handsome one, the great dancer, came strutting into the village in his doeskin shirt and deerskin leggings. The manito in human form was on his way to see the men of the village, although he knew they disliked him. They often called him idler, coward, and gambler. Their special name for him was Storm Fool, because he often stirred up trouble.

He was on his way to the lodge of old Iagoo, the storyteller. On his way there, Pau-Puk-Keewis made an angry face as he passed Hiawatha's empty lodge. "Bah! I'm tired of hearing about brave Hiawatha! Wise Hiawatha!" he growled. "I hate the very sound of his name!"

Then Storm Fool reached Iagoo's lodge and stepped inside. There he found the village men seated and listening to one of Iagoo's many wonderful tales.

"Hark!" shouted Storm Fool. "Aren't you tired of this old man's stories? Now here is something better to amuse you!" With a wicked twinkle in his eye, he took out the game of Bowl and Counters. Four of the thirteen little counters were round. Others were shaped like serpents, a fish, a war club, and other objects.

Iagoo and the others watched with growing interest. Storm Fool shook the counters in the bowl and then sent them flying to the ground. "Ha!" he cried, clapping his hands. "Thirteen tens and eight are counted!" Then he proceeded to teach the interested men the game of chance.

The wrinkled storyteller leaned forward. "Ha! I can beat you. I can even give you some lessons," he exclaimed. "The man who plays with me must have nimble fingers!" Then he and all the others laughed and began playing the game.

Past midnight and into the early morning hours they played. And when dawn came up, only Storm Fool was smiling. He'd won all the men's ermine robes, crests of feathers, and other treasures. These lay in heaps before him on the ground.

The mischief-maker yawned and looked around. He could see the men's eyes glaring up at him like those of angry wolves.

"Well, now," he said. "I need a servant and a pipe-bearer. I'll gamble all my winnings on a single throw. If I win, Iagoo's nephew must come with me."

Iagoo looked at his sixteen-year-old nephew, a slim youth called Face-in-a-Mist. Then Iagoo studied the faces of the troubled men. "So be it," Iagoo mumbled at last. He seized the bowl and shook it fiercely. But when the counters lay on the earth before him, his eyes grew dark with worry. Iagoo had scored only five points!

Grinning, Storm Fool knelt to take his turn. He shook the bowl and tossed the pieces lightly into the air. The men leaned forward as he made his count. "Five tens!" he cried. "The game is mine!"

Then Storm Fool rose and left the lodge, followed by his new servant carrying all the trickster's winnings. Smiling, Storm Fool said, "Take everything to my wigwam far to the eastward. Go now! I will remain here for a while."

The handsome one's eyes were red and hot after a night of gambling. Yet he was in a good mood. Smiling, he waved his fan of turkey feathers before his face as he walked through the village. But when he caught sight of Hiawatha's lodge, his smile disappeared. And he frowned when he saw Hiawatha's pet raven sitting on the top pole of the lodge.

Grinning in an evil way, Storm Fool looked about. After that, he leaped up and seized the screeching bird. He whirled it around and around like a rattle until it grew silent. The mischief-maker left the bird's limp body hanging from the top pole.

Next, Storm Fool crept into Hiawatha's lodge. Like a sudden wind, he began tossing things about. Bowls and kettles went crashing to the ground! Blankets and skins went flying through the air! And when all these things were piled in wild disorder, the trickster hurried away and went whistling into the forest.

Later on, he climbed to the summit of a rocky headland jutting out into the Big-Sea-Water. Stretched upon his back he lay there, watching Hiawatha's mountain chickens wheeling above and almost brushing him with their wings. Suddenly he reached up and began slaying bird after bird!

A sea gull perched on a rock saw the terrible thing that was happening. "It's Pau-Puk-Keewis! He's slaying us by the hundreds! A message must be sent to our brother! To Hiawatha!"

Not long after that, a young man came racing into the village. Hiawatha, son of the immortal West-Wind, was so swift that he could shoot an arrow into the air and then race ahead so that the arrow fell behind him!

With eagle feathers standing up in his dark hair, the youth stood slim and strong as he listened to his people tell about Storm Fool's visit. Then words of anger buzzed like hornets through Hiawatha's teeth. "My wrath shall reach him," he cried. "No matter how long the way or how rough the road!" Turning, he went bounding into the forest with some braves racing behind him.

Hiawatha and his men followed Storm Fool's trail to the top of the rocky headland. But the mischief-maker wasn't there. Then Hia-

watha looked down into the lowlands far beneath them and spotted the trickster racing away. So with mighty leaps, Hiawatha went springing down the rocky hillside.

Through field and forest, Storm Fool bounded along like an antelope. Soon he reached a beaver dam in a forest stream. "Friends!" he called to the beavers. "Let me rest in your lodge! And change me into a beaver!"

The kind beavers agreed to help him. So down into the water Storm Fool sank, changed into a beaver. Yet he wasn't satisfied. "Make me larger," he demanded. "Larger than all the other beavers!"

Soon after that, he was ten times larger than the others in the underwater lodge. Indeed, he was so big and strong that the beavers quickly made him their king and fed him well. However, the new king didn't have much time to rule. For Hiawatha and his men soon began kicking in the dam. Water went gushing down through the cracks as the frightened beavers sought to escape the hunters. They began rushing out through the small doors. But Storm Fool, puffed up with pride and food, couldn't squeeze through any of the doors.

The hunters came crashing through the roof. Then they beat the trickster with their clubs until he lay still. After that, they carried the giant beaver back to their village on poles. But Storm Fool's ghost didn't remain inside the beaver body. It rose like a mist and then took the trickster's human form as it went gliding into the soft blue shadows of the pine tree forest.

However, sharp-eyed Hiawatha had seen everything. He dashed into the forest in pursuit of the trickster!

Panting heavily, Storm Fool raced like the wind until he reached a large lake. Black-billed birds with shiny necks were swimming calmly among the water lilies.

"Oh, my brothers," Storm Fool called to the wild geese. "Change me into one of you! And make me large! Ten times larger than all the others!"

The geese were pleased that he wanted to be like one of them, so they did as he asked. And soon Storm Fool was a huge bird, swimming calmly in the sky-blue lake. But it was only moments later that Hiawatha appeared at the shore. The startled birds took to the air with loud cries. Storm Fool, the largest bird, flew off with them.

"Be careful! Don't look down!" the birds called to Storm Fool. Then on they flew, through mist and sunshine all through the day. Only when the stars came out did the tired creatures stop to sleep among the reeds.

On the next day, the birds flew off again, lifted by the south wind. And as they soared along, the sound of human voices reached them.

Far below them lay a village. People were pointing up and shouting. At once, Storm Fool began trembling because he recognized two of the voices. The voices of Hiawatha and Iagoo! Startled, he forgot about the birds' warning. He bent his neck to look down. And when he did this, the wind caught his tail feathers. The giant bird was thrown off balance!

He went spinning and wheeling downward. He could hear people's laughter growing louder and louder, and he could see the village getting nearer and nearer. Then with a loud cry, he crashed to the ground!

The body of the giant bird lay very still. Yet Storm Fool's ghost survived. Once again, the trickster's spirit took on human form and rushed away. And once again, eagle-eyed Hiawatha saw this and pursued the mischief-maker.

"My wrath shall overtake you!" shouted the young brave. "No matter how far the way or how rough the road!"

Moving swiftly, Hiawatha reached out to grab his enemy. But Storm Fool began whirling about. He fanned the air into a storm, a roaring whirlwind! Dust and leaves danced about. They hid him as he sprang into a hollow tree. There he changed into a serpent, and then glided out unseen among roots and fallen leaves.

In the meantime, with one hand Hiawatha smashed the tree into shreds and splinters. But he didn't find Storm Fool there. "He's escaped again," he groaned. However, as Hiawatha turned to go, he caught sight of the trickster speeding along in the gust and whirlwind.

He was again in human form, and Hiawatha set out after him. On and on they raced along the banks of Gitchee Gumee, westward near the Big-Sea-Water, until at last they reached the rocky headlands.

Looking over his shoulder, Storm Fool trembled to see Hiawatha so close behind him. "Manito of the Mountains!" the frightened creature cried aloud to the Old Man of the Mountains. "Open wide the rocky doorways! Give me shelter in your dark caves!"

The old manito took pity on the handsome one, and opened up the sandstone walls. And the weary trickster was safely hidden away when Hiawatha arrived seconds later.

"Open! I am Hiawatha!" he shouted as he beat his fists against the stone walls. "Open wide the rocky doorways!" But the wrinkled old manito wouldn't open the sides of the mountain for him.

Angry and determined, Hiawatha looked skyward and lifted both arms high. "I call upon the tempest!" he shouted toward the clouds. "I call upon thunder and lightning!" His voice and eyes were filled with pleading, and the mighty forces heard the noble leader's call. The powerful forces came sweeping down from the distant Thunder Mountains. Fiercely they came rushing over the Big-Sea-Water.

Trembling from head to foot, Storm Fool heard the booming, the footsteps of the thunder. And he crouched in terror before the red eyes of the lightning that struck the rocky doorways. Then the thunder came roaring into the caverns causing the crags to shake and go crashing down.

Among the shattered rocks Storm Fool lay dead, slain in human form. Ended now were his days of wild adventure.

Hiawatha stood over him. "Nevermore in human form shall you search for adventure! Nevermore shall you dance the dust and leaves into whirlwinds!" exclaimed Hiawatha. "You shall bother my people no longer. From this day on you will be changed into a great war eagle. You shall be the chief of all the fowls with feathers. You shall be the chief of Hiawatha's chickens!"

Now in winter, people laugh when the wind whistles and snowflakes whirl around outside their lodges. "Here comes Storm Fool dancing through the village again," they cry. "Here comes Storm Fool, gathering in his harvest!"

# QUESTING FOR INFORMATION

## A. Getting the Main Idea and Facts

Write the letter of the answer that best completes each statement.

1. This story is mainly about how _____ .
   a. gamblers lost their treasured possessions
   b. an evil force was pursued and destroyed
   c. a mischief-maker became king of the beavers
2. Hiawatha's father was the _____ .
   a. Manito of the Mountains
   b. West-Wind
   c. storyteller, Iagoo
3. Hiawatha smashed a tree to splinters with _____ .
   a. one hand      b. a war club      c. help from some braves
4. Storm Fool caused himself problems because he insisted on being _____ than the beavers and the birds.
   a. wiser      b. larger      c. faster
5. Storm Fool was finally changed into a _____ .
   a. sea gull      b. pet raven      c. war eagle

## B. Going Beyond the Facts

Write the letter of the answer that best completes each statement.

1. We may infer that news brought by a horrified _____ brought Hiawatha racing to his village.
   a. beaver      b. manito      c. bird
2. From Face-in-a-Mist's behavior, we may conclude that he was very _____ .
   a. stubborn      b. obedient      c. jolly
3. We can tell that Storm Fool really _____ the men to gamble.
   a. tempted      b. forced      c. disliked
4. It seems correct to say that Storm Fool was both _____ .
   a. playful and gentle
   b. silly and harmless
   c. proud and jealous
5. We may conclude that only in _____ form could Storm Fool finally be stopped and lose all his evil powers.
   a. ghostly      b. human      c. animal

## QUESTING FOR MEANINGS

Write the letter of the word that best completes each sentence below.

a. mischief   b. summit   c. nimble   d. tempest   e. harvest

1. The pianist's _____ fingers seemed to fly over the keyboard.
2. Snow covered the lofty _____ of the mountain.
3. Hail driven by the violent winds of the unexpected _____ ruined some crops.
4. This year many farmers gathered a rich _____ of wheat.
5. The child's _____ almost caused an accident on the stairs.

## QUESTING FOR UNDERSTANDING

1. Hiawatha, like many heroes in other epic tales, was gifted with some unusual abilities and even some magical powers. Name at least three of these gifts and tell how he made some use of each in his efforts to help his people and his animal friends.

2. To many people, Hiawatha stands as a symbol of a noble man and leader. By making use of the information from both the story and its introduction, show how he was each of the following:

a. a caring person
b. a determined man
c. a wise leader
d. a lover of nature

## QUESTING FOR ENRICHMENT

The English language makes use of many words borrowed from other languages, including American Indian languages. For instance, squaw, papoose, tepee, pow-wow, chipmunk, possum, Mississippi, and many other words from American Indian languages have become part of the English language.

Write the letter of the Indian word in column B next to the number for its English word in column A. Then do the same for the words in columns C and D.

## A
### (English)

1. pecan (a tree; nut from that tree)
2. pone (bread made with cornmeal)
3. raccoon (furry animal with black stripings on its head)
4. squash (fruit of gourd or cucumber family)
5. toboggan (flat sled without runners)

## B
### (American Indian)

a. tobogan
b. pakan
c. askutasquash
d. achpoan
e. arakun

## C
### (English)

1. hominy (coarsely ground corn used as cereal food)
2. moccasin (sandal of soft leather)
3. persimmon (a tree; orange-red fruit from that tree)
4. skunk (small furry animal with white stripings)
5. succotash (corn and lima beans boiled together)

## D
### (American Indian)

a. msiquatash
b. rockahomine
c. mohkussin
d. squnck
e. pasimenan

# Evangeline's Incredible Journey

The Canadian peninsula called Nova Scotia was once called Acadia. After years of conflict with Britain, France gave up its claim to this land. During the years that followed, some French settlers in Acadia supported France's attempts to reclaim the land. This caused a great problem for all French Acadians in 1755.

The poem *Evangeline,* published in 1847, was written by the American poet, Henry Wadsworth Longfellow. It tells of the sufferings of the young and innocent Evangeline and other French Acadians. In this tale we see how the troubled young woman suddenly fears that she may indeed be on the trail of a ghost.

## Major Characters

**Evangeline**   a beautiful maiden

**Gabriel**   engaged to Evangeline

**Basil**   a blacksmith, Gabriel's father

**Benedict**   a rich farmer, Evangeline's father

**Michael**   a fiddler

**Father Felician**   the village priest

**Baptiste**   the notary's son

## Vocabulary Preview

**bayou**   a marshy, slow-moving stream flowing into or out of a river or lake
After drifting slowly on the *bayou*, the empty boat reached the river.

**betrothal**   an engagement to marry
The couple's *betrothal* was celebrated at a surprise party.

**epidemic**   a widespread disease
Victims of the *epidemic* filled the hospitals.

**lowing**   the mooing or soft bellowing of cattle
The evening air was filled with the *lowing* of cattle.

**phantom**   a ghost or specter
Listeners trembled at the tale of the *phantom* hunter who walks through the woods when the moon is full.

# I. Unwelcome News

"**H**ow charming!" sighed the woman sitting at her spinning wheel before her thatch-roofed cottage. She smiled as little Evangeline and dark-haired Gabriel went hurrying by. From earliest childhood they had grown up like sister and brother. These close friends who even learned their letters from the very same book were now on their way home after lessons. Soon they'd stop to watch the sparks flying in the shop of Gabriel's father, Basil, the stocky blacksmith.

In the years that followed, many young men hoped to win Evangeline's heart. However, the maiden with eyes as black as berries cared only for one youth. She went walking only with Gabriel, and so it came as no surprise to the people of Grand-Pre when they were invited to a betrothal party for the happy couple.

One evening, Evangeline and Gabriel stood together, holding hands near a window in Evangeline's home. Gabriel was slim and handsome, and the seventeen-year-old girl was more lovely than ever. Indeed, people often spoke of her kind and lovely face, and of the light that shone from it.

Nearby, Basil sat with Evangeline's father, Benedict, the richest farmer in the valley. Though the white-haired farmer was seventy years old, he was as sturdy as an oak tree covered with snowflakes. Puffing on his pipe, he sat talking with his best friend as they waited for the village notary to arrive with his inkhorn and paper. He was to write up the marriage contract, and a betrothal party was to be held early the next day.

Basil puffed on his pipe and sighed deeply. "There are English ships in the harbor with their cannon pointed at us. And tomorrow we are ordered to meet the British commander in the church," he said. "There is something evil in the air!"

At this, good-natured Benedict just smiled. "Be calm, my friend. Perhaps there was a poor harvest in England," he said. "The ships may just be here to take away more food and grain from our bursting barns to feed cattle and hungry children."

Basil lowered his thick eyebrows and shook his head. "Not so! The British have never forgotten how the French here in Acadia battled with them over the ownership of this land. Every day we are treated unjustly, and now they've taken all our weapons from us! Surely, they no longer trust us at all because of our French blood," he declared angrily. "I tell you, my friend, there is something evil in the air!"

And so the two old friends continued to speak until the notary arrived. Then, after the wedding contract was signed, Basil and Benedict laughed and played checkers until nine. In the meantime, Evangeline and Gabriel sat whispering together, watching the moon rise and the stars come out one by one.

The air was sweet and the nearby ocean was calm on the next morning in 1755. The cornfields and green meadows were bathed in a golden glow. Happy people came pouring into the huge orchard owned by Benedict Bellefontaine. And the women wearing their holiday best looked especially pretty in their white caps and long dresses of scarlet and blue and green.

Under the open sky, the betrothal feast was spread for all to enjoy. Music filled the air as old Michael, the fiddler with snow-white hair, played tunes from France, the land from which so many Acadian settlers had come over the years.

Michael's jolly face shone like a glowing coal as he beat time with his wooden shoes. The old folk and young danced together, whirling about merrily to the lively music. Evangeline, beautiful in her swirling blue dress, was dancing with Gabriel. Her golden earrings and long tresses shone brightly in the sunshine as she and Gabriel went spinning around and around. The happy couple smiled at everyone, but they really saw only each other.

But then all at once the music stopped. Everyone stood still and looked toward the distant church, listening to the sound of the tower bell and to the beating of a drum. It was time for the meeting with the British commander! So, with worried looks, the people of Grand-Pre hurried toward the church.

Before long, all the men were crowded inside the small building. The door slammed shut behind them as the British commander stood on the stairs of the altar.

"Men of Grand-Pre, listen well. You are called together today at His Majesty's orders!" said the commander. "You have not been grateful for King George's kindness. You know in your hearts what I mean!

"The task I must now perform is painful to me, but I must bow and obey my king. You and your families are now the king's prisoners! All your lands, homes, and cattle now belong to the crown! You are all to be sent away to other lands, and the ships to carry you off are even now in the harbor!"

The men stood in speechless wonder for a moment. Then they turned and rushed as one toward the door, but armed troops blocked their way. Seeing this, Basil raised his arms and roared, "Down with the tyrants of England! Death to these foreign soldiers who seize our homes and harvests!" And he would have gone on shouting, but a tall soldier struck Basil in the mouth and sent him tumbling to the floor.

Now grown wild with anger, Basil's friends began shouting and pushing forward toward the commander and his men near the altar. But just at that moment a deep voice called out, "Stop! This is madness!"

The men halted in their tracks as Father Felician went on. "Have you forgotten where you are? Have you forgotten all that I've taught you?" Father Felician then walked among the confused and angry men to comfort them.

The terrible news soon reached the women and children waiting outside the church. Screams filled the air, and everyone wept. "Where will we go?" sobbed a little boy, clinging to his mother's hand. "Will we stay together? Will they put us on the same boat?"

The men remained locked in the church, while their families were sent home. And five days later, the women and children took a long, last look at their homes. Then the tearful women began driving wagons filled with household goods down to the seashore. The children ran beside the wagons, urging on the oxen. And some children clasped fragments of playthings in their little hands.

Later that day, the men were turned out of the church. Like weary pilgrims, they sang to lift their spirits as they marched down to the harbor. Evangeline quickly ran among them. Finding Gabriel, she clasped the pale youth's hands and laid her head on his shoulder. "Be cheerful, Gabriel!" she cried. "For if we love one another, nothing can harm us!"

Moments later, Evangeline spied her father. Benedict no longer seemed as sturdy as an oak tree. The light was gone from his eyes. Evangeline rushed over and embraced the stooped man. "Have courage, dear Father," she cried. "We are still together." Then she helped him find his way down to the restless sea.

There was much confusion on the crowded shore. People were being pushed and ordered about. Some were already being taken away in small boats to the high-masted ships in the harbor. From time to time, wild screams filled the air. Wives were torn away from husbands! And parents, too late, saw their weeping children with arms outstretched left on the shore!

Gabriel was seized and hurried away to a ship. "Evangeline! Evangeline!" he shouted over the gray waters. But Evangeline didn't hear him because she was too busy caring for her father.

The gentle girl spoke words of love and comfort to the old man, but he made no answer. He just sat on the ground and stared into a small fire. Evangeline wept, and thought that her heart would break.

Suddenly, a great light filled the evening air. Evangeline looked up, filled with horror. The village of Grand-Pre was burning! Flames went reaching toward the sky like the hundred fiery hands of a giant. The barking of dogs and the sad lowing of cattle left behind on the farms filled the smoky air.

Tears filled Evangeline's eyes as she turned to comfort her father. But Benedict had slumped to the ground. He lay there without moving. Kneeling beside him, the young woman wailed in sorrow until she fainted; and she lay in a deep slumber all through the night.

Early the next morning, Evangeline sadly agreed that her dear father should be buried there by the sea. And after this was done, she was hurried away to a waiting ship.

"Gabriel! Oh, my beloved!" she sobbed. But Gabriel was nowhere around. The unhappy youth was on a vessel already far out at sea. And Evangeline shed bitter tears as her own ship set sail.

# II. The Search

Far apart, on separate coasts, the exiles landed. They were scattered like snowflakes in the wind. Homeless, they wandered from city to city, from the cold lakes of the North to the hot grasslands of the South. Many wandered in rags from place to place in search of lost loved ones. And some of the unhappy people perished along the way.

Evangeline refused to settle anywhere. Eager to find Gabriel, she traveled on with some friends, some of whom were also searching for lost loved ones. Among Evangeline's companions were Father Felician and curly-haired Baptiste, the notary's son. This young man had always loved Evangeline. He still hoped that one day she'd marry him.

However, Evangeline's one dream was to find her lost love. She searched everywhere for him. And as she passed through towns, she'd even stop in their cemeteries. Filled with fear she would gaze at the tombstones. And sometimes she would just sit quietly near a nameless grave for a while before going on.

Years went by, yet the brave young woman pushed ahead. Wherever she stopped she would ask people if they had seen or heard about Gabriel Lajeunesse.

"Oh, yes," said some people. "We've seen him. He's with Basil, the blacksmith. They've gone west to the prairies to hunt and trap."

"Why, yes," said other people. "We've seen him. He's traveling south in the lowlands of Louisiana."

Evangeline was confused and unhappy. Her companions felt very sorry for her. Finally, a kind woman took Evangeline's hand in hers. "Hear me. You've been traveling for a long time," said the woman. "Why don't you give up this search? Why don't you marry young Baptiste? Surely you know that he loves you dearly."

But Evangeline just shook her head. "No, kind friend, I must find Gabriel," she answered. "Where my heart has gone, there I must follow. It's like a lamp lighting the way."

And so Evangeline went on with her search. At times her feet were bare and bleeding, yet she pressed forward. Then, in the month of May, she and her friends boarded a raftlike boat. It carried them down the Ohio River. After that, the exiles rowed past the mouth of the Wabash River. Then they floated into the golden stream of the broad Mississippi.

Day and night they moved along. Finally, they entered a bayou in Louisiana. On they journeyed, and soon they saw little islands all around them. The air was filled with the sweet perfume of magnolias and roses. It was all so beautiful that the weary travelers pulled their boat ashore and rested under a tree on one of the islands. Evangeline's eyes were so heavy that she was soon fast asleep.

Just then, a boat moved swiftly past the island. With his head bowed, Gabriel sat in the prow of the boat. His dark and shaggy hair fell over his sad eyes. The unhappy man was on his way to the northwest to hunt and find relief from sorrow.

Evangeline slowly opened her eyes and sat up with a smile on her lips. "Something in my heart tells me that Gabriel is near," she told her friends. Then filled with new hope, she and her companions moved on.

Before long, they noticed a thin blue column of smoke rising from a house on a nearby shore. They could see a man on horseback, and they could hear the distant lowing of cattle. So the tired travelers pulled their boat ashore. At once, Father Felician and Evangeline began advancing toward the man on horseback.

Suddenly the man sprang down from his horse. With a joyful shout and outstretched arms, he ran forward. It was Basil, and this was his huge ranch!

Laughing and weeping, Basil and the other exiles embraced each other. "How wonderful to see you!" cried Gabriel's father. "It's been such a long time since we were parted." Then he led his two guests into his cool and colorful garden to sit and talk. It was there that Basil noted the doubt and fear in Evangeline's eyes. Sensing her unasked question, he looked a little embarrassed. So he said, "How is it that you didn't meet my son's boat on the bayous today?"

Tears filled the young woman's eyes. "Gone? Is Gabriel gone?" she cried out. Then she buried her face on Basil's shoulder and sobbed as though her heart would break.

However, Basil just smiled as he tried to comfort her. "Be of good cheer, my child. Gabriel just left today," he said. "Thinking of you, he was always sorrowful. So I sent him to a nearby town to trade for mules from the Spaniards. Then he'll travel on to the Ozark Mountains to hunt and trap for furs. He's not far off yet, Evangeline. I know the inn he plans to visit before he sets off for the mountains. We'll follow him fast in the morning, and bring him back tomorrow!"

These words brought a happy gleam to Evangeline's eyes. Color returned to her pale lips. And she smiled with joy when the other exiles came up from the shore with Michael, the old fiddler, on their shoulders. He had been living under Basil's roof in Louisiana for a long time, like a god on Mount Olympus, with no other care but to give music to mortals.

Evangeline and Father Felician greeted Michael warmly, while Basil hailed his old companions with laughter, and with embraces for the mothers and daughters! Then he led everyone into his huge and comfortable house, where everyone rested and feasted well.

When the wonderful dinner was ended, Basil calmly lit his pipe and stood at the head of the table. "Welcome once more, my friends. Welcome to a new home," he said. "Orange groves are in blossom here all year round. Herds of animals go unclaimed, and lands here may be had for the asking. There's no King George here to drive you away from your homes and steal your farms and cattle!"

The hearts of the smiling exiles were filled with new hope. And their hearts were made even gladder when they heard some familiar voices at the door. A number of Basil's distant neighbors, people who had once lived in Grand-Pre, came bursting into the dining room. Basil had sent word to them at their ranches, and now they and old friends stood hugging each other joyfully and asking countless questions.

A short time later, the sound of Michael's fiddle was heard filling the air. At once, people broke into merry laughter and began dancing about like delighted children.

However, Evangeline just stood like a person in a trance. Old memories rose in her mind. Through all the music she could hear the mournful sound of the sea, and sadness filled her heart. Then stealing unseen into the moonlit garden, she wandered about. "Oh, my love, are you so near me, and yet I cannot see you? When will I hold you in my arms again?"

And to Evangeline it seemed that Nature was answering her. "Patience!" whispered the oaks through the night. "Tomorrow!" a sigh answered from the moonlit meadow, filling Evangeline with new hope.

But the young lady's joyful hope was not to last very long. For when she and Basil arrived at the inn the next day, Gabriel was already gone.

# III. Journey's End

Kind Basil tried to comfort Evangeline. He agreed to travel to the West with her. With their Indian guides, they followed Gabriel's trail right up to the base of the Ozark Mountains. There they thought they saw the smoke from Gabriel's campfire some distance ahead. But when they reached the spot they found only embers and ashes at an empty campsite. Yet the fire of their love drove them on.

One night, a young Indian widow came to visit the travelers. She was a Shawnee woman with a soft, low voice. Sitting by the campfire she told Evangeline the story of her lost love, her Canadian husband who had been slain in the wilderness. And Evangeline wept for another unlucky heart like her own. Then she in turn told the gentle widow her own sad tale, and of her long search for Gabriel.

The dark-eyed Indian woman sat silent with wonder at Evangeline's story. Then, as though filled with horror, the woman told two Indian tales.

"Mowis, a bridegroom made of snow, married a lovely maiden. But when the bright sun appeared, Mowis melted away. The unhappy maiden never saw him again, though she searched everywhere for him."

Evangeline sat wide-eyed, listening to the flow of magical words as the woman went on. "There was a maiden who heard a phantom of the forest breathing like the evening wind through the pines. He whispered words of love to her and she went to follow him. Through the forest she followed his green and waving plume, and her people never saw her again."

Evangeline trembled. A sense of pain and terror crept like a poisonous snake into her heart. She felt for a moment that she, like the Indian maiden, was chasing a phantom. And with this thought she went to sleep.

When she awoke, she found that her fear had vanished in the morning sunlight. So once again the determined woman started out on her march. The Indian woman traveled with her for a while. Then before they parted, Evangeline was given a ray of hope by the lovely lady. "You should go to see the Black Robe chief," said the lady. "He knows much. His tent is on the western slope of these mountains."

Evangeline gladly took this advice, and hurried to find the Black Robe chief. He was a French missionary priest. And from him she learned that she'd just missed Gabriel by six days! However, she was told that Gabriel would return to the mission in the fall.

Happy at last, Evangeline settled down to wait for her lost love, while Basil turned homeward. Slowly the days, weeks, and months went by as Evangeline waited. But when the autumn came, Gabriel did not appear.

The kind missionary felt pity for the disappointed woman. "Patience," he said gently. "Have faith and your prayer will be answered. Look at this plant that lifts its head from the meadow. See how its leaves are turned to the north, as true as a magnet. It's called the compass flower, and it helps to direct the traveler here in the wild.

"Brighter flowers, like some of our wants and desires, may lead us astray. But faith, like this humble plant, can truly guide us along."

And so Evangeline waited. Autumn and winter went by, and spring returned to the mission, but Gabriel did not. Then just as summer was beginning, Evangeline heard a welcome rumor. She heard that Gabriel was living in a lodge on the banks of the Saginaw River in Michigan. However, her long trip there ended sadly, for she found Gabriel's cabin empty and falling down.

Evangeline was older now. Some gray streaks were beginning to show among her lovely tresses, yet she went on searching everywhere. Finally, her travels took her to Philadelphia.

The city was clean and peaceful. The people spoke politely and treated all others as equals. "This place reminds me of Grand-Pre," said Evangeline to herself. "Here I will end my search. Here I'll live and seek a way to be helpful to others."

Of course, her love for Gabriel didn't die. Though she spent lots of time helping people as a Sister of Mercy, she always remembered her beloved Gabriel. Within her heart his image remained as youthful as when she last saw him. But somehow her pain began to grow lighter and lighter day by day as she helped the poor and the sick.

Evangeline's heart was at peace. She was happy with her new life and work in Philadelphia. Then a terrible thing happened. The city of brotherly love was struck by a horrible epidemic. People in every part of the city were dying of the plague. The very poorest people had no place to go but to the almshouse, a place for the homeless.

Even the sickest people would smile with pleasure when the sweet lady walked into the room. She cheered them up, gave them cool water, and bathed their feverish brows. Sometimes it was her sad duty to close the eyes of the dead.

One sunny morning, Evangeline stopped to pick some flowers for her patients. And as she approached the almshouse, a voice within her said, "Your trials are ended." Suddenly she felt calmer than ever. Smiling, she then entered the building and held up the bright flowers for all to see. But suddenly her mouth fell open! Trembling, she dropped the flowers and screamed!

Stretched on a bed lay the thin, gray-haired Gabriel! Yet in the glow of the morning light, his face for a moment seemed young once more.

"Gabriel! Oh, my beloved!" cried Evangeline. The dying man heard her voice, and stirred in his bed. Then in a dream he beheld once more his childhood home. Green meadows and rivers among them! Village and mountain and forests! And he could see a girl smiling up at him as they walked along.

Tears filled his eyes. Slowly he lifted his eyelids. Seeing Evangeline, he tried to call her name, but he could not speak. And when he tried to sit up, Evangeline quickly knelt beside him. She kissed his lips and held him in her arms.

Joy and peace filled Gabriel's heart. Sweet was the light in his eyes! But then it suddenly sank into darkness, as when a lamp is blown out by a gust of wind.

All was ended now—the hope, and the fear, and the sorrow. Meekly Evangeline lowered her head. "Father, I thank thee," she whispered softly.

In the years that followed, the gentle woman continued her work of helping others. Then, when her life and work were done, she was placed in a little churchyard. And there Evangeline still rests, near Gabriel, having completed her long and incredible journey.

## QUESTING FOR INFORMATION

### A. Getting the Main Idea and Facts

Write the letter of the answer that best completes each statement.

1. The line "_____" spoken by Evangeline tells best what this story is about.
   a. "Have courage, dear Father; we are still together."
   b. "Something in my heart tells me that Gabriel is near."
   c. "Where my heart has gone, there I must follow."

2. The notary visited Benedict's home to _____ .
   a. plan a betrothal party
   b. write up a marriage contract
   c. ask Evangeline to marry his son, Baptiste
3. We were told that the exiles were scattered like _____ .
   a. glowing coals　　b. blackberries　　c. snowflakes
4. After her long search, Evangeline finally settled in _____ .
   a. Michigan　　b. Philadelphia　　c. Louisiana
5. Upon hearing Evangeline's voice in the almshouse, Gabriel
   _____ .
   a. dreamed of home
   b. called out her name
   c. regained his health

## B.  Going Beyond the Facts

Write the letter of the answer that best completes each statement.

1. We may conclude that the British _____ .
   a. needed the Acadians' weapons
   b. feared an uprising
   c. wanted the Acadians to settle in Louisiana
2. Probably, Evangeline's main reason for visiting cemeteries was to
   _____ .
   a. find Benedict's grave
   b. pray for all the dead
   c. see if Gabriel had perished
3. It would seem that the Shawnee woman's tales about Mowis and
   the forest phantom were meant to _____ Evangeline.
   a. delight and amuse
   b. frighten and warn
   c. encourage and console
4. Which of these events occurred *first?*
   a. Evangeline missed Gabriel at the mission by just six days.
   b. Evangeline found Gabriel's empty cabin on the Saginaw River.
   c. Evangeline slept as Gabriel passed her on the bayou.
5. We may infer that right after Gabriel's death and in the years following, Evangeline felt _____ .
   a. content　　b. useless　　c. angry

## QUESTING FOR MEANINGS

Write the letter of the word that best completes each sentence below.

a. lowing   b. phantom   c. betrothal   d. bayou   e. epidemic

1. The townspeople claimed that a _____ haunted the old house.
2. The young lady was happy with her _____ gift.
3. Doctors hoped the new medicine would halt the _____.
4. We heard the _____ of the cows walking back from the pasture.
5. Two youths rowed their boat on the _____ to reach their water-front home.

## QUESTING FOR UNDERSTANDING

1. What do Evangeline's efforts to find Gabriel tell us about her as a person? Do you think she was foolish to continue her search for so long? Discuss.

2. What *physical* suffering did Evangeline endure in this story? Starting with the end of her betrothal party, discuss some events that caused her to endure *mental* anguish (fear, disappointment, sorrow, etc.). Finally, discuss one or more examples of how and when the troubled lady found peace and contentment.

## QUESTING FOR ENRICHMENT

A. Most probably you've seen close-ups of faces filling movie and television screens. Imagine that you are studying "Evangeline" close-ups for a movie you're helping to produce. Write the name of the character that belongs in each close-up below. Use each name only once. Then be ready to tell what feelings (joy, anger, etc.) should be expressed on each face, and why.

*Close-ups for "Evangeline" Film*

1. wide-eyed face of someone shouting, "Down with the tyrants of England!"
2. dull-eyed face of someone staring blankly into a small fire near the sea
3. pale face of someone gazing at a nameless grave

4. glowing face of someone being carried on men's shoulders
5. firelit face of someone telling unusual tales
6. morninglit face of someone just waking up after dreaming

B. Imagine that you've been asked to help a film editor put scenes for the "Evangeline" movie in proper order. For column A, decide on the order in which the interior (indoor) scenes appear in the story. Write the letters of the scenes in that order. Then do the same for the exterior (outdoor) scenes in column B.

# A
### Interior Scenes

_____ a. men waiting inside a locked church
_____ b. Evangeline tending the sick in an almshouse
_____ c. children watching sparks fly in a blacksmith's shop
_____ d. Gabriel and Evangeline holding hands near a window as the stars come out
_____ e. the exiles dining in Basil's Louisiana home

# B
### Exterior Scenes

_____ a. exiles sailing on a raftlike boat
_____ b. people dancing merrily in an orchard
_____ c. women driving wagons down to the seashore
_____ d. Evangeline picking flowers for patients
_____ e. a village burning in the distance

# Glossary of Names

Achilles, uh-KIL-eez

Aeneas, ih-NEE-us

Aeneid, ih-NEE-id

Aeolus, EE-oh-lus

Agamemnon, ag-uh-MEM-non

Alfonso, al-FON-soh

Anchises, an-KY-seez

Andromache, an-DROM-uh-kee

Antinous, an-TIN-oh-us

Anu, AH-noo

Aphrodite, af-ruh-DY-tee (called
Venus by Romans)

Apollo, uh-POL-oh (called
Phoebus Apollo by Greeks)

Aragon, AR-uh-gon

Ares, AIR-eez (called Mars by
Romans)

Argos, AHR-gus

Artegall, AHR-teh-gal

Artemis, ART-uh-mus (called
Diana by Romans)

Aruru, ah-ROO-roo

Ascanius, as-KAH-nee-us

Ate, AYT-ee

Athena, uh-THEE-nuh (called
Minerva by Romans)

Augustus Caesar, aw-GUS-tus
SEE-zer

Bammana, bah-MAH-nah

Baptiste, bap-TEEST (or bah-
TEEST in French)

Basil, BAZ-il

Bellefontaine, bel-fon-TAYN (or
bel-fon-TEN in French)

Benedict, BEN-eh-dict

Beowulf, BAY-uh-wolf

Breca, BREK-uh

Briseis, bry-SEE-iss

Britomart, BRIH-tuh-mart

Burdama, boor-DAH-mah

Busirane, BUS-ih-rayn

Buthrotum, buh-THROH-tum

Calchas, KAL-kus

Carrion, kah-ree-ON

Carthage, KAR-thij

Cassandra, kuh-SAN-druh

Castile, kas-TEEL

Cerberus, SUR-bur-us

Charlemagne, SHAR-luh-mayn

Charon, KAR-un

Charybdis, kuh-RIB-dis

Chou Yu, CHOW-YOO

Chryseis, kry-SEE-us

Chuko Liang, ZHOO-kuh
LIYANG (or JOO-kuh
LIYANG)

Colada, koh-LAH-da

Crete, KREET

Creusa, kree-YOO-suh

Cumae, KYOO-mee

Cupid, KYOO-pid (called Eros by
Greeks)

Cyclopes, sy-KLOH-peez

Cyclops, SY-klops

Dardanus, DAHR-dan-us

Delos, DEE-los

Diana, dy-AN-uh (called Artemis
by Greeks)

Dido, DY-doh

Diego, dee-EH-go

Discordia, dis-KOR-dee-uh (called
Eris by Greeks)

Djinar, JIH-nahr

Drepanum, DREP-uh-num

Duessa, doo-ES-suh

Durendal, der-en-DAHL

El Cid, el SID

Elizabeth, e-LIZ-uh-beth

Elvira, el-VEER-uh
Elysian Fields, ih-LIZH-un
    FEELDZ
Enkidu, EN-kee-doo
Enlil, EN-lil
Eris, ER-iss (called Discordia by
    Romans)
Eros, ER-us (called Cupid by
    Romans)
Eumaeus, yoo-MEE-us
Eurycleia, yoo-RIK-lee-uh
Evangeline, ih-VAN-juh-lin (or eh-
    vonj-LEEN in French)

Fates, FAYTS
Felician, feh-LISS-ee-un (or feh-
    lees-ee-AN in French)
Felix, FEEL-iks
Fernando, fer-NAN-doh

Gabriel, GAY-brih-el
Ganelon, GAN-uhl-on
Gilgamesh, GIL-guh-mesh
Glauce, GLAW-see
Goroba-Dike, goh-ROH-bah DEE-
    kay
Grand-Pre, grahn-PRAY
Grendel, GREN-del

Hades, HAY-deez (called Pluto by
    Romans)
Hamadi Ardo, hah-MAH-dee
    AHR-doh
Harim, ha-REEM
Harpy, HAHR-pee
Hector, HEK-tur
Helen, HEL-un
Helenus, HEL-uh-nus
Hephaestus, hee-FES-tus (called
    Vulcan by Romans)
Hera, HEE-ruh (called Juno by
    Romans)
Hermes, HUR-meez (called
    Mercury by Romans)

Hiawatha, hy-uh-WATH-uh
Humbaba, hum-BAH-bah
Human, yoo-MAN

Iagoo, YA-goo
Ida, AHY-duh
Iliad, IL-ee-ad
Ilium, IL-ee-um
Ilmarinen, EEL-mah-ree-nun
Ionian Sea, ahy-OH-nee-un SEE
Iran, ih-RAN
Irus, AHY-rus
Ishtar, ISH-tar

Jimena, hee-MAYN-ah
Jove, JOHV (also called Jupiter
    by Romans; called Zeus by
    Greeks)
Julius Caesar, JOOL-yus SEE-zer
Juno, JOO-noh (called Hera by
    Greeks)
Jupiter, JOO-pih-tur (also called
    Jove by Romans; called Zeus
    by Greeks)

Kahindo, kah-HEE-ndoh
Kalevala, kah-luh-VAH-luh
Kode Ardo, KOH-dee AHR-doh

Laocoön, lay-OK-uh-wahn
Latium, LAY-shee-um
Lavinia, luh-VIN-ee-uh
Lavinium, luh-VIN-ee-um
Leon, lay-OHN
Lethe, LEE-thee
Louhi, LOO-hee
Lu Su, LOO SOO

Manito, MAN-i-toh (also Manitou,
    MAN-i-too)
Mars, MARZ (called Ares by
    Greeks)
Marsiles, mahr-SILL-eez
Massina, mah-SEE-nah

Menelaus, meh-neh-LAY-us
Mercury, MUR-kyuh-ree (called
   Hermes by Greeks)
Merlin, MUR-lin
Minerva, mih-NUR-vuh (called
   Athena by Greeks)
Morocco, muh-RAHK-oh
Mwindo, MWI-ndoh

Navarre, nuh-VAHR
Neptune, NEP-toon (called
   Poseidon by Greeks)
Nova Scotia, NOH-vuh SKOH-
   shuh
Nyamitondo, nya-mi-TOH-ndoh

Odysseus, oh-DIS-us, or oh-DIS-
   see-us (called Ulysses by
   Romans)
Odyssey, OD-ih-see
Oliphant, OH-lee-fant (or oh-lee-
   FON in French)
Olympus, oh-LIM-pus
Ozarks, OH-zahrks

Palinurus, PAL-ih-noor-us
Patroclus, puh-TROH-klus
Pau Puk Keewis, paw-puk-KEE-
   wiss
Peleus, PEEL-yus
Pelion, PEE-lee-on
Penelope, puh-NEL-uh-pee
Phoebus Apollo, FEE-bus uh-
   POL-oh (called Apollo by
   Romans)
Pluto, PLOO-toh (called Hades by
   Greeks)
Poseidon, poh-SY-dun (called
   Neptune by Romans)
Priam, PRY-um
Pyrrhus, PIR-us

Romulus, ROM-yuh-lus
Roncevaux, RONS-eh-voh
Rustem, ROO-stum

Samangan, SAM-an-gan
Saragossa, sar-uh-GOHS-uh
Sariam, sah-REE-ahm
Sarpedon, Sahr-PEE-duhn
Scudamore, SKUD-uh-mor
Scylla, SIL-uh
Shahnamah, shah-NAH-mah
Shamash, SHAH-mash
Shemwindo, sheh-MWI-ndoh
Sibyl, SIB-il
Sicily, SIS-uh-lee
Sinon, SY-non
Sohrab, SOH-rab
Sol, SOHL
Ssuma Yi, SOO-MAH YEE
Styx, STIKS

Tahmineh, tah-MEE-nuh
Tartarus, TAHR-tuh-rus
Telemachus, teh-LEM-uh-kus
Thetis, THEE-tiss
Tiber, TY-bur
Tizonia, tiz-OH-nee-uh
Tsao Tsao, TSOW TSOW
Tubondo, too-BOH-ndoh
Tuoni, TWAW-nee
Turan, too-RAN
Turnus, TUR-niss

Ulysses, yoo-LISS-eez (called
   Odysseus by Greeks)
Unferth, UN-firth
Uruk, OO-ruk

Valencia, vah-LEN-shih-uh
Venus, VEE-nus
Vulcan, VUL-kin (called
   Hephaestus by Greeks)

Yangtze, YANG-tsee

Zaire, zah-AYR
Zeus, ZOOSS (called Jove or
   Jupiter by Romans)